George Wood

The Gates Wide Open

Scenes in Another World

George Wood

The Gates Wide Open
Scenes in Another World

ISBN/EAN: 9783744708685

Printed in Europe, USA, Canada, Australia, Japan

Cover: Foto ©Thomas Meinert / pixelio.de

More available books at **www.hansebooks.com**

THE GATES WIDE OPEN;

OR,

SCENES IN ANOTHER WORLD.

THE GATES WIDE OPEN

OR

SCENES IN ANOTHER WORLD.

BY

GEORGE WOOD,

AUTHOR OF "PETER SCHLEMIHL IN AMERICA," "MODERN PILGRIMS," ETC.

> What if earth
> Be but the shadow of heaven, and things therein
> Each to other like, more than on earth is thought?
>
> MILTON, P. L., Book V.

> SOCRATES, before drinking the cup of hemlock, said to his disciples,
> " It is especially suited to one who is on the eve of departing to another
> world, to inquire into and speculate upon his migration thither — of what
> nature we suppose it to be."
>
> SANDFORD'S PHÆDO, p. 8.

BOSTON:
LEE AND SHEPARD,
149 WASHINGTON STREET.
1869.

ADVERTISEMENT.

——◦◦◦——

An edition of this work, entitled "Future Life; or, Scenes in Another World," was published by Derby and Jackson in the fall of 1858. The firm failed in the spring of 1859, and the plates were resold to the author, and have remained in his possession unused until the present time, when the recent popular and attractive book of Miss Phelps, entitled "The Gates Ajar," suggested its republication and the change of title which is now made. The Author hopes his readers will be gratified with this attempt to picture the Scenes and Society of Another World.

Washington, May 1, 1869.

(v)

TO THE READER.

THIS work was designed by the Author as a manuscript tale for a young friend; but, as "stories somehow lengthen as they run," and being pleased with the labor, the work grew under his hands, and took its present shape.

All our ideas of the future must be formed out of the present life; nor can we reach outside of a physical theory. The vehicles of thought and representations of The World to Come, found in this volume, are the same which have been adopted by the inspired writers of the Holy Bible, and by Dante and Milton.

Jeremy Taylor, speaking of a poor widow who labored hard to procure the means of subsistence, says, "her ideas of heaven were few and simple. She rejected the doctrine that it was a place of constant activity, and not of repose; and believed that when she at length reached it, she would work no more, but sit in a clean white apron and sing psalms."

In like manner we all have our own ideas of heaven, which have been forming from the day-dawn of existence, and result from a combination of all the varied influences that have ever been brought to bear upon our physical as well as our spiritual nature.

The Author, after the book was written, in order to meet objections as best he could, sought for passages from Dante and Milton to countenance his imaginings, assured that under the shelter of their great names he would be safe from misconception and censure. The eminent English essayist, JOHN FOSTER, has thus given his judgment of such an effort as this: "I am very far from disliking philosophical speculation, or daring flights of fancy on this high subject. On the contrary, it appears to me strange that any one firmly holding the belief of a life to come should not have both the intellectual faculty and the imagination excited to the utmost in the trial, however unavailing, to give some outlines of definite form to the unseen realities." And SOCRATES, addressing those by whom he had been condemned, spoke of his death as a departure to the society of the good in another world, and asked: "If this be true, O my judges, what greater good can there be than this? At what price would not either of you purchase a conference with Orpheus or Musæus, with Hesiod and Homer? What would not any one of you give for an interview with him who led that mighty army against Troy; or with Ulysses, or ten thousand of others, both male and female, that might be mentioned? For to converse and associate with them would be an inestimable felicity. Truly I should be willing to die often, if these things be true."

In a work of the Imagination, which, so far as his knowledge extends, is the first to portray after this manner the *possible* scenes of a future life, the Author may not hope to satisfy his readers; yet, if its perusal shall be suggestive, and if, by antagonism even, thoughts in their souls before dormant, or undefined and shadowy, shall become operative ideas, his wishes will have been so far attained.

Heaven is the true happiness of the human soul; presenting the attractions of every excellence and the fruition of every desire. The Author's aim has been to awaken in his readers new aspirations of hope for "the glorious appearing of the great God and our Saviour Jesus Christ."

CONTENTS.

CHAPTER I.

CHAPTER II.

CHAPTER III.

CHAPTER IV.

CHAPTER V.

CHAPTER VI.

CHAPTER VII.

CHAPTER XI.

CHAPTER XII.

CHAPTER XIII.

CHAPTER XIV.

THE GATES WIDE OPEN.

CHAPTER I.

It was at the close of a summer's day, that a female form, arrayed in robes of light, floated in the atmosphere of a world of loveliness and grandeur. Upon her beautiful brow shone the halo of immortality, whose pure rays resembled the scintillations of stars. Her robes and vesture

———"Sky robes spun of Iris' woof,"

were classic in their fashion, and fastened around the waist by a girdle studded with gems of rare brilliancy. Her eyes were lit with intense delight as she gazed long and ardently upon the varied landscape mapped out beneath her.

On this globe were vast continents, with mighty mountain chains, and oceans gemmed with islands, whose peaks were lifted high above the clouds. All around were scenes of rarest combinations of luxuriance and loveliness. Cities of vast size were seen, whose domes rose like gold and silver-capped clouds.

Sweeping above the earth, like an eagle on wings of even poise, did this shining one circle over the plains below. And while thus occupied and absorbed, angel forms from the empyrean, appeared in the distance, with the suddenness of falling stars. Arrested by the vision of beauty, with a swoop high in air, they staid their flight, and floated amid the clouds.

This squadron of angels, descending, left one of their number above. He, too, bore the flame of the Redeemed, shining like the morning star over his forehead. By a law of sympathy, as undefined in heaven as on earth, these two shining ones drew nearer and nearer, until, in immediate proximity, they awoke to the consciousness of each other's presence. After graceful salutations, as befits the courtesies of all worlds, the man, for such he was, addressed the woman thus: "Fair sister, are you, like myself, a stranger here?"

She replied, "I am, and have but just reached this beautiful world. Can you tell me anything of its history?"

"My companions in travel, who have just left me, tell me that this world is one of the centres of the Fine

Arts, to which many of the redeemed of earth are sent
to be initiated into the love of Music and the Arts of
Design."

"I am most happy to know this. I have never heard
of such a world, but as God, our Creator, is the author
of Beauty, I knew he must sympathize with the feeblest
efforts of his children, in whatever scale of existence,
and however rude their attempt to realize the Ideal." *

As the woman spoke, there was a flash of mutual
recognition, and with a burst of joy the friendships of
earth were now renewed. †

All that the reader need know of the lives on earth of
these persons, thus introduced to his acquaintance, is
told in a few words. Mrs. Anna Jay had been the wife
of an eminent citizen of New York, still living in that
city, with his only child, Miss Augusta Jay, now a young
lady: and the male spirit was none other than Mr. Peter

---

* PLATO, in his book "Against the Atheists," which is the "10th Book of Laws,'
with wonderful acumen makes an argument *à priori*, derived from inward consciousness, in which he demonstrates that the Supreme Being is the God of beauty
and love. His words are " God is Beauty and Love itself."

† RECOGNITION OF FRIENDS IN HEAVEN.—Baxter says, "I must confess, as the experience of my own soul, that the expectation of loving my friends in heaven
principally kindles my love to them on earth. If I thought I should never know,
and consequently never love them after this life, I should number them with tem
poral things, and love them as such; but I now delightfully converse with my
pious friends, in a firm persuasion that I shall converse with them forever; and I
take comfort in those that are dead or absent, believing that I shall shortly meet
them in heaven, and love them with a heavenly love."

Schlemihl, whose adventures in this country are well known to the readers of his book, entitled "Peter Schlemihl in America."

After the surprise of this unexpected meeting was over, Mrs. Jay proposed that they should alight, saying, "I have a thousand questions to ask you."

Leading the way, Mrs. Jay descended gently down the skies to where a beautiful little Doric edifice stood on a shaft of granite, which rose out of the centre of a lake, the shores of which lay about a mile distant. These were covered with villas whose velvety green ornamental grounds ran down to the water. In front of them, and standing upon a bold rocky bank, rose a magnificent temple, whose golden spires and lofty dome were reflected in long lines of light upon the glassy surface of the lake, with all the gorgeous clouds of a summer's eve, lit up by the great setting flame. Here as they sat admiring the scene before them, Peter thus addressed his companion :

"How unspeakably happy I am, Mrs. Jay, to meet you here in these realms of life and immortality; 'redeemed, regenerated, disenthralled!'"

Mrs. Jay, with her eyes lifted to heaven, replied: "Free, Peter! yes, my soul, complete in the circle of its powers, has but one aspiration, to be God-like." Recovering herself, she continued: "Now, Peter, tell me of your escape out of the body?"

Peter replied: "Dying was to me, Mrs. Jay, as it is

to most men, a matter of painful apprehension. Not
only because of 'the pains, the groans and dying strife,'
but most of all, lest, after all, I should find myself self-
deceived, and forever lost. It was on Friday night,
now six weeks since, that I went to bed with a chill. I
had spent the evening at your house with your husband
and Augusta, and not feeling well, I left at an early
hour. That night I had a hot fever, and the strangest
of dreams. In the morning, my excellent friend, Dr.
Hall, came up to see me, and prescribed. My fever
raged with violence for five days, and I began to realize
the possibility that this was to be my last sickness, and
that soon I should stand before God. Satan was near
me to accuse me, and I was made to look down into
the immeasurable abyss of my depravity. Such was
the activity of my soul, that the retrospection of
my life now is not more vivid than it was at that
time. My reply to all these accusations of conscience
was this: I repeated all the exceeding great and precious promises of the word of God, and all the verses
of hymns I could recall, and these flowed into my soul
with such sweetness that I was kept, for the most part,
in perfect peace. I say for the most part, for there were
moments when my sins rose like mountain waves,
impending over me. I knew I was wading through the
Jordan, and though the waters rose very high, I was
assured of my safety; so that when the anxieties of
those around me increased, mine had all ceased. I was

perfectly passive, suffered little, and was only sorry to see those about me in tears. The ninth day, and it was the Lord's day, about noon, I was aware of those around me expressing a wish for me to give them some token of my consciousness. I felt the pressure of their hands, but could not return it. My soul was now bathed in perfect repose, when, my sight failing, I saw but dimly those near me, and became conscious of the presence of my guardian angel. 'Give me,' said Augusta, 'one last pressure;' I did so, and then sunk away into a blissful sleep. From this I woke, and found myself clad in the robes of immortality, the morning star shining above my forehead.

"I lingered awhile, anxious to manifest myself to those who stood around my bed weeping. It was all in vain that I spoke to them; and thus I grew into the full consciousness of my separate existence. 'Let us depart,' said my angel; and with the last emotion of sorrow I shall ever know, I found myself rising into the heavens, and soon suns and stars fled by me with the rapidity of meteors, as we mounted upwards on our way to the Holy City, there to be presented to our great Redeemer as a new trophy of his victory. The rapture of that glad hour I have no words to express, and happily you need none. It was to me, and ever will be, a glory unutterable. After my audience with our great God and Saviour, I was sent by him, under the conduct of my guardian, to this world, here to begin my studies. By permission of my angel, I have remained above to witness the beauty of the landscape, and, to my great joy, I have met you."

"Were you not surprised, Peter, to find in the Holy City no Scripture personages, and no one of whom you had read in the history of the church?"

"I was greatly surprised. I inquired for them, especially for the apostle Paul, but was told by my angel that they had all long since been made meet for the high service of messengers of the grace of God, and were now telling the tidings of the redemption of a lost race by the sufferings and death of Christ. He told me this was the last attainment of a glorified soul: that, in order to this, after long practice in the schools of eloquence, the languages as well as the sciences of the world to which the missionary is sent were to be acquired; and then it demands the greatest possible range of illustration to make sinless beings comprehend the mysteries of the renewal and sanctification of a lost soul."

"And what was the newest of your joys, Peter, after you were clothed upon with immortality?"

"It was the absence of sin—no more sin! A soul saved I knew must be happy, but the manner in which happiness came was new to me. The great unappreciated weight of sin, which, like our earth's atmosphere, once weighed me down, was now no more. And then, such was my joy in the exercise of my new-found faculties of knowing and loving. Gladly did I task my angel into the development of my soul's energies, and yet I was surprised to find myself, though disembodied, and after so great a change, so little changed. And this thought was present to me, when I felt in my soul the consciousness of power to wing my flight to the very verge of creation, if such there be. But it was not long before I found myself, as on earth, a child of limited powers and in the infancy of my being. I had everything to learn, and could not reach my longings any more than an infant who cries for the moon; but then I was docile, and made the glad discovery that I had now none of the repinings of earth clinging to me." *

* The Author respectfully requests the attention of his readers to this note. Archbishop Whately, in his recent work on "A Future State," presents these views: "Vast as must be the difference, in many respects, between the glorified condition of the saints, and everything they have experienced here, yet I doubt whether there may not be more resemblance between the two states—the earthly and the heavenly—than some suppose. Sins and infirmities will of course be excluded from that better world; the enjoyments and perfections of sincere Christians will be immensely heightened; but if we look on the highest and purest spots of human nature and human life, as it is here, we may be led to form, I think, no unreasonable conjectures as to some things that will be hereafter. For, we should remember, that both worlds are the work of the same Author—this present world of trial, and the eternal world,—'the new heavens and the new earth wherein dwelleth righteousness.' All that is suitable to this world alone will be removed from that other, what is evil will be taken away, what is imperfect will be made complete, what is good will be extended and exalted; but there is no reason to suppose that any *further* change will be made than is *necessary* to qualify the faithful for that improved state, that their human character will be altered any further than it *wants* altering, and its dispositions and whole constitution unnecessarily reversed."—*Lecture X.* "*Occupations and State of Society of the Blest*," p. 20.

"One of the glad surprises which filled me with **joy**," said Mrs. Jay, "was my recollection of all I had ever thought, or said, or did. I had read of a French metaphysician who says, 'a thought is more substantive than a post,' and in studying mental philosophy I had learned that thoughts were eternal, but the recovery of all these at will has filled me with delight. And now your presence brings back to me all we have said and done from our first acquaintance; but after all, I cannot ask you a thousand questions at once, and I find I am, as you have just now suggested, still the subject of time and space."

And while they thus sat conversing the sun of that world was making a golden set, and distant songs of praise from a multitude of voices were borne by the evening breeze over the surface of the lake, from out of the cathedral, and with such a flood of harmony as at once arrested the attention of Mrs. Jay and Peter. The last note was hushed, when the hymn to the Trinity came to them on the wings of the wind, and reverently rising, they joined in the song of saints and angels.

"Let us go down to meet these children of the highest," said Mrs. Jay; for now the multitude of worshippers were seen thronging out, and returning, in family groups to their villas. By a volition they alighted on the greensward in front of the temple, and stood aside, to see these new-found creatures of their Heavenly Father, who, in passing, saluted them with the profound deference due to their superior race. Last of all, there came thronging out of the temple a bevy of youth of both sexes, wearing the halo of the redeemed, who were crowding playfully around two mature persons who seemed to promote the amusement of these happy beings. There was a gracious smile on the handsome face of the man, whose merry sayings provoked the mirth of the group, while his wife (as they supposed her to be) looked around with a pleased air, the very type of goodness and gentleness. It reminded Mrs. Jay of the playfulness of boys and girls around beloved teachers.

As these drew near, Peter, to his great joy, discovered in these seniors, his well beloved friends, Deacon and Mrs. Colgate.   With extended arms he advanced towards them, and they, recognizing him, came towards him with glad expressions of delight. This over, Mrs. Jay was presented and then the deacon called his son Thomas, and after him the whole school came forward and were introduced. The young folks then left them to enjoy their sports on the green, and on the lake. "Do you not wish me to tell you whose these are?" said the deacon as they stood looking, watching their antics and frolics.

"Certainly, Deacon Colgate," said Mrs. Jay.

"These all died in childhood or infancy, and they have been sent here to be trained into the science of music. They are the choristers of this great cathedral as we should call it on earth, while they pursue their various studies in the academy whose dome you see yonder," pointing to it in the distance.

"Come," said the deacon, "let us have the pleasure of your company for the night. I have many inquiries to make of our world, and here we have homes as wide and spacious as our hearts."

"You have always had such a home, deacon," said Peter.

"Let us lead the way, Mrs. Jay," said the deacon, offering his arm; and Mrs. Colgate and Peter followed after.

The Palace of the Redeemed stood on a gentle slope of land bordering on the lake. The grounds were beautifully laid out and were adorned with statues, which, seen in the shadows of twilight amid the shrubbery of the garden, were often mistaken for living beings of sur passing grace and beauty. The building stood in the centre of the grounds, and rose before them a splendid palace. There was a lofty pillared porch over the grand entrance, and, having ascended its marble steps, they entered a vestibule so beautiful in its adornments, as to make them pause and look up and around in wondering amazement. The frescoes were to their eyes living realities, and when they entered the spacious saloon they found themselves surrounded with works of art, the ceilings covered with forms of loveliness, and the walls hung with paintings which riveted the attention of beholders so newly arrived as were both Mrs. Jay and Peter.

They were permitted to indulge their admiration to the full, when the deacon, addressing Mrs. Jay, said, "I see, madam, you love art. That is something I have now to acquire, and I am taking my first lessons in drawing. In the utilitarian world in which, when a boy, I lived, Art was not regarded with much favor. Indeed, an artist, whether in music, painting or sculpture, was considered as a worthless fellow who wanted to live without labor. All we desired then was just enough of music to turn a tune, and of painting, to make a portrait, where every feature was caricatured into what is called "a striking likeness." And as for sculpture, all we asked was a carver to make figure-heads for our ships, or gravestones with horrid cherubs, to mark the place where our dead lay buried. But a great change had been effected, and at the end of the first half of the nineteenth century, I was fearful we were getting on too fast with our love of art, and spending money on works of taste which ought to have been devoted to works of benevolence and the cause of missions."

"'Offences must needs come,' deacon," replied Mrs. Jay. "Man, sinful as he is, will never do anything as it ought to be done. Perfect symmetry of life and action is not of earth but heaven. For myself, I always loved art, for I felt that next to Holiness, God must love Beauty. I use the language of earth in so speaking, for in the mind of God there are no sequences."

"You will have your longings fully met in this, God's

world of art and beauty," said Mrs. Colgate, "for here, Mrs. Jay, the struggle is to reach to the full comprehension of what meets the eye wherever it rests, whether in the creations of God, or of his creatures.

"Let us now take a survey of our home here," said this good woman; which they did under her guidance and the deacon's. The grandeur of the saloons and halls, and the splendor of the furniture, and beauty of the drapery, all were subjects of Mrs. Jay's especial admiration.

When they had walked through the saloons, returning, they took seats at windows opening upon the lake, where they saw many gilded skiffs gliding along under the guidance of the children of the palace. Some were running boat races, striving for the goal, and followed by many as lookers-on; and others were playing along the banks. While they sat gazing on the sports of these shining ones, the deacon asked many questions concerning his children and the city, and finally, as to the state of political parties. He asked after the progress of liberty, and was happy to be informed that every advance was in favor of freedom.

"I doubt not it is so," said the deacon. "The Gospel of our great God and Saviour Jesus Christ is leavening the whole lump, but how slowly. It seems to me the advance of Christianity and civilization (and these I regard as identical), is like the swaying of a pendulum, first one way and then another; but there is a rack movement high over all, beyond the control of rulers, whether kings or congressmen, which carries the world forward." And pausing a moment, the deacon, with one of his merry smiles, continued, "I think, Peter, the world every now and then makes a sudden lurch, and the advance of a generation seems lost; but it is not so, for the world's history shows that the subversion of the eternal laws of God and humanity are overruled for the advance of the kingdom of Christ; for which alone, my friends, the world is kept in being."

"All you say is true, Deacon Colgate," said Mrs. Jay, "but you would not preach the doctrine of submission to evil-doers if you were on earth."

"By no means. Let every man be zealously affected in a good cause, and if, by mistake, good men even knock each other's heads off, it only hastens them in their pilgrimage to the celestial city." This unexpected turn given by the deacon to the discourse was followed by one of his merry laughs that shed its sunshine, as they were wont to do, over the circle about him. It was beautiful in the eyes of Peter, to see these dear friends once more, and to hear the wise sayings of the good deacon, and to enjoy his grave, genial and becoming mirth, illustrated and heightened by the silvery laugh of Mrs. Jay.

At this point of their discussion, supper was announced, and the deacon led Mrs. Jay, Peter and Mrs. Colgate following, across the central hall into a spacious saloon, where they found a hundred youth or more assembled, and the table covered with a service of gold of exquisite workmanship, and vases filled with fruits and flowers; grapes just gathered, and fruits of various hues, before unseen. The "Gloria" having been sung, they seated themselves. A lovely girl of fifteen, whose lustrous eyes bespoke her origin in eastern lands, sat next Peter, and made herself agreeable to him, helping him to select the fruits to be eaten, and replying to all his inquiries.

"Have the Fellahs of Egypt yet awakened the sympathy of the European churches?" asked the girl; to which Peter replied he had not heard of any such missions.

"Pray tell me," asked Peter, "are you from Egypt?"

"Yes, I was born at Philæ, and was thrown to the crocodiles. I was born but to be born again unto the kingdom of heaven; and after having received the blessing of our God and Saviour, I was brought here by my angel to be educated. See that girl conversing opposite; she was born in Hindostan, and was exposed to vultures; and you see here representatives of all lands."

"Are there many such homes for infants in this world?"

"O, yes, we are scattered everywhere; not only in this world, but in other worlds of Art and Beauty, of which there is an inconceivable number."

The scene was one of singular interest to Peter, as he sat looking up and down the table and saw this lovely company, all arrayed in robes of light and wearing the halo of immortality, feasting with playfulness and joy on fruits which might have satisfied the palate of Raphael, the angel of God, in Paradise.*

On rising from the table, as the evening was advanced, the deacon proposed to Mrs. Jay and Peter, to go out and see the starry heavens. They did so, and looking up were filled with admiration and awe. There was a broad belt of light circling the heavens which reflected the sun's

---

* Lest some of his readers may deem this as "of the earth earthy," the author deems it wise to call on Milton to give him his aid and countenance. In the *Paradise Lost*, book v., we read of Raphael's visit to Adam and Eve in Paradise. Raphael being invited to the banquet prepared by Eve, Adam apologizes for its quality, saying:

> ———" 'unsavory food, perhaps,
> To spiritual natures."
> To whom the angel : 'Therefore what he gives
> (Whose praise be ever sung) to man in part
> Spiritual, may of purest spirits be found
> No ingrateful food: *and food alike those pure
> Intelligential substances require,*
> As doth your rational; and both contain
> Within them every lower faculty
> Of sense, whereby they hear, see, smell, touch, taste,
> Tasting concoct, digest, assimilate,
> And corporeal to incorporeal turn.' "

After further discourse, Raphael, speaking of heavenly fruits, tells Adam:

> " ' Yet God hath here
> Varied his bounty so with new delights
> As may compare with heaven; and to taste
> Think not I shall be nice.' So down they sat
> And to the viands fell; *nor seemingly
> The angel,* nor in mist, the common gloss

rays, and four moons were visible, one at the full over head, another just emerging from behind the ring, and two others showing the cusp of a coming and of a waning moon. These, and stars which hung down from the dark depths of the sky like burning lamps, forming glorious constellations, filled the souls of our travellers with adoring rapture.

They remained in the open air, walking along the shores of the lake, accompanied by deacon and Mrs. Colgate and the Egyptian girl, who held the hand of Peter, and described to him the cosmography of this system of worlds with which she was familiar from having personally visited every planet and every moon in sight; and this she did in the most pleasing manner conceivable.

The chimes of the cathedral reminded them of their hour of worship and rest. Returning skiffs freighted with shining ones were seen now hastening to land, and soon this Community of Love were assembled in the grand hall, as it was called by preëminence, when the choir

Of theologians; but with keen dispatch
Of real hunger. . . . . . .
. . . . . Meanwhile at table Eve
Minister'd naked, and their flowing cups
With pleasant liquors crowned."—Line 445.

In Gen. xviii. we read of a visit made by the angel Jehovah and two attendant angels to Abraham. It is written—"Abraham ran unto the herd, and fecht a calf, tender and good, and gave it unto a young man; and he hasted to dress it. And he took butter and milk, and 'he calf which he had dressed, and set it befor) them; *and they did eat.*"

with one consent began their song of praise. This service ended, with graceful adieus, they separated. The deacon consigned Mrs. Jay to his wife, and Peter to his son, to be conducted to their several apartments.*

Peter was again surprised at the beauty of his chamber, and its furniture. The couch was of classic form and the filmy curtains were held up by cherubs wrought in gold, whose faces were beautiful beyond description. It was late, and Peter, a little weary with his long flight, laid himself down to sleep.

Now the state of repose to the redeemed is bliss unknown on earth; for then the soul in vision rises with a flood of light, into the sensible and immediate presence of the Saviour, and holds with him the most intimate communion; asking him every question love can inspire, and receiving his gracious answers, as did the disciple whom Jesus loved while leaning on his bosom. It was the belief of the saints of all ages, and this was sustained by those most learned in the science of the soul, that this state of exaltation was the highest life; when the soul found its repose in God, the ocean of the Infinite, where all is light and love; to each soul the perfection of being, defined by no line, bounded by no circle, but in which the soul was represented to itself as the centre and God the circumference. Such was the communion of the

---

* Satan, (*Paradise Lost*, book I, line 325) reproaches his fallen legions, lying entranced upon the burning lake:

"To slumber here, as in the vales of heaven!"

redeemed with God and Christ, alike to all capacities, the mightiest mind and the infant heir of glory who but breathed and was exhaled to heaven; and shared too by archangels, those who stood with Lucifer, son of the morning, when the almightiness of God was first manifested in the creation of suns and systems, innumerable.

Happy sleepers! whose beautiful activity is thus suspended to wake to visions of a more beatific existence.

CHAPTER II.

Morning Scenes—Deacon Colgate's account of this New World—Colloquy concerning this World in contrast with Earth—Breakfast—Servitors described—
Peter receives a Message from his Angel to hasten to the Metropolis to hear a
new Oratorio by Handel, Haydn, Mozart and Beethoven—The Messenger
tells the Story of his Life.

Our travellers arose with the song of earliest birds, and
met each other on the terrace leading to the grounds
bordering on the lake. The morning breeze was just
waking the waves to life. If the sunset was glorious,
the rising sun, whose coming was foretold by the
reflected light from the vast zone circling this world,
was magnificent, and filled their souls with emotions of
sublimity which kept them silent.

They were brought down from heaven to earth by the
song of birds, whose plumage was paradisiacal, while
their notes, running through the sweetest inflections,
won their admiring attention. And looking round they
were delighted to see flowers of unknown fragrance, and
new combinations of hues; and above and around were
trees of great height and beauty of foliage whose

pendent boughs, far drooping, waved gracefully over them.*

"How beautiful!" was an exclamation ever rising to their lips.

While thus occupied, Deacon Colgate and wife joined them, and after morning salutations, Mrs. Jay asked the deacon to tell them something about this lovely world.

"We are told, madam, that this is a very ancient world, and has been peopled many cycles of centuries. It is one of worlds of Beauty and Art, or, as my son has it, of the True and the Beautiful in Art. If you have circled it before alighting here, you have seen its many and vast cities, filled with glorious temples and edifices devoted to galleries of paintings and sculpture, and museums of natural history, so various and bewildering, that walking through them even, wearies the attention of new comers; and when you shall visit them, as I have done, you will come away as I did, with a feeling that ages would be exhausted in the attempt to know all that is to be known of this one world."

"How the glory and greatness of God widens! When I was on earth, and thought of eternity, I sometimes speculated whether the time would not come when I should have exhausted all that was knowable."

"And so, Mrs. Jay, you thought you might become a

* "Many are the trees of God that grow
In Paradise, and various yet unknown
To us." . . . .—*Paradise Lost*, book ix., line 618.

fit subject of *ennui*," said the deacon, smiling. He con·
tinued, "Heaven is certainly somewhat different from
what we have dreamed; but however that may be in our
experience, our hopes are realized in that we have no
tears to be wiped away, no more of sin to taint the conscience and wound the soul."

Mrs. Colgate, with her sweet smile, followed her
husband, saying, "To be holy, forever pure as God is
pure, is the completeness of heavenly felicity. And yet
we all feel that we are but in the beginning of our blissful
existence. To grow into the likeness of God—'one
with God as Christ and God are one'—means more
than we can now conceive of, and the ages of eternity
will come to us full freighted with the blessings of our
adoption, and 'a far more exceeding and eternal weight
of glory.'"

"It must be so, dear Mrs. Colgate," said Peter,
" and yet, for myself I speak, I have no power to apprehend these great thoughts from the completeness of my
present existence. The measure of my capacity will
doubtless be enlarged, but no measure can be more than
full."

"Pray do not perplex my mind, Peter," Mrs. Jay
exclaimed, " with such vain imaginings; soap bubbles of
philosophers! I am happy now, and shall be forever
happy. What more can be desired, deacon and Mrs.
Colgate? And yet, deacon, I can guess at the per-
plexity and embarrassment you felt while wandering

through a vast collection of natural history, which was new to you, and which you could not but strive to arrange into some order which would be available to you hereafter."

"My dear madam," said the deacon, "you do not begin to guess the embarrassments that await you. Here is a world, one of fifty-two planets, that belong to this system, whose history goes back many millions of years, and every age an age of progress. Their authors' works are written in a language forever changing, making the literature of one cycle unintelligible to those of the next, and all these changes are to be studied and attained before the books piled up in public libraries can be read. Then there are as many eras in Art as in literature, and in the same age, in different lands, are contending schools whose works to be appreciated must be studied in the light of the period when they were originated. So that I, who when I reached here, knew nothing of such matters, felt myself overwhelmed with the variety of knowledge to be acquired. Happily I have no lack of industry and docility; and under the kind tuition of able masters, aided by my son, Mrs. Colgate and I have begun at the alphabet of science, and we hope to comprehend what now only inspires us with wonder."

A scampering of some sort was heard in the shrubbery, and turning round, our friends saw a flock of fawn-like animals bounding over the bushes. So soon as they discovered strangers they stood at gaze, and when Mrs. Jay ran towards them with kind words and extended hands, they drew back, till coming to a wall of shrubbery, they turned and giving a leap were out of sight. Shortly the Egyptian girl joined the party, and at the deacon's request she gave a whistle, when the troop came bounding once more over the bushes and ran up to her to receive her caresses. Encouraged by her voice, the animals stood while Mrs. Jay stroked their smooth skins, spotted with white. "How beautiful!" said Mrs. Jay, and turning to the deacon, she inquired, "Of what use are they?"

"How much that smacks of earth, madam. In our world everything is regarded as valuable or otherwise for its utility. An animal for his fur or his flesh, but here are animals whose only use, outside their own joy of living, seems to be to fill the mind with forms of beauty, and to give play to the loving affections of the soul. I doubt not there is a use in all things God has made, but I doubt if the inhabitants of this world ever had this inquiry of yours in their heads. You will find, Mrs. Jay, that all your ideas are to be read backwards in worlds where sin and sorrow are unknown."

"Is there no death here?" exclaimed Peter, "and if none, what saves you from a redundant population?"

The deacon replied with a smile, "I assure you, Peter, we do not need English laws to discourage matrimony, nor any aid from Mr. Malthus, as to population."

"Do explain yourself, Deacon Colgate," said Mrs. Jay; "for this world wears a look of spaciousness, and from the bird's-eye view I have had of it, though cultivated as a garden, it has no sign of being crowded; indeed, there are vast areas yet in nature's virgin soil to be seen in every continent and on every island."

"The germ of population commenced here as on earth, only as their Adam and Eve ate no apple, so their Paradise now covers the entire globe. There are here two classes—the commoners, who are many, and the select few, who are born, as in England, lords of the soil. These all have their appropriate training in their several schools of literature, art and science, and when they attain to perfection here, they are translated to a higher sphere, where they are placed in worlds analogous, but of greater glory, and thus they go onward in endless progression."

Mrs. Jay asked, "Do they not dread this change? Is there no hesitancy, nothing like that which we feel when leaving

> ———' the warm precincts of life's cheerful day,
> We cast one longing, lingering, look behind?' "

"O, never!" replied the deacon. "I have witnessed several translations. When the angel comes for them, all their children and friends are gathered together with joy and gladness. After a season of festivity, the father and mother (for here these ties are indissoluble), are taken up into the air by the convoy of angels, and their songs of thanksgiving are sent back by those they leave behind."

"And do children never hear from their parents? Are there no telegraphic lines to link these far-off worlds together?" asked Peter.

"No, Peter, we have no such vehicles of thought, though we are constantly receiving visits of angels who bring messages from those 'not lost, but gone before.' But though we have no such lines as you ask after, you will find each of our great cities the centre of a net-work of wires; for though these people are in advance of us by cycles of ages in all our discoveries of printing, steam, and the like, yet Professor Morse's discovery of sending a *written* message with the speed of lightning was a surprise; and it was at once introduced into this world. There are no such pitiful jealousies here, as has kept Wheatstone's *visual* telegraph in being in England, while the continent of Europe is covered with Morse's instruments, writing by Morse's alphabet."

"Have they made no improvements upon Morse?" asked Peter.

"None," replied the deacon, "and for this reason, Professor Morse, at a single bound, reached the *ne plus ultra* of alphabetic signs, since nothing is so simple as a *line*, nothing can be less than a *dot*."

Mrs. Jay, who had been listening with great attention, asked if they used steam on this globe, for, she said, "I thought I saw vast steamers, crossing the ocean in all directions, but I could see neither smoke-stacks nor smoke; and yet they went forward with amazing celerity."

"Steam has long since been superseded by the discovery of a very simple and safe process of liberating the inconceivable power of electricity latent in water. This is done with perfect ease, and a wineglass of water is found to contain as much electric force as is evolved in the heaviest of thunder storms; and this latent electricity has been made as docile as the electro-magnetic fluid in sending messages from New York to New Orleans."

"Is it possible!" exclaimed Mrs. Jay; "and is this dreamed of on our earth?"

"Yes," replied the deacon, "I am told this great idea has been started by Michael Faraday, and it will not now be permitted to remain undiscovered." *

"To change the topic of our discourse," said Mrs. Jay, "will you please tell me what number of the Redeemed are residents of this world?"

"The number varies daily, madam, but probably fifty to seventy-five thousand are scattered over this globe, in its hamlets, villas, towns and cities."

"So few! John saw in heaven a great multitude,

* The author quotes from memory. The paper by Faraday is in the printed Transactions of the Royal Society, from 1835 to 1845.

which he says, 'no man can number, of all nations, and kindreds, and peoples, and tongues, clothed in white, singing the anthem 'Salvation to our God.'"

"Yes, Mrs. Jay, but who can number the worlds of light that burn in the depths of space, in all which God reveals his love of science and art? Are you good at figures, Mrs. Jay?"

"My mental arithmetic, Deacon Colgate, was quite equal to the sum of fifteen and a half yards of silk for a dress, at two dollars and eighty-seven and a half cents a yard; and I think Mrs. Colgate will confirm me in saying, that this is more than most, ladies can do who buy their silks at Stewart's. But why do you ask me such a question, deacon?"

"I thought, perhaps, you could have told us the number of Noah's family, upon the ratio of increase which has been fixed upon by statisticians of our times. When you shall have studied numbers, as you will do hereafter in some world devoted to this wonderful science, you may make up the mighty sum, and have a capacity to grasp it. The only interest it now has to us, children of immortality, in this the infancy of our heavenly existence, is, to show the folly of the opinion which obtains with many persons, that our earth is to be made up anew for the habitation of the Redeemed." *

* Archbishop Whately, page 192, Lecture ix., on the "Condition of the Blest and their Abode in Heaven," says: "The eternal habitation of the blest is described by the apostle as 'new heavens and a new earth;' meaning by

"That thought was never pleasant to me," replied Mrs. Jay, "and the moment I was free from the body, at one volition I was beyond the system of our earth, and as my angel told me, surrounded by the suns of the Nebula in the belt of Orion. And I have not the least desire to go back even for a short stay."

"You will never return unless God wills it," said the deacon, "and then your will and his will be one."

"May I ask what are your studies here, deacon?"

"Well, Peter, I have of course begun with the language of this people at the present day, and I have now a good command of their vernacular, so that when I meet with the common people I can converse with them. The higher classes usually speak English with great beauty. This arises from so many being sent to this world who are natives of Great Britain and North America. My first study in art has been in drawing and perspective, preparatory to the study of architecture. You remember, Peter, my brick front to the old tabernacle. *That* stands a monument of my skill. My

'heavens' the air we breathe and sky over our heads, as he means by 'earth' the place on which we dwell. As this description must be understood, in a great degree at least, literally; since the blest in the next world, having real material bodies as now, though different from their present bodies, must inhabit some *place* fitted for the reception of such bodies; though exempt, of course, from the evils of the world they now dwell in, and from all the temptations that could lead them into sin; 'righteousness,' says the apostle, will dwell in the new heavens and the 'new earth' which God has promised."

In order to show the impossibility arising out of numbers, the author requests the attention of his readers to Appendix A.

son, Josey, amused himself by calling it 'Colgate's front,' and I am sure Michael Angelo, or Sir Christopher Wren, would give it their sanction. It was an old building, and needed a front of some sort; and for the money it cost, I do not believe it could be bettered. I was not a little proud of it, and I may have talked more about it than it merited; but I am sure I committed greater follies in my lifetime than by advocating free pews and my brick front, which, even now, contrast favorably with marble-pillared porticoes, which frown upon the poor, as they in passing cast a stealthy look into a luxurious church which contains no free seats for them. I thank God, that I have left behind me a building for the worship of God and Christ which is free to all."

The hour of morning worship now sounded from the belfry of the cathedral, when the inhabitants in all their homes assembled for the adoration of their Creator and bountiful Benefactor. Our friends all rose to go into the chapel, as it was called—a large hall in the eastern wing, fitted up with an organ. Not only the Redeemed, but all the servitors of the palace were present, when

> ——" with preamble sweet
> Of charming symphony they introduced
> Their sacred song, and wakened raptures high.
> No voice exempt, no voice but well could join
> Melodious part : such concord is in heaven." *

* Milton—*Paradise Lost*, book III., line 370.

After the morning service, followed the sweet morning congratulations of the Redeemed, and with a mirthfulness alike graceful and pleasing, they all proceeded to the great saloon, where, as before, a table was spread, whose magnificence was, to Peter and Mrs. Jay, amazing. Fresh fruits and fresh flowers, and grapes just gathered, were placed before them by servitors whose every movement was a new surprise of grace to our new comers. These were as numerous as the company. Various were the topics discoursed of at the table, and Peter listened with delight to tones that seemed to him spoken music.

The servitors were all young, and far surpassed the Redeemed in beauty and figure; and then, the slightest act, whatever it might be, was the perfection of grace. These servitors regarded it as a high distinction conferred upon them, though they all belonged to the nobility, thus to stand associated with the children of God.

After breakfast, they separated; some to one studio, and some to another; some to paint on a picture, another to chisel a statue. Often several of both sexes were at work on the same group of marble; and others again, set off for the schools of science and literature.

Deacon and Mrs. Colgate offered to devote themselves for the day to Mrs. Jay and Peter, but as this would interrupt their studies, Mrs. Jay insisted that she should be left to the care of Peter, and that they would make a near survey of this lovely world, and return in good time for evening worship in the cathedral.

While thus engaged, one of the Redeemed entered the saloon where they were sitting, and, addressing Peter, said to him, "The angel of Peter Schlemihl has sent me: he wishes you to accompany me to the metropolis, where a new oratorio, by Handel, is to be performed this day, at twelve, in the Academy of Music." This at once settled the question as for the day's occupation, for Mrs. Jay asked permission to go with Peter, which was promptly granted by the messenger; and the deacon and wife were also earnestly invited, but the deacon declined, for, he said, "Neither Mrs. Colgate nor myself have yet attained to such knowledge as will enable us to comprehend this oratorio."

The excellent deacon and his lady walked with them to the portico, and there took leave of Mrs. Jay and Peter, with warm invitations to return whenever it should please them to do so. It was a bright day; the air warm and full of fragrance, and with a joy only known to the Redeemed, they rose gracefully into the air, until they had reached a pleasing height, and which afforded the best bird's-eye view of the country over which they were floating.

"It is somewhat surprising, sir," said Mrs. Jay to their guide, "that any one can leave such a world as this without one sigh of regret."

He replied: "To us, of earth, it is wonderful; but

their wills are one with God's; and then they know that every change is one of progress, and that joy is their heritage. How unlike our earth! but then our joy is heightened by contrast."

"Doubtless," replied Peter; "but it is learned in a school of temptation and trial."

"It is a source of terrible apprehension even now," replied the guide, "to think of the precipices of destruction upon which we once stood, unconscious or reckless of the fiery billows burning below us, and from which we were saved by the ministry of angels, thus perfecting the love of God our Saviour. These people, in common with all intelligences unfallen, listen with delight to the stories of the redeemed, especially of those who have come out of great tribulations, and washed their robes white in the blood of the Lamb. They but feebly comprehend what is the height and depth of the love of God in the redemption of sinners; and the chiefest vehicle of these great ideas is music. This is, therefore, the method adopted by the glorious men of our world to make known to other worlds, such as this, the mystery made manifest in the life, sufferings and death of the Lord Jesus Christ. To-day we are to listen to a new labor of Handel's genius, aided by others as gloriously endowed, which is to tell of the Nativity of Christ. I am sure you will be amply repaid for your visit."

"May I ask, sir, where were you born, and in what age?" asked Mrs. Jay.

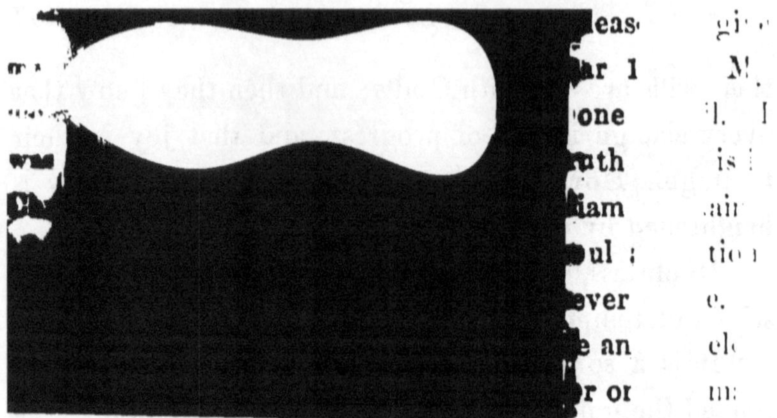

sion of the Earl of Stafford. For the first time in my life I entered a gallery of sculpture and paintings. Then it was I began to breathe. My soul took its first flight, and I was lost in the visions of beauty that I saw all around me; but it was all too brief, for my opportunities of seeing paintings and statuary were like gleams of sunshine on the dark and desolate wastes of existence. The temple of art was closed upon me in time, but here it has been thrown open to me heaven-wide."

CHAPTER III.

A Day spent in the World of Art and Beauty—Of the new St. Peter's built by Michael Angelo—Mrs. Jay and her friend Peter meet with their neighbor, Mr. Laurens —The new Oratorio by Handel is performed, aided by Haydn, Mozart and Beethoven—Of the Language and Literature of the World of Art—They reach the Happy Valley—Trial of Skill with a Mocking-bird—The Enigmas of Faith Discussed—Laurens introduces his friends to St. Perpetua—They attend Vespers— The Temple and Worship described.

As they thus floated along in pleasant converse, they often paused in their flight to look down on cities, crowded with edifices, the work of many centuries. After circling this globe for more than four hours, they reached the Metropolitan City, which covered an immense plateau of high land, surrounded with mountains capped with snow; in the very centre of which lay a glassy lake of pure water, forever supplied by rivulets trickling down the sides of these mountains. Though situated near the equator of this globe, the atmosphere was cool and bracing, and this city was regarded as admirably well situated for the prosecution of the higher branches in art, because of the purity of its climate.

Led by their guide, they alighted upon the tessellated

pavement of a grand square. On either side of them, as they stood gazing about, were sculptured fountains, throwing up plumes of crystal water into the air, which came down in diamond drops. Slender obelisks rose to a great height, in front of a majestic temple, which filled up one side of the square, surpassing all they had conceived as possible for created beings to have built.

"This grand temple," said the guide, "is in the form of the Greek cross, and is a reproduction of St. Peter's, by Michael Angelo.* He was made happy by being appointed architect on his arrival here, which happened immediately after his death; and on its completion, he was sent to a more glorious world, where his lofty genius will find scope for yet higher conceptions of his art—*the art of arts*," said Godfrey with emphasis.

"Is architecture so regarded here?" asked Peter. "I remember to have seen this claimed for it by Vitruvius; but it was not so regarded in our day, certainly not in the United States."

"For the good reason," replied Godfrey, with warmth, "that there are but few men capable of comprehending all the demands made by the art. It is all that Vitruvius has said of it, and Michael Angelo has

---

* St. Peter's was first designed by Bramante, who was followed by Sangallo, who was associated with Raphael. On the death of these eminent men, in 1546, Michael Angelo Buonarotti was appointed sole architect. His design was a Greek cross. It was changed by Carlo Maderno, internally as well as externally, to the shape of the Latin cross.—*Letters of an Architect*, by Jos. Woods. London, 1828.

shown to the world the intimate relations of the
builder and the sculptor and painter. But any builder
of dwelling-houses, even, is allowed to call himself an
architect; and when a man of varied learning and
science and skill arises in the providence of God to bless
the nation to which he is given, his genius is cramped
by the ignorance of those who hold the purse."

"There will be no more grand labors of the archi-
[illegible]," continued Godfrey, "since the world has become
[illegible] and when every man holding office
[illegible] competent to control and direct men of
[illegible]

[illegible] with feeling," said Mrs. Jay.

[illegible], and with reason. I made a brief
[illegible] since to our world, and was so
[illegible] wretched imitations of the ancients, and
[illegible] dark, ill-ventilated, pigmy places of
[illegible] 'Gothic churches,' that I came away
[illegible] determined never to visit the earth

[illegible] Mrs. Jay, smiling, "it is nothing but bad
[illegible] ables will come to their senses and go
[illegible] of building fitted for the worship of
[illegible] twenty years after, their shallow imi-
[illegible] their example."

[illegible] conversing, they walked towards the
[illegible] A multitude of citizens, with their fami-
[illegible] the entrance. Their robes and ves-

tures were of various hues, and worn with a grace of
movement, and a mien so beautiful, that both Peter and
Mrs. Jay paused to witness a sight so novel. Every face
was bright with anticipation, and their steps were eager
and elastic; but there was no vulgar hurry, no jostling,
but the utmost courtesy prevailed. On their approach,
these citizens, with a smile and graceful recognition,
stood aside with deferential courtesy, to make way for
their entrance into the vestibule of the temple. Here
new wonders awaited them. On the walls so vividly
were pictured scenes from the life of Christ, that it was
as if the forms before them were instinct with life, and
statues, too, looked down from their pedestals as if about
to open their marble lips.

On all sides of this vast temple were seats as in an
amphitheatre, which were already filled with an expec-
tant audience. At the entrance, Mrs. Jay and Peter
were met by Peter's angel, who led them to seats of eminence, already occupied by numbers of the Redeemed,
and of women "native here."

It was with breathless delight that Mrs. Jay and Peter
found themselves seated next their lost and gifted friend
and neighbor, Mr. Alexander Laurens, who had discovered them as they were being led up.

Rising, Mr. Laurens gave his seat to Mrs. Jay, and so
sat between Mrs. Jay and Peter, turning from one to
the other, exchanging glad congratulations at meeting
each other under such happy circumstances. He had a

hundred questions to ask of Peter, who, having left the world last, could best inform him of the welfare of his wife and children. While these hurried questions were put and answered, the choir and orchestra were entering and taking their several seats, filling up that portion of the temple which would be called on earth the altar or chancel. There stood the great organ, in all respects equal to the building, and beside all known instruments there were others whose forms were as new as the sounds they made.

Laurens whispered to Mrs. Jay and Peter, "that the oratorio which was about to be performed was the joint production of Handel, Haydn, Mozart and Beethoven; all of whom would aid in the performances. Music, and the Arts of Design," he said, " are the best of all vehicles for revealing to the minds of sinless beings the mystery of man's redemption. In *this* world, music is not regarded as a sign of the decline of a race, but rather as the nearest approach to the God-like that creatures can attain unto."

"Very unlike the world we have left," said Peter.

Laurens smiled and replied, "Our quartette parties will have given you but a faint idea of the music you are about to hear. On earth, eloquence of words is regarded as the highest attainment of man ; but here the glorious capacity of harmony to reach the soul is felt and acknowledged. Indeed, music is here in some sort a universal language. If the voice of Clay, of Calhoun, or of Webster, glowing with eloquence, could thrill the souls of a listening multitude, what must be the electric force of such a choir as you see collecting, aided by such performers, when, too, every note is pregnant with meaning, with which the choir, orchestra and auditors are alike inspired, as by the overshadowing of the omniscient Jehovah. And then the theme is worthy the galaxy of genius that has been tasked in the composition of this grand oratorio; for it is the story of the birth of Christ."

"Pray tell me, Laurens, how long *you* have been here?" asked Peter.

"After my arrival at the Holy City, and my presentation to my glorious Saviour, I sought for my infant boy, and was informed that he had been sent to the World of Art and Beauty to commence his studies. Now of all worlds, that devoted to the science of harmony was attractive to me; and so it was, that after a short stay in the Celestial City, I was brought here by my angel, and found my son, a beautiful spirit, whose loveliness of form and admirable skill and attainments filled me with delight. You see him now near that gentle featured man, whose sweet smile comes from a heart full of goodness—that is Mozart."

Both Peter and Mrs. Jay looked with eagerness to see the lovely son of their friend, and the gentle Mozart.

Handel, Haydn, Mozart and Beethoven now had taken their several stations, when the organist began playing the grand overture. As the overture proceeded the orchestra slid into the *Thema*, and gradually the intensity of high and holy thoughts conveyed by the soul-entrancing harmony, so thrilled the audience that they rose as by one impulse, when the choir burst into the opening anthem—"Holy, holy, holy art thou, Lord God Almighty: the earth is full of thy glory!" These words were reduplicated in multiform ways, and with every new modification, new impressions of the stupendous thoughts arose in the soul of every auditor, until it seemed beyond the power of even angelic natures to endure such harmony as this.

This anthem sunk away in far-off echoes, as if distant worlds had caught the flame of enthusiasm, and the rebound came back in murmurs, till all was hushed. Then the silence of night on the plains of Bethlehem was painted to the mind's eye through the ear. The bleating of the lambs, and the buzzing of the insects of a summer's night were distinctly heard, and the dull tinkling and pastoral voices of night were so closely imitated that the imagination was captivated by the soothing sounds.* Then a new movement showed the souls of the shepherds

* Weber says, he never saw a beautiful landscape that did not produce in his mind a train of corresponding musical associations.

" A universal sympathy, and the faculty of expressing it in forms as multifarious as the aspects of nature—remote ideas instinct with truth—the power of awakening in a phrase of melody a long train of dormant feelings, which seem before to have wanted their true expression—these are the qualities to account for the rarity of high musical genius ; and especially so when it becomes necessary to suppose them refined by a tedious education, and an experience in the details of art the most painfully minute "—Southgate's *Many Thoughts.*

full of lofty aspirations as they gazed upon the stars burning above them; and in recitatives they spoke to each other of the promises made in the holy oracles of God, of the Messiah that was to come. Then suddenly blazed forth the glory of God from out the dark heavens, and the words of the angel were sung—"Fear not: for, behold I bring you good tidings of great joy, which shall be to all people. For unto you is born this day in the city of David, a Saviour, which is Christ the Lord." Then came the glorious chorus—"Glory to God in the highest, and on earth peace, good will toward men."

Such were the familiar words which formed the themes of harmonies which thrilled this vast audience with emotions no words can express. Peter, forgetful of everything, turned to the lady who sat on his right, and exclaimed, "How unspeakably glorious!" She smiled as she bowed graciously and replied in a language unknown to him.

The assembly was a long time in dispersing. There were so many words to be spoken in admiration of the new oratorio, and of the glorious theme, that Mrs. Jay and Peter had time allowed them to look about them. They were charmed with the child-like innocency in the face of Mozart; as for Beethoven he had not yet descended from his open vision of the throne of God, and sat gazing upward as in a trance. Haydn with smiles received the congratulations of the choir gathering about him, while Handel, in a rapt state of soul, stood looking up to the frescoed roof, as if those angels ever bright and fair, floating in the heavens above, were answering back his beautiful appeal to take him to their arms.

It was hard to quit this glorious creation of genius. They wanted hours to satisfy their wish to look up at the dome, painted by native artists who had here labored to give color and expression to the cartoons of Michael Angelo. Laurens was impatient of delay, and wished them to tear themselves away, saying, "You can come to-morrow and see this to your heart's content." "To-morrow!" exclaimed Mrs. Jay. "No, there is none in this life, as there was none in the past. What we wish to see we must see as it passes before us ; for with infinity of worlds all around us full of wonders, we shall, perhaps, never return to this again."

"Oh yes! this world will probably be the school to which you will be sent to take your first lessons," replied Mr. Laurens.

"I shall be most happy if it be so," said Mrs. Jay ; "but as yet I have been allowed to go wherever I will to be. This large liberty of action is my delight now. It is so delightful to say—'I will,' and I am."

As they thus stood gazing up and around, Peter's next neighbor passed, and with a bow of recognition and a lovely smile, spoke to him a few words as she swept by with her party.

Peter touched Laurens' arm, and asked, "What did that lady say as she passed us?"

"It was the usual salutation of this people expressing their pleasure in meeting friends," replied Laurens.

"Tell me how do you get on here, where all tongues and dialects are new to you? Is it not very embarrassing?"

"It would be were it not that our English tongue is generally spoken in the higher circles. And you are doubtless conscious of the fact, that the Redeemed and angels are possessed of the power of intuition; so that in whatever language the idea is conveyed, it is represented to the mind of the listener in his mother tongue; and to your apprehension angels and the Redeemed all speak the English language."

"I never guessed they did not speak English, and the choicest of English, Laurens. How is it with you, Mrs. Jay?" asked Peter.

"The thought never presented itself before. As it was represented to my mind, so I supposed it was spoken; but now I see the goodness of God in thus constituting our minds for receiving and conveying ideas. Let me ask, do you speak the language of this world, Mr. Laurens?" asked Mrs. Jay.

"I have a command of all their familiar words, which combine the power of the language, as the Saxon does the English. They, however, amount to many thousand. You can have little idea of the opulence of their vocabulary, as well as of the grace and elegance of their thoughts. I am told there are famous worlds where every symbol signifies not a sound but great and mighty thoughts, forged from brains of beings who hold rank in those worlds, as Homer, Virgil, Dante, Shakspeare and Milton do with us. Their works are the classics of these distant and ancient worlds. But even here they surpass all our ideas of grace and eloquence of expression.* I met recently a Christian, from Athens, belonging to the first century; a man learned in all the wisdom of his age, and who was converted by the ministry of St. Paul himself. He has resided here for nearly a century, devoting himself to the acquisition of the language and literature of these people; and he tells me, that with all the enlarged powers of a redeemed soul, he has but begun to drink into the deep fountains of their literature. 'Nothing,' he says, 'had inspired him with such a sense of their angelic goodness as their condescension to the poverty of his ideas. But then they regard us as the sons of God, and as such, we are objects of their admiration and love. Our histories are more wonderful to them than was the story of Sinbad, the sailor, to us in our childhood. Only our tales are real, and

---

* In the German edition of the "Seeress of Prevorst," by Justinus Kerner, there is a specimen of the writing of the spirit-world into which Frederica Hauffe (known to the world as *Seherinn von Prevorst*) was admitted, and which she wrote while in her trance-state. This plate was shown by the late Rev. Dr. Eliakim Phelps to his son, while in one of his singular states of suffering, when he took the book and cried out with astonishment, "Who wrote these characters? They are the symbols of great thoughts—thoughts I have no words to express." His father asked him "if he could not give him some idea of these symbols?" After thinking, his son replied, "No; they transcend all our ideas."

they often ask questions as to our intentions and motives of action in our lives on earth, which lie beyond all our capacities to answer. We are, indeed, infants in comparison, but in their regard, we are, all of us, *Infantas* of the King of kings and Lord of lords."

They were now joined by Peter's angel and Godfrey, who accompanied them in their walk down the long aisles of this magnificent temple, and detained them, calling their attention to objects of interest worthy their special regard. On reaching the open air, Mr. Laurens asked leave of the angel to take his friend Peter home with him—a request which was cheerfully granted.

"He is at liberty to follow his intuitions here without any further guidance," said the angel.

After taking leave of Godfrey and the angel, with many thanks for the pleasure they had derived from attending this oratorio, Mrs. Jay and Peter, at the suggestion of Laurens, rose with him into the air, to a height whence they could look down upon the city and its inhabitants, as from some tall monument.

Laurens pointed out the many great public edifices encircling vast areas and gardens filled with fountains and works of art. "That massive structure is the Vatican of this Rome; but, unlike the Vatican of our Rome, there are no bars and bolts to be drawn to give the freest access to its spacious halls, and when these are opened, no envious lock is put upon the doors of the cases which contain the books collected in the Vatican for show, in this

Alexandrian library for all people. That noble building, to the right of the library, is the Academy of Art; the left wing, which extends five hundred yards, is devoted to the school of Sculpture, and the right wing to the school of Design. Students are supported at the public expense; for the citizens of this world regard painting and sculpture as the chief agencies of refinement and progress." *

* Dante thus speaks of sculpture and its uses in his Vision of Purgatory, Canto X. On being admitted to the gate of purgatory, Dante, accompanied by Virgil, ascended a winding path. On the side of the mountain was seen, in white marble, stories of humility, and whilst they were contemplating them, there approached the souls of those who expiate the sin of pride, and who are bent down beneath the weight of heavy stones. The bass-reliefs are thus described :

———" I discovered that the bank, around,
Whose proud uprising all ascent denied.
Was marble white ; and so exactly wrought
With quaintest sculpture, that not there alone
Had Polycletus, but e'en nature's self
Been sham'd. The angel (who came down to earth
With tidings of the peace. so many years
Wept for in vain, that op'd the heavenly gates
From their long interdict), before us seem'd,
In a sweet act, so sculptured to the life
He look'd no silent image. One had sworn
He had said ' Hail !' "—Line 38.

In Canto XII., Dante thus describes the wonderful Mosaics he saw in Purgatory while traversing the first cornice :

" What master of the pencil or the style
Had trac'd the shades and lines, that might have made
The subtlest workman wonder? Dead, the dead ;
The living seem'd alive : with clearer view,
His eye beheld not, who beheld the truth,
Than mine what I did tread on."—Line 62.

"What can that immense pile of building contain?" asked Peter, pointing to a quadrangular building that inclosed miles of area.

"That is their museum of ancient art and history. You will find it extremely interesting to study the growth of art from the earliest age to the present."

"I think I shall like to make my home here," said Mrs. Jay, "so soon as I have done with our earth."

"Do you expect to survive your sympathies at an early day?" asked Laurens. "I have seen those who lived centuries since as deeply concerned in the affairs of our world as we are who have left our loved ones behind us."

The city, and its wide suburbs having been fully scanned, Laurens proposed they should hasten their flight, and with the swiftness of angels they swept over plains and mountains until they came to the happy valley of the Redeemed. This lay within an amphitheatre of mountains whose peaks pierced the clouds. The palace with its wide-spread wings and many pillared porticoes, stood in the centre of a paradise filled with wildernesses of shade and sunshine. Sculptured fountains threw up high into the air vast plumes of crystal waters, flashing brightness all around. Groups of statuary filled the walks with beauty. Some stood on pedestals so low and with such life-like action as to arrest the eye and inspire the doubt whether they were works of art. But if all stood instinct with life, it was a life of love and beauty. No Laocoon and his sons writhing in agony—no dying gladiator, with eyes swimming in death, was to be seen, recalling the miseries of a fallen world. Nothing of all this, but all that art, and skill and labor could create was here, combining to make this one of the "many mansions" prepared by the Saviour for the home of his disciples. Nor was this all; in the distance was seen a lake of many miles upon whose surface lay islands of differing area, covered with classic temples filled with statuary. Laurens told his friends, it was accounted a glorious achievement for a native artist to make a group worthy of a place in this home of the Redeemed.

These beautiful grounds were filled with guests—some threading the shaded walks, some sailing on the lake, others gathered in sweet converse beneath trees of transcendental beauty. Music from far-off choirs, who were seated in the arbors and on the turf, mingled sweetly with the melodies of birds.

Alighting in the gardens of the palace, the attention of our friends was attracted by a singular trial of skill between a beautiful creature, "native here," and a mocking-bird which sat on the highest branch of a lofty tree. The bird would trill and rise with a transition of lightning speed, and then, as in circles, come back to the note from which it started. The young girl would repeat every trill, rise to the same note, and with like circling melody return to the point of departure. Then again the bird would strive with new and more difficult notes to surpass all competition; and as the contest went on, flights of singing birds gathered in the branches; and when the bird could go no higher, it rose on its wings and flew away. Then as with one consent all the birds burst forth into joyous song, filling the air with heaven-inspired harmonies.

Mrs. Jay and Peter were delighted. They approached the young girl, and in the choicest phrase they could command, told her of their admiration of her powers. Mrs. Jay said, "she had been charmed by the beauty of her notes. On earth she had had the pleasure of listening to the notes of Malibran and Jenny Lind; but their notes were not to be compared with hers." And Peter, not to be outdone by Mrs. Jay, assured the girl that "there were thousands on earth who would be glad to exchange their golden eagles for her winged notes, which had this advan tage that *they* would '*pass current*' everywhere; defying, as they did, both competition and counterfeit."

The girl looked up, reading their meaning in their eyes and the tones of their voices, while Laurens stood listening with an amused air at the elaborate compliments of his friends, Peter's especially. When they had finished, the girl made a graceful courtesy and ran toward her friends who were awaiting her return; to please whom this trial of skill with the mocking-bird had been attempted.

"Those were very pretty compliments," said Laurens, "and it is to be regretted that that sweet creature did not understand a word you said."

"Pray tell me," said Peter, "is there no universal language understood by beings of all worlds?"

"I know of none," replied Laurens, "unless it be musical sounds.* That sweet girl, though she did not understand the precise thoughts expressed by Mrs. Jay and yourself, yet guessed your meaning in your tones—the intuitive sympathy which pervades sinless beings of all worlds."

"My previous conceptions are so unlike what I find to be real," said Peter; "and yet in many things there is a delightful realization of my day-dreams on earth. But this learning various languages in various worlds is all new to me. I had supposed we would have been born into the knowledge of language just as Adam was. By the by—have you met with Adam and Eve, and where are they to be seen?"

* Mendelssohn, on his return from Scotland, was asked by his sisters to tell them something of the Hebrides. "That cannot be told," said he, "it can only be *played*," and seating himself at the piano, he improvised the beautiful theme which he afterward expanded into the "Overture to Fingal's Cave."—*Quarterly Review.*

"The art of music, whose power has been acknowledged by the most powerful thinkers of all ages, is of later growth than her sisters—poetry, sculpture and painting; and its means of communicating ideas are also less positive and direct; but the principles which govern its manifestations are strictly analogous, and we cognize in its very vagueness that yearning after the infinite, that feeling of ineffable loveliness, which, by the electrical rapidity of its action upon the mind, the slow deductions of reason and all powers of analysis, approaches the divine in its bright mystery and inexplicable influence upon our sentiments and emotions."

Sir J F. W. Herschell says (Discourse on the study of Natural Philosophy, p. 186), "the sense of harmony is perhaps the only instance of a sensation for whose pleasing impression a distinct and intelligible reason can be assigned."

"No, I have not," replied Laurens; "indeed, I have met with no one of the celebrities of the Holy Scriptures. I have inquired very diligently after the apostle Paul, whom, of all redeemed men, I have longed most to see; for Paul has ever been regarded by me as my ideal of a Christian, and a man.* I want to ask him about those questions 'hard to be understood' by St. Peter himself."

"And do you think" asked Mrs. Jay, "that St. Paul can succeed any better in heaven than on earth, in doing away with all difficulties in religion?"

"Perhaps not," said Mr. Laurens, "but I would like to hear him pour out his eloquence, discoursing to the beings of other worlds of the love of God in Christ. As for the paradoxes and enigmas of human life, they remain to my mind now what they ever were, inexplicable. Paul, in his Epistle to the Romans, fairly stated the question of questions when he made his interlocutor Jew say, "Why doth God find fault? for who hath resisted his will?" to which Paul had no other reply to make than this, "Nay, but, O man, who art thou that repliest against God? Shall the thing formed say to him that formed it, 'Why hast thou made me thus?' Is there unrighteousness with God? God forbid!"† And why did he end thus, but

* Archbishop Whately, "Future State," p. 215, says, "The highest enjoyment of the blessed will be the personal knowledge of their great and beloved Master; yet I cannot but think that some part of their happiness will consist in an intimate knowledge of the greatest of his followers also; and of those in particular, whose peculiar qualities are, to each, most particularly attractive."

† Rom. ix., 20.

because that was, for earth certainly, and it may be in heaven too, the end of the discussion. In time, this great stone of stumbling and rock of offence, was the test of docility of the soul. If the proud heart of man would not submit itself to God, and to such evidence of his attributes as were made manifest in his works, his ways, and his word, he perished of necessity."

"Necessity!" exclaimed Mrs. Jay—"there's another of those mystic words which on earth have made my head ache with thinking."

"And would forever," replied Laurens, "if you could again entertain those rebellious thoughts which gave rise to all such speculations. The answer here is, as there, 'Shall not the judge of all the earth do right?' When I say I long to see Paul, it is to listen to his glowing eloquence as he discourses of the height, and depth, and length and breadth of the love of God in Christ Jesus—which passeth knowledge. That was his theme in time, and it is that which burns and brightens and hallows in his great and glorious soul; and he is now, in far-off worlds, making known to principalities and powers in heavenly places, the mystery of the manifold wisdom and love of God in the redemption of the world; mysteries angels have desired and still desire to look into; hid in the ages that are past and now revealed *in us* and *by us* to unknown realms. Everywhere, as here, humanity is the most glorious mystery of God's greatness and goodness. We are not so beautiful nor so gifted as those around us; we have little of their grace of movement, little of that surpassing intelligence beaming in their lustrous eyes, and finding expression in voices ever changing in melody, and in forms of speech inexpressibly sweet. But they recognize us to be sons of God, by the robes of light we wear, by the halo which burns upon our foreheads, and by powers put forth by us which fill them with wondering admiration."

"I am sure there exists a universal language, though you may never have heard of it," said Peter. "And how convenient it would have been had I known it this morning, when I addressed my next neighbor."

Laurens, smiling, replied, "It is not God's way of working. We are not *born* to the knowledge of anything, and Adam and Eve probably had no vocabulary taught to them beyond their immediate wants. You must not mistake Milton's epic for Bible truth. I am sure it will be our happiness to be forever pupils in the schools of creation, providence and grace."

"It may be so," said Peter, with some reluctance, "but I had my own notions of these matters from my earliest days, and always believed when I reached heaven I should be endowed with all knowledge by intuition, and that I should speak all languages and understand all science and art—in a word, that I should know all things comprehensible to a finite being. But here I am, a child new-born, with powers unknown, and with demands upon my time which will absorb eternity itself. I am astounded at the outset, in view of such multitudinous objects which demand my attention."

"Ah, wait, and you will become teachable," said Laurens. "When we find ourselves free from earth, like birds let loose in eastern skies, we rise high into the air, and wheel round and round in vast circles, as if in doubt as to our pathway; but we are soon satisfied with our large liberty, and are sweetly led to trace that luminous path of progress towards the Infinite which our Saviour selects for us. It seems to me of all worlds my lot is cast in the one I love best; but so every one says."

"Mr. Laurens," asked Mrs. Jay, "will you please tell me what difference exists in your perceptions in this life, as contrasted with the past? Let us hear what you have to say, for you always loved metaphysical investigations, and I want to compare notes."

"I do not see any difference in kind," replied Mr. Laurens. "In the world, we lived with God all about us, without the consciousness of his omnipresence; as, while we saw objects in the light of the sun, for days it may have been, we never once looked up at the sun. But here all is changed; with every new development of science the Infinite is present to us, and in every new manifestation of loveliness, in art or nature, we see the Author of Beauty. In those lovely forms," pointing to a group of statuary, "we see the attempt of the artist to realize an ideal existing in God. And thus it is we live in the conscious presence of our Creator, Redeemer, and Sanctifier—Father, Son, and Holy Ghost—one God!" and so saying, Laurens folded his hands over his bosom, and bowed his head.

Recovering himself from his high rapture, Laurens led his friends to a beautiful marble pavilion, and while ascending the steps, they discovered a lady engaged in reading. She rose with graceful dignity, and with a smile of courtesy welcomed their coming.

Laurens leading the way introduced Mrs. Jay and Peter to this splendid woman as St. Perpetua.

Mrs. Jay looked her surprise at hearing such a title conferred in a world where all are alike saints; and after they had taken seats on a sofa together, she said to the lady: "It is the first time I have heard this title conferred upon any one since leaving our world."

St. Perpetua, with a smile, replied, " I was an inhabitant of heaven for three centuries before I ever dreamed of having any peculiar claims to this title, which is here used only because it has become historical on earth. I perceive you are no Romanist?"

" No, indeed, madam. I am most Protestant, and a member of the Anglo-Saxon, American Protestant Episcopal Church."

"Do you claim to be still a communicant of Trinity?" asked Peter.

"I claim to be a member of Trinity Church still,"

said Mrs. Jay in tones of voice a little brusque. "I do not lose my fellowship with saints on earth by becoming a saint in heaven. What says St. Perpetua?"

This lady at once assured Mrs. Jay of her entire concurrence with her views, though she never had the matter presented to her mind in just these terms.

"May I inquire, St. Perpetua," asked Mrs. Jay, "why you said I was no Romanist?"

"With pleasure," she replied, "for had you been familiar with the Romish calendar, you would have seen my name set against the seventh of March, and in any edition of the 'Lives of Saints,' you would have read some account of my martyrdom under Emperor Severus."

"Will you not, in pity of my ignorance," said Mrs. Jay, "tell me by what sufferings you reached this crown of glory, to be a Roman saint?"

"Do you not prefer the epithet, this 'bad eminence?'" asked Perpetua, smiling.

"O no," replied Mrs. Jay; "it may be that the Romish church have canonized bad men, but I have always believed such must have been but exceptions, and that piety—eminent piety, has worn this crown of glory in all ages."

"To-morrow," said St. Perpetua, "I will with pleasure tell you of my early history. Now the hour has come for our vesper songs. Let us go to the temple. See! the Redeemed are all in motion."

They rose, and Perpetua taking the arm of Mrs. Jay led the way. From every direction, from the palace and garden walks thronged a multitude of persons all tending with elastic steps towards their place of worship.

Perpetua led them by a mazy walk through deep shades, out of which they emerged in front of a pile whose magnificence exceeded all their powers of imagination. It was another Milan cathedral, whose niches were filled with statuary and whose façade was covered over with frost-work of the chisel. Its high spire and many minarets flamed with polished gold; and grand and sublime as was the new St. Peter's of Michael Angelo, this far surpassed it in splendor. Perpetua enjoyed the surprise of our friends; and allowing them ample time to make all their exclamations of delight, she aided them to a glimpse of the arcana of architecture to awaken sentiments of sublimity. This occupied some little time; for both Mrs. Jay and Peter were slow to realize the relations of form and color and ornament in a great edifice to fill the soul with a sense of grandeur. As yet they were beginners in the science of beauty and art.

"Let us go on," said Perpetua. "At some future period I will help you to an idea of the laws of relation which make every line, curve, window, moulding, niche, ornament, statue and minaret, up to the lofty spire, symbolic and necessary to completeness; that this temple may meet the soul's aspirations after the sublime.

These laws were felt and sought after by the architects of Greece and Italy, and builders of later days. The structures you see on this globe have in some measure succeeded; but what perfection is, we do not know and never can attain unto."

When they entered the spacious vestibule, and thence into the temple, they were tempted to pause at every step to gaze with wondering admiration on every side. The ceiling was upheld by pillars of marble, veined with glittering ores. These were spiral and covered with sculptured vines, and flowers and fruits—resembling nature in her most perfect forms. Nor was this all; the roof hung down with the lightness of a grove of majestic elms, and the rays of the setting sun poured down upon the multitude already assembled like stealthy rays through rich foliage. To Mrs. Jay the interior looked like a magnificent arbor of tall trees, stems, fruits and flowers, green and golden, rather than a work of labor and art.

The choir, as it would be called on earth, occupied the altar and transepts. The organ with its pipes rose like a wall of gold; and the orchestra and singers were more numerous than at the Metropolitan Temple. Handel, Haydn, Mozart and Beethoven were already in their places, and crowds thronged in through the many entrances and swept onward to their appointed places.

No sooner had Perpetua seated her companions, and

was giving Peter and Mrs. Jay some explanations of the scene before them, than a beautiful boy and girl came threading their way up the aisles to where they sat, and delivered a message from St. Cecilia to Laurens, inviting him to play her violoncello. This high distinction, Laurens, with his wonted modesty declined; but St. Perpetua laid her commands on him, speaking as one who had a right to decide for him his course of action, and with a pleased reluctance he was led by these graceful messengers, each one holding him by the hand, to the orchestra. As he ascended the steps, he was met by the beautiful saint, whose fame for music has filled the world. She was a being of dazzling beauty.* With a smile of inexpressible sweetness, she took Laurens' hand, and led him to his seat, when she presented him her violoncello. This done, she at once ascended the

---

* St. Cecilia has been the admiration of the world for her beauty. That old Protestant, Fox, in his Martyrology (book 1., A.D., 222) says of St. Cecilia, that having converted her husband, Valerien, and her brother, Tiburtius, to the faith of Christ, she was apprehended and brought to the idols to sacrifice, and refusing, was condemned to death. "In the meantime," says Fox, following the legends of the Roman church, "the sergeants and officers about her beholding her comely beauty, began with many persuasive words to solicit her to favor herself, and such excellent beauty, and not to cast herself away. But she replied to them with such reasons and godly exhortations, that, by the grace of Almighty God, their hearts began to kindle, and at length to yield to that religion which before they persecuted." She converted upwards of four hundred persons, and among them a noble named Gordian, before her martyrdom by the axe."

The tale of St. Cecilia is closely copied by Chaucer, in "The Second Nonne's Tale," from the golden legend of Jacob Jannensis. She was also the theme of St. Aldhelm's panegyric in his poem in praise of Virginity.

pedestal assigned her as the Corypheus of the choir. The overture was overpowering to both Peter and Mrs. Jay. They sat in breathless astonishment as they listened. Then came recitations celebrating the glory of Christ, not less eloquent in the thought than its expression, both alike perfect in the rendering. Of the themes sung, Perpetua kindly acted as the interpreter to her new-found friends.

There sat Laurens, his ear fondly inclined to his violoncello, listening with a pleased air to the sounds it gave forth at the sweep of his bow. It was nearly two hours, and it may have been more, the vesper service lasted, and yet no sign of weariness or exhaustion was shown by the choir or orchestra; for indeed none was felt, but rather a fresh inspiration of strength from on high. And when the whole audience rose in singing the Hymn to the Trinity, the divine presence was made manifest by a halo of light which filled the temple with ineffable glory.

Time was no more. The entire audience of saints and servitors rose and sang "Gloria in Excelsis." This ended, the Redeemed, unaided and alone,* sang their song, forever new—"Unto Him that hath loved us and washed us from our sins in his own blood, and hath made us kings and priests unto God and His Father; to him be glory and dominion forever and ever. Amen."

On leaving the temple, to their surprise, Perpetua and

* Revelations, xiv. 3.

our friends found it was night. The heavens were lit up with stars and moons. Filled with awe and love at what they had just witnessed, they went to the palace. Perpetua, having first commended Mrs. Jay and Peter to the hospitalities of the mayor of the palace, who received them with great consideration, left them for the night. They were shown into a spacious hall splendidly lighted, where they sat down conversing with Laurens on all they had seen during the day, till servitors of both sexes came to show them to their several apartments. Thus ended with our friends their first day spent in the delightful circles of this new world.

CHAPTER IV.

St. Perpetua sends Persis to Mrs. Jay with a Message—Their Conversation—The Idea of Married Life entertained by Persis—Her Admiration of Mrs. Jay—Scenes on Silver Lake—Mrs. Jay joins Perpetua, who relates the Story of her Martyrdom at Carthage—Of her appearance before Hilarion—Scene in the Amphitheatre—Her Companions in Martyrdom—Of the Fathers of the Church—The Similarity of Pagan and Papal Religions in Social Life—St. Perpetua and Mrs. Jay are joined by Faustinus and Calliste, just returned after an Absence of fourteen Centuries—Their Colloquy with Mrs. Jay—Their Surprise at hearing of the Discovery of a "New World"—Mrs. Jay describes her meeting Satan, the "Architect of Ruin"—Faustinus's Account of the New World whence he has returned—Public Opinion in Rome, A.D. 330—Roman Society of the Fourth Century—Calliste tells the Story of her Conversion; her Interviews with St. Paul, of her Trials and Martyrdom.

THE next day, Mrs. Jay, as she was walking through a long gallery of paintings, was waited upon by a young native girl, with a message from St. Perpetua, to bring Mrs. Jay to an island, which was a favorite haunt of hers, in Silver Lake.

As she walked with the sweet girl through the garden, Mrs. Jay inquired of her her name and duties in the palace. The girl replied, "My name is Persis, which name St. Perpetua gave me while an infant. I have grown up under her care, and she has taught me your tongue, that it might be useful to such of our visitants as come from England and America."

"What is your age, Persis?"

"I am almost eighteen, and then I shall be marriageable."

This was said with a joyousness which spoke more of earth than anything Mrs. Jay had heard for a long time.

"Is it possible that your happiness can be enhanced by being married?" cried Mrs. Jay, with much astonishment. "I thought," she continued, "angels neither marry nor are given in marriage."

"O yes, angels; but I am so glad I'm not an angel; for I cannot conceive how any one can but be happier for loving and being loved," said the girl with earnestness.

"It may be so in this world," replied Mrs. Jay; "but in my world the wider the target of our bosoms, the more sure are the shafts of death to pierce the heart."

"What a world that must be!" said Persis, with a look of painful surprise. "All such ideas are so terrible to me, if indeed I do rightly appreciate the thoughts expressed. No skill of mine can reach the profundities opened to my mind while I listen to what is told of your world; only this, that by some surpassing manifestation of the mercy of God, outcasts from holiness and heaven have become by adoption, 'one with God, as Christ and God are one!'" And Persis's look, as she fixedly gazed upon the face of Mrs. Jay and its halo, and thence at her iridescent robes which fell in graceful and ample folds at her feet, showed the intensity of her awe and admiration of beings so mysteriously endowed by the great Creator.

On reaching the shore of the lake, Persis pointed out to Mrs. Jay the island, and asked her to take a seat in a little skiff which she unfastened from a rock, to which it had been held by a golden chain.

"It is unnecessary, Persis; I can will myself across the water," said Mrs. Jay.

"Yes, but I shall be pleased to accompany you, and I want to sit and listen to your conversation with my lovely lady. Then, too, you will lose the pleasure only to be enjoyed by sailing over our blue and beautiful lake. You see others, who could as readily as yourself reach their places of destination by a volition, rowing their skiffs, or who, by raising silken sails, are wafted across the surface of the water. Will you permit me to row you over?"

"Oh, certainly," said Mrs. Jay; and Persis ferried her over in her skiff; her every motion was the perfection of grace, and Mrs. Jay was pleased to think she had not lost the pleasure of witnessing such beauty. The island lay a mile distant, and as they glided over the rippling surface, skiffs of various forms, all alike beautiful in shape, and managed with equal skill by others as young and graceful as Persis, passed rapidly by them, piloted to one of the many green gems of the lake; some freighted with many, some with few of the Redeemed, who, thus surrounded by the loveliest of His works, were keeping a new holiday with God.

As they neared the island, which was almost covered by a temple of purest marble, they discovered Perpetua seated with a golden lyre, which gave forth sweet chords as her fingers swept over the strings, soft as if waked to life by whispering zephyrs. As they ascended the marble steps, Mrs. Jay saw that Perpetua was rapt in far-off visions; and her face, always full of sweetness and majesty, was now angelic. The strain ended, and resting the lyre on her lap, she covered her face with her hands, and sat for a while silent.

Persis spoke, and Perpetua, rousing herself, received Mrs. Jay with a graceful smile. "I have been indulging myself with lofty and far-reaching thoughts of the love of God in the redemption of the world. 'O the heights and the depths of the riches both of the wisdom and knowledge of God! how unsearchable are his judgments, and his ways past finding out!'" *

This said, Perpetua took a seat beside Mrs. Jay, while Persis placed herself at the feet of her mistress. After calling the attention of her guest to a fragrant flower which twined about the pillar near her, Perpetua

* Romans, xi. 33.

explained its structure, and spoke of the botany in the world around them in contrast with the world they had once inhabited.

"And now, my dear lady, you may ask me any questions you please. What shall I tell you of myself?" said Perpetua.

"Tell me, my kind friend, the story of your life, or if that be tasking you too far, of your martyrdom. When a child I was delighted to read in a black letter folio edition of Fox's Book of Martyrs, of those who witnessed a good confession and won the crowns of martyrdom and immortality; and now you are the first of all that noble army that I have met with since I was born into eternal life."

With loving courtesy, Perpetua, taking the hand of Mrs. Jay, which she held in both of hers, began. "I suffered at Carthage, with others, in the year of Christ 205.* My martyrdom was the more notable because I belonged to the nobility of that city, where I lived a young and happy wife and mother, surrounded with the luxuries of that age, beloved by my husband and idolized by my father. There had arisen in the minds of the people of the great centres of the empire, a feeling of bitter hatred to the sect called Christians; which was the necessary antagonism of irreconcilable religions. This had been overlooked at first, for the emperors and people of Rome were not hostile to religionists, ' setters

---

* So says Baronius in his Annals, book II. Others say, A.D. 210.

4 *

forth of strange gods;' but Christianity knew nothing of compromise, and it gradually became a question *which* should live. While Christian teachers claimed a religion from God, Roman philosophers believed they had a purer code of ethics in their divine philosophy. Then, too, the vulgar mind was full of prejudices, inspired by vile stories of the Christian mysteries; because they sought, from necessity, to worship Christ in the vaults of catacombs and caverns of nature, where they held their love feasts, and partook of the Communion of the Lord's Supper. Nor were these prejudices lessened by confident prophecies made by mad zealots that the world was soon to be burned up; and too, the eloquence of great men had created in the minds of Christians an indifference to life and its pursuits: for as the world was soon to be consumed, there was no worth in wealth, and by the ardent and ill-advised, the crown of martyrdom was sought for as the highest honor, inasmuch as all who suffered entered into the paradise of God and were crowned with glory."

"How were you brought to the knowledge of Christ?" asked Mrs. Jay. "What great Christian father had for his crown of rejoicing your enlightenment?"

"It was no great orator of the church who brought to me the knowledge of the gospel of the Son of God, but a lovely boy whom my husband brought home to me from the slave-market as a gift. He was about fifteen years of age, and his face beamed with gentle-

ness and goodness. He took his place with other of
my servitors, and these were many. He was most
happy to be near me, and devoid of the artifices of other
of my pages, was diligent, dutiful and exact in every
duty. He sought for no indulgences from me; and
when not waiting upon me, or discharging some duty,
was always to be found in the apartment assigned to
him. His beautiful countenance shone with that seren-
ity of soul, that I loved to gaze upon. Nor was I alone
in this, for Claudius, my husband, felt this silent attraction of the beauty of my boy Julius. One day, sitting
alone together, we asked him of his parentage and
education, and were told he had been born a slave
and was brought up in the family of his master as
the companion of his only son. The master and son
had both suffered as Christians, and he had been brought
to the forum to be sold by their relatives. This was
all he had to say at that time; and it was of little interest
to us, except that he had been once owned by one of
the sect of Christians. Claudius was attracted by this
fact, and made many inquiries as to Christ and his
disciples, and the philosophy which made Julius so
serenely happy—for so we called it. Julius was glad
to tell us all he knew. It was wonderful how well he
could repeat the Gospels and the Epistles. He never
owned a copy, but had committed to memory most of
the Gospels of Luke and John, and portions of the
Epistles of Paul. We were both interested in his

recitations for their singular beauty and precision. Then Claudius began to talk of this religion, and was led by Julius to attend the midnight meetings. He then procured a copy of the Gospel of John and Paul's Epistle to the Romans, which he read daily to me. In a word, my dear lady, we unawares became converts to the Christian faith.

"Our conversion was soon known; for such were the demands made by Roman rites, that when these ceased to be conformed to, it was at once known to our household and all who shared our hospitalities, that we had become Christians. Every kind entreaty was made by our relatives and friends to save us from being denounced to the magistracy. It was told us we should be forced to recant. Claudius lost no time to manumit Julius, and to send him, under conduct of one of our friends going into Greece, to Athens, where he was born. We made every possible preparation for whatever should betide us, in the disposition of our property and our slaves. This done, we awaited the action of Hilarion, then Pro-Consul of Carthage, hoping if we were to suffer the ordeal of the Amphitheatre we should stand together. Hilarion did not think I could endure this furnace of affliction alone. He had shared the hospitalities of our palace, and had ever expressed a warm friendship for us both.

"My first trial was being torn from my husband, and taken with my infant son to prison. There were five of us led through the narrow streets on foot, followed by a rabble. A young disciple, named Satur, joined us, ambitious of sharing our fate. Such heroism was not unfrequent in those days. *

" When I had reached the vaulted prison in which we were to be confined, and seated on a block of stone, surrounded with dirt, was nursing my boy, my venerable father came to visit me, and in an agony of tears besought me to have pity on his grey hairs. He kissed my hands, praying me to have compassion on my infant boy, who must die if deserted by me; to pity my husband; and falling on his knees, weeping, called me no longer his daughter, but the mistress of his fate. Oh, it was sad, very sad; but I had the joy of knowing that, except my dear father, my husband and all I loved best, rejoiced in my confession of Christ."

Perpetua ceased. "And is that all? Pray go on," said Mrs. Jay, earnestly.

"Do not let me weary you," said Perpetua. "The days following my arrest were days of intense anguish; for I was a daughter, a wife, and a young mother, accustomed to all the luxury of a most luxurious age. But I endured all the miseries of my prison without flinching. Then my child was taken from me, and I was brought

* In the persecution which commenced in the tenth year of Severus (A.D. 202), Leonidas, the father of ORIGEN was beheaded. Origen, then a boy, was very anxious to share with his father the glory of martyrdom, and his desire was frustrated by his mother, who hid away all his clothes and so prevented him from leaving home.—*Smith's Dictionary, Article, "Origen."*

before the governor in open court, surrounded by a vast
crowd. My imprisonment had become a matter for the
wonder of Carthage, and my martyrdom was to be to
all ·classes a holiday. It was, therefore, a question of
interest whether I would confess or recant. My poor
father brought to me my infant, as I stood on the
scaffold before this immense concourse, and besought me
to have pity on my son. I kissed my child, who was
held up in his hands, but I would not come down. Seeing this, my father caught hold of my dress, and strove
to pull me from the scaffold. Hilarion at once cried
out to the guards to beat back my father, which they
did; and every blow he received upon his head fell upon
my heart. In this hour of intense agony Christ was
near me. I knew that my martyrdom was a necessity
in Carthage, for the success of the religion of God and
my Saviour; and that it was mine, not only to suffer,
but dying to uphold the fainting faith of those in like
condemnation. The day following was the festival day
of the birth of the emperor, and it was to be made joyous to the multitude by my martyrdom. My companions were Felicitas, a young wife and mother like myself,
and a nameless slave; so as to heighten the contrasts,
and make the spectacle the more remarkable. With
every possible indignity we were led from the prison to
the Amphitheatre.

"This vast edifice was crowded with people; bench
above bench, to the flat where the multitude stood, and

had stood for hours, while many who occupied the benches had been there all night, so eager were they to witness the spectacle. For, my dear lady, I may here tell you without vanity, that I was known not only for the gifts of rank and wealth, but what attracted this crowd more than all, was the fame of my beauty; and Felicitas, too, my female companion, was not without her attractions, and had become a mother since her imprisonment. When led into the centre of the circle, we stood awhile, to satisfy the gaze of the audience. This done, we were seized by the gladiators and stripped naked. Our shrieks at this indignity thrilled the breasts of the multitude, and while we were being placed under nets, preparatory to our exposure to wild beasts, their cries rose to such a pitch of fury, that the gladiators withdrew the nets and threw us back our garments loose, to cover us. This done, a cow, made wild, was let into the arena, and attacked us, wounding and maiming, but not killing us. The audience, weary of this torture, demanded the termination of our lives. One of the gladiators came forward and drove his sword into my ribs. In my agony, I offered him my throat, and he gave me a blow which set my soul free. The story of my martyrdom has been told with many variations by Beda, Usardus and others. I have told it to you without any of their ornaments." *

* The story of the martyrdom of Perpetua has been related with no other

"And now I want you to tell me, Perpetua, if your death was necessary? The pro-consul was a personal friend of yourself and family; and was it necessary you should inflict such misery upon your father and your husband, and then, too, to desert that infant boy? Could it be that all this was demanded of you?" asked Mrs. Jay, with a shuddering emotion. "My dear Perpetua, I have the impression that those 'old men eloquent' of the early church, inspired Christians with a mad zeal for martyrdom; and that Roman magistrates were taunted to become their murderers."

"I have never doubted that my pouring forth was a duty I owed to my Saviour," replied Perpetua, with great solemnity. "He died on the cross for me, and had a right to claim my martyrdom in the Amphitheatre at Carthage."—This said, Perpetua assumed her usual sweet and lovely air and manner, adding, "The early fathers doubtless erred in many things, and their eloquence did produce the effects you have named; but, madam, what age is free from error? Not your age, certainly, and how much less mine. And I must say in its defence, I have never seen an age like that which produced Athanasius, Basil, Gregory, Ambrose, Chrysostom and Jerome; men whose ardor led them to reach after impracticable virtues, and to regard marriage itself, in the language of St. Gregory of Nyssa, himself

change, than the incident of her clothes being given back, which, though not true of *her*, is a fact in Martyrology.

a married man, as 'the prologue to all the tragedies of life.' " *

"There are hundreds of thousands upon earth at this very moment, Perpetua, both men and women, who hold the same opinion as St. Basil, though I never before knew it had been upheld by such eminent authority. What is your opinion, *now*, St. Perpetua?" asked Mrs Jay.

"In life," answered Perpetua, with a look of love, raised up to heaven, "I was a happy wife and mother, and the happier in heaven for the loves of earth. My love reaches to the remotest links of the chain of existence derived from me; they are all mine, and as truly

* St. Gregory, of Nyssa (A.D. 372), was a younger brother of St. Basil. He deplores the condition of married life with great force and eloquence in his writings, while he delineates with a brilliant pencil the delights of virginity. In his exegesis of Genesis, chap. iv., he says: "Since marriage was the last step which separated us from Paradise, I would advise those who are ambitious of returning thither, to begin by relinquishing marriage, the last stage, as it were, in the road between earth and heaven." The age of St. Basil and the Gregorys was eminent for its talents rather than for its piety. We read in writers of the Oxford school much in praise of the church in the fourth century. Milner in his Church History says, the character of the church at the close of the third century resembled the Episcopal Church of England during the reigns of Charles II. to George II. (vol. i. p. 464). It is certain that a deep declension from Christian purity had taken place. This is abundantly shown in the Epistles of Cyprian, who describes a state of morals, and tests of character, which cannot in these days of refinement be so much as alluded to. The licentiousness of confessors, men who did not die, gave the bishops great trouble. The lapsed were numerous, and on the approach of persecution, Cyprian says, "Many ran and sacrificed to the gods, and the crowds of apostates was so great that the magistrates wished to delay numbers till the next day, but they were importuned by their wretched suppliants to be allowed to prove themselves heathen that very night."—*Ep. of Cyprian*, 31.

embraced by me as when my boy-babe lay in my lap, the sole fond object of a mother's love. Our circle of sympathy and love widens like ripples on a glassy lake, and the outmost wave is as truly of that circle as is its very centre."

"That is a new thought to me," said Mrs. Jay, "and it oppresses me. I cannot conceive of it. I do not want such a wide circle of loves; but I, too, may share in like joy when I have lived to see a grandchild. How odd it seems to me now! The fact of the case with me is this: I was so glad to get away from my body and the world about me, that the moment I was free, at a single bound, I found myself threading with my angel, the nebulæ in the belt of Orion, on my way to the Celestial City, and have never been back to earth since; nor have I met with any one, till I was joined by my friend, Peter, from whom I could make a single inquiry after my husband and only child, Augusta."

"That surprises me, Mrs. Jay," replied Perpetua, "for I spend some portion of every century in revisiting the homes of my children. My boy grew to manhood, and was sent to Britain with the cohort he commanded. There he remained, and had children, and died, and of those children there are now living representatives in every clime; not one of whom is unknown to me. My Claudius is now in India with one of our boys, who is engaged in civil war with the Sepoys before Delhi."

"Will you tell me, St. Perpetua, if the condition of society in Carthage in your lifetime was like to that of Rome, as described by St. Paul in the opening chapter of his Epistle to the Romans; if so, from what a maelstrom of depravity you escaped!"

"It was indeed a vortex of splendid vice; and it is to illustrate the wonderful goodness of God to me, that I love to dwell upon my early life in Rome and my married life in Carthage. You are, doubtless, familiar with the adroitness and cunning of the priesthood of the papal church in taking charge of a child so soon as he comes into the world and sealing him with the cross of baptism; and next with childhood comes confirmation, and before marriage the first confession and communion; and so on, step by step in life's progress, the priesthood have their hand upon the man from the cradle to the grave, nor leave him there; for the future of his soul ceases not to be a fountain of wealth to the coffers of the church. You know as a Protestant something of this. You may have seen others thus crushed by the Church of Rome, though happily you have been exempt from such spiritual despotism."

"Yes indeed, Perpetua," replied Mrs. Jay with flashing eyes, as she recalled the memory of the past. "I have had in my service poor Irish women whose hard earnings have been absorbed, anticipated even, to pay their priests for their prayers for the dead as well as their sacraments for the living. How strange it is, that these men should be venerated, instead of being execrated; who say they can release lost souls from the miseries of purgatory by their prayers, but will not do it unless they are paid for it. What would be said of a man in a life-boat who should refuse to rescue a child drowning, until he was paid for doing so? He would be called a monster indeed; and yet Roman priests of the present day live without offering up a single prayer for a lost soul, unless they have the price paid in hand."

"Yes, I am aware of it. I have witnessed the rise of the papacy from its beginnings, though its seeds were sown in the days of Paul. I saw the ripening of the germs to their full fruit, and it is one of the subjects of my inquiries, in every visit I make to earth, to see its latest developments. My motive in alluding to this wonderful net-work wrought out by the papal priesthood was to illustrate to you the like meshes of superstition woven by the religion of Pagan Rome about a Roman child; and to show you how hard it was, in my time, for a mother, or a maiden, to become a Christian."

As Perpetua was speaking, two of the Redeemed, a male and female of resplendently beautiful forms, alighted from the skies upon the steps of the temple, and with bright and beaming looks of joy came up the steps. Perpetua, rising, received them with a warm welcome, exclaiming, "What strangers you are!" This done, she presented them to Mrs. Jay. "Let me introduce to you, dear sister, my beloved Faustinus and Calliste, and to you, Calliste and Faustinus, our newly-arrived sister, Mrs. Jay, of New York, North America."

Mrs. Jay was greeted with all the charming courtesies of the world of Art and Beauty, and Persis having set couches for them, the strangers took their seats; and turning to Mrs. Jay with smiles of welcome, Faustinus spoke: "Tell us, where is North America? That is a new name to us."

"North America," said Mrs. Jay, not a little surprised and somewhat at a loss how to make herself understood to these unlearned guests of Perpetua, "is separated from Europe by the Atlantic ocean."

"Ah!" exclaimed Faustinus, "then the Atlantis has been discovered at last. In our day, Perpetua, it was thought to be a fiction of Plato in *Timæus*."

Perpetua smiled at the surprise to be seen in Mrs. Jay's face, and turning to her said, "Since the departure of these dear friends of mine, the New World has been discovered."

"A new world!" exclaimed Faustinus, "pray explain."

Perpetua was amused, and addressing her friends told them that since they had left this world, a Genoese, named Columbus, had in the year 1492 discovered a continent which had been called America, the northern section of which had been settled by Britons, and the southern by Spaniards and Portuguese. That this "new world," as it was called, in its area was as large as Europe and Africa, and was found peopled with natives now known as Indians, and much more that need not be repeated.

"But where on the plane of the earth's surface is this wonderful continent?" asked Faustinus.

"O! there again," said Perpetua, "you will have to learn that the earth is not a plane, but a globe, and that the doubtful sayings of Nicetas, Heraclides and Ecphontus as to the possibility of the motion of the earth and the hypothesis of Aristarchus of Samos, that the earth revolves in an oblique circle round the sun, and daily on its own axis, has been demonstrated by a German, known to all the world as Copernicus."

"A German and a Genoese! pray what have Romans been doing, that such discoveries as these have been made by men of obscure provinces?" asked Faustinus.

Perpetua replied with a tone of deep emotion—"There are no more Romans! Those who now people Italy are no longer known as Romans, but as Italians, and as such they have been dispersed over all lands, and are known as the pastrycooks and organ-grinders of the world. The Church of Rome has become the seat of Anti-Christ.* Her priesthood

* In the Homily of the Church of England for Whit Sunday we have the follow-

have made themselves notorious for their skill in cruelty. They have created a secret tribunal, known as the Inquisition, for the suppression of the gospel of Christ. In their dungeons Christians are tortured with such exquisite refinement of cruelty that the last throb of agony is extorted before the soul is permitted to escape them. And as for the nobles of Rome, they are all gone, and Italian princes, so-called, have taken their places, rich only in titles and recollections of the past."

Faustinus and Calliste sat horror-struck at such a picture of their country; for they were of the proud senatorial families of Rome in the days of Nero.

"We shall have ample time to tell you of all the events which have elapsed since you left us; and now tell me briefly where you have been for the last fifteen hundred years," said Perpetua, wishing to change the current of their thoughts.

"We have been most happy in seeing a new world resembling our earth, peopled with a race of beautiful beings, to whom we have been ministering spirits," replied Calliste.

"I hope Satan may not find it out and carry ruin and desolation into it," said Mrs. Jay.

"O, never!" exclaimed Calliste. "Satan has been

ing testimony, which is of force with all who hold the doctrines of the Episcopal church—The Homily says, "If it be possible to be where the true church is not, then it is at Rome."

chained ever since Christ rose to his throne of everlasting Dominion."

"You must be mistaken, madam," said Mrs. Jay, "for I met him with legions of fallen angels not long since, and left them at work destroying a world of beauty; ripping up continents with horrible combustions."

"Can it be so?" said Calliste, with a look of terror, in which Faustinus sympathized.

Mrs. Jay was earnestly requested to tell them of all she had seen, for both Faustinus and Calliste said they had supposed Satan had been shut up in hell since the resurrection of the Saviour.*

Mrs. Jay replied: "It is only a short time since I was roaming the wastes of space; a solitude so vast that no ray from far-off stars reached it, when suddenly a baleful glare rose out of the depths. Coming straight on I saw a multitude of mighty forms, and stood awaiting their approach. I was soon surrounded with a legion of angels of darkness, who encompassed me as in a circle of red flame. Then came forward their

---

* That Satan has been in some way restricted in his power on earth since the coming of Christ, is an opinion very generally received. Milton thus alludes to it, in his sublime poem, "On the morning of Christ's nativity"—Hymn, stanza xvIII

———————"For from this happy day
The old Dragon under ground,
In straiter limits bound,
Not half so far casts his usurped sway,
And wroth to see his kingdom fail
Swindges the scaly horror of his folded tail," etc.

chief to where I stood, gazing with wonder, but without one throb of fear, on this globe of faces whose flaming eyes were all bent upon me with fierce glances of anger. How well he bore himself! I recalled the Milton's description of Satan, and I knew in whose presence I stood.*

"'Who and whence art thou?' he asked in tones which would have once filled me with horror. I replied, 'I am a child of earth, for whom Christ died, and who now stands before you, redeemed from the curse and dominion of sin. Would I could tell you of like mercy and pardon; of a restoration to happiness and heaven.' He replied, 'Know, child of God, I could mount up from the pit of hell to the highest throne of created existence, and be once more Lucifer, son of the morning, if I so willed to be?' 'Ah!' I replied, 'you could as easily create a world as to will to be what you once were. Would it were possible that your enmity could be changed to love.' Oh, how he swelled with pride and rage as I said this. 'Never! penitence precedes pardon, and I hate God and all his works, and will mar if I cannot destroy, and will forever task omnipotence to renew what I reduce to ruin and chaos.'

"In a twinkling these baleful flaming angels broke their

* "He, their dread commander, above the rest
    In shape and gesture proudly eminent,
    Stood like a tower: his form had not yet lost
    All her original brightness, nor appear'd
    Less than archangel ruin'd."—*Paradise Lost*, book I. lines 590.

circle and I saw them rushing deeper into the night of unfathomable space. The sound of such a moving multitude was like the roar of mighty waters upon the air of midnight. I stood awed, when an angel of light joined me, to whom I told all I had seen. 'Come with me,' said the angel, "and you shall see by what agencies worlds are made." As we flew with the speed of the messengers of the Almighty, the angel told me, that a far-off world had reached a condition when a cataclysm was required. 'It has been,' he said, 'the home of lower forms of life, and is about to assume a higher development. Satan, as the 'architect of ruin,' does but fulfill the behests of Infinite wisdom.'

"A bright star now sent its rays across the wastes of night, for which we steered our course, when a splendid solar system came into view. It was a galaxy of glories and worlds filled with Paradises. We had only time to survey a beautiful world soon to be made desolate, when the corps of destroying angels came and circled the globe. The heavens gathered the blackness of darkness, and suddenly great thunderbolts, hurled by Satanic power,* broke through the crust of the earth and down rushed the ocean, when flames of concealed fires burst forth, and towering mountains were ripped open and melted, like icebergs in a sea of flame. It was a scene of terrible sublimity!"

Perpetua, after a silence which seemed the effect of

* See Job, I. 16, for examples of Satanic power.

terror upon the minds of Mrs. Jay's auditory, with her eyes raised, spoke: "Great and marvellous are thy works, Lord God Almighty; just and true are thy ways, thou King of saints!" Then, turning to Faustinus, she asked, "What description of world is this where you have been residing, and what species of intelligences are these new-made creatures of God's goodness?"

"The system is so very like our own planetary system," replied Faustinus, "that to us it seemed a reduplication of the sun and earth and planets; only the constellations were all different, as you may readily suppose they would be. The new Adam and Eve were just beginning their labors in the Paradise of their own Eden, when we reached them. At that time they were being taught the uses of words and the value and qualities of things about them. There is no death known in that world, for there is no knowledge of sin. After living about a century of our years, they are translated to some higher sphere.

"We were thus permitted," said Callisto, "to live with them the life of our first parents; as they would have lived had Satan and sin never entered Paradise."

"It must have been full of interest to you, thus to minister to the development of the faculties of an unfallen race of human beings," said Mrs. Jay.

"It has been," said Callisto; "and now that you tell us Satan is let loose once more, we must return and help to guard this happy home from his wiles."

"Oh, there can be but one fallen race in all the universe," said Peter. "Christ has died once for all. The mystery of man's redemption has been revealed, and as our great Redeemer said on the cross, 'It is finished!'"

"And do *you* think so, Perpetua?" asked Mrs. Jay.

"So far as assurance can be mine, I am confident that our race, and the 'angels who kept not their first estate,' are the only intelligences to whom sin is known by bitter experience. How sin came to be, is the enigma of enigmas, before which we must bow and be silent—believing and resting in our knowledge of God and his attributes, that 'He will do right.'"

"Perpetua, you speak of the origin of evil," said Faustinus, "as being the enigma of enigmas. When we left on our mission to this new world, which was in the year of Christ 330, just after the Synod of Nice had dissolved, the great stumbling-block in the way of the progress of the church was that of the Holy Trinity.* Pray tell me is that now an established article of faith in the churches of Christ."

"It is of all *Christian* churches. There are in Germany, Britain and Gaul, churches, so called, which reject

* The Athanasian Creed was left out of the Book of Common Prayer, by our House of Bishops, in adapting the Liturgy of the Church of England to our country: an omission, which, for one, the author has ever regretted. He has always felt deep sympathy with this creed for its intensity of zeal for the divinity of Christ, and the reduplications of its claims for the personality of the Holy Trinity. It was the work of a mighty mind, and will stand up, like a peak of the Cordilleras against a clear sky, unapproachable in its sublimity.

Christ as the Son of God and the Redeemer of the world."

"Has there ever been a solution of the enigma, Perpetua?" asked Calliste. "I had supposed God's mode of existence must of necessity be incomprehensible."

"As it was, so it is, and ever will be, Calliste. Modern science has helped us to a glimpse of His mode of existing as Three Persons in One God. A ray of light has been decomposed into three distinct colors, red, yellow and blue, known as primary colors, and these when recombined, make one pure ray. Now we are told by inspiration, 'God is light!'"

"We were speaking, just as you joined us, my dear Faustinus and Calliste," continued Perpetua, "of the condition of Roman society in the days of Paul, as described in his Epistle to the Romans; and Mrs. Jay was expressing her wonder and admiration, how Christianity could have gained access into Rome. And to show her some of the barriers to the Gospel, I was about to tell her how Paganism bore upon females in all the relations of life. Now, Calliste, as you lived in the days of Paul, you can best render her this kind service."

"I do not know how better to fulfill your wishes, and these of our new-come sister," replied Calliste, bowing to Mrs. Jay, "than by telling her briefly the story of my life. I was born on the 5th of the Kalends of May, in Rome, while the people were celebrating the Floralia, in the year of Christ 40. I was the only child of a senator of wealth and influence, and in due time was affianced to my beloved Faustinus, and was married on my eighteenth birthday. All went happily with us, and we were made rich by the possession of five lovely children, when sickness came, and in a few months we were childless. For a change of scene we went out to our villa, which was beautifully situated on the banks of Lake Albanus, at Alba Longa, about ten miles from Rome. The nurse of our children was a Christian slave of mine, who had feared to avow her faith in Christ, lest she should be denounced and delivered up to the lions. But when Myrrha saw me broken-hearted and in deep despair, she spoke to me, little by little, of the life and immortality brought to light in the glorious gospel of the blessed God. It was like water to a lost wayfarer on the desert. It was life to the dead. The wealth of the world was less than nothing and vanity in comparison with such hopes. In all this Faustinus profoundly sympathized with me. He sought out the teachers of the church, and went to the caverns of the catacombs to listen to the preaching of the Gospel, which he rehearsed to me again and again. This was hazardous, for it was after the conflagration of the city, and Christians were being sacrificed to appease the people of Rome, who were made to believe that Christians were the incendiaries by whom so large a portion of the city had been laid in ruins.

"It was at this time the great apostle of the Gentiles was brought again to Rome a prisoner, and was bound

in the Mamertine prison.* We hastened back to our
palace, which was near the Amphitheatre of *Statilius
Taurus,* and some distance from the prison; for at all
hazards we purposed to see St. Paul. Disguised as best
we could to resemble the poorer class of the common
people, we sought admission, which was readily granted
to us. We found Paul seated on a block, near the base
of the pillar to which he was chained. He was wrapt in
his cloak, and some rolls of parchment lay at his feet.
He seemed in deep meditation when we drew near. He
addressed us in Greek, in reply to our salutation in that
tongue. This was safest for us, as there were prisoners
bound in like manner as Paul to other pillars, not far off.
Our tale was a short and simple one, and it told him how
the longing love of being restored to our lost ones had
opened our hearts to receive the gospel of the grace of
God by Christ Jesus. Paul listened with earnest attention. He read our souls, and discerned our spirits as
an apostle only can do. He had no reproofs to make,
but taking up the theme of eternal life, brought to light
in the Gospel, he preached unto us Jesus; showing how
all ancient prophecies had been fulfilled, and mysteries,
hid from the foundation of the world, had been revealed
in the coming, the death and the resurrection of Christ,
who had ascended upon high, where he ever lived to
make all prevalent intercession for his disciples. We

* According to the legends of the Mediæval Church, St. Paul was imprisoned in
the Mamertine prison.—CONYBEARE AND HOWSON'S *Life of St. Paul,* vol. II. p. 438.

forgot everything while we listened, and his face, like Stephen's, was full of the glory of heaven.

"It was our privilege to minister to the necessities of Paul, while he opened to us the glorious Gospel. One day Luke the beloved physician was with us, and to him Paul told the story of our life. Luke asked us, 'If we were willing to take up the cross of Christ, and bear it into the Amphitheatre of Nero.' He was abrupt, and we were staggered at the thought of being sacrificed. Paul reproved Luke, and told him we were as yet but babes in Christ, and then directing us to kneel before him as he sat, with a fervor of soul that was heaven-inspired, laying his hands on our heads, he prayed for the descent of the Holy Ghost to enlighten and uphold us; and when he had made an end of praying, the peace of God and the love of Christ was shed abroad in our hearts—a joy unspeakable and full of glory! By direction of Paul, and upon confession of our faith and repentance, St. Luke baptized us in the name of Christ, in the prison tank, in presence of all the prisoners. This, however attracted little attention from them, for it was of daily occurrence, and was regarded by them as some superstitious washing of these new religionists. And yet the person of Paul was awe-inspiring; felt and acknowledged by every one, bond or free, soldier or centurion.

"The day dreaded by all the disciples at last came, when Paul was to be exhibited in the Amphitheatre.

We received notice from the palace of Nero that the nobility of Rome were expected to be present. It was perilous to be absent, and on that dark day we took our seats in the gilded balcony of our rank, which hung over the walls of the arena; and there we sat and witnessed the pouring forth of the life-blood of the most glorious of men—the Apostle to the Gentiles.

"The day of our trial was not distant. One of our freed-men, named Felix, a man whom we trusted without limit, a year before had robbed me of a casket of jewels. He was taken and punished. It was at our earnest entreaty his life was spared. We could not have saved him from the stripes inflicted upon him, had such been our wish. Returning to us, he could no longer be trusted, but was compelled to take his place among our menials of the lowest class. This he resented as an affront, and then it was that he became a spy upon us. He watched us as narrowly as he could from the distance to which he had been removed by his new duties, and noticed our frequent absences from our palace. It was our custom to leave our grounds disguised as plebeians of the poorer class, through a remote postern gate opening into a vacant lodge, and thence to the nearest assembly of Christians held in some upper room, or dark vaulted chamber; for in those days the Word of God was most precious, and the courage of Christians rose with the exigencies of the trial. The words of Christ came home

to our souls with the clangor of the last trumpet—
'If any man will come after me let him deny himself
and take up his cross and follow me; for whosoever
will save his life shall lose it, and whosoever will lose
his life for my sake shall find it *—Whosoever shall
be ashamed of me and my words in this adulterous
and sinful generation, of him shall the Son of man be
ashamed when he cometh in the glory of his Father
with the holy angels.† For what is a man advantaged
if he gain the whole world and lose himself, or be
cast away.' ‡ Our worship was real, and our prayers
so fervent and effectual, that heaven seemed open to us.

"It was the custom during our exercises of devotion,
to be told of those who had been offered up on that
day; and we received from spectators usually their
messages of love and dying exhortations.* We were
told of those apprehended, or who had been denounced
to the magistrates by their slaves, their neighbors,
familiar friends, and sometimes, as in the martyrdom
of St. Christine,§ by their parents. The prophecy of
Christ was already verified—'The brother shall deliver
up the brother to death, and the father the child; and
children shall rise up against their parents, and cause

* Matthew, xvi. 21.   † Mark, viii. 88.   ‡ Luke. ix. 23.
§ St. Antonius, according to Baronius, has told the story of this young saint.
Her day on the Roman calendar is the 24th July. She was imprisoned by her own
father Urbanus, and after various modes of torture, yielded up her soul to God,
A.D. 295, in the reign of Diocletian and Maximinus. St. Isidore says, "sl e took
the name of Christine of Christ, because she was a Christian."

e hated of all
foes shall be
as not a meet-
three only were
did not bring
who had wit-
was full of the
walked, as it

life from the observation of our households. In many little matters, as in the customs of every-day life, the paganism of Rome was interwoven, and a failure of compliance with its established usages was at once observable. Indeed, concealment was not possible; and we could but confide in the devotion of those who were about us at table and in our private apartments. In those days, Nero illuminated his gardens at night with disciples who had refused to sacrifice to the gods. These were wrapped in rolls of linen and pitch and seated on pedestals, all to be fired by a signal at the same instant. It was our sad duty to visit these disciples and supply them with food and drink; to whisper the promises of God for their consolation and support. Often these martyrs, thus wrapped up like so many Egyptian mummies, were surrounded by their parents and brothers and sisters, and slaves, all weeping and praying them to consent to pour out oil upon the altar before any one of the gods of the capitol; while near by, enclosed in shrouds covered with pitch, stood those neglected or unknown—nameless on earth, but whose names were written in the Lamb's Book of Life. How often have I found such weeping, not for themselves, but for those thus tempted to deny the Lord Jesus. Oh, how often have I sat down upon a pedestal just vacated by one whose heart had melted at the prayers and tears of those they loved, and who was being led away to the temple of Jupiter near by, followed by the plaudits of her relatives and friends, and have asked myself—'Can it be that God, my Saviour, demands such sacrifices as these? Is not that sweet girl whom I call apostate, to be commended?' and then came the question of Christ to Peter, sounding its dreadful appeal to my conscience, 'Will ye also go away?' and I rose in haste out of my fearful revery, and asked, 'Lord to whom shall I go? thou only hast the words of eternal life!'

"My dear lady," continued Calliste, after the pause of a moment, as if living over the past in her memory, "you may never have known anything like this fearful conflict of doubt. It was the agony of our existence, and forever present to our minds. How wisely and cogently and convincingly did our hearts reason against what we every day witnessed in the martyrdom of the young and the beautiful; of those endowed with all that can make life lovely and themselves the centres of happiness. But in despite of all such terrible conflicts in our souls, toward the close of the day, during the banquet hour, when we were least likely to be missed from the palace, Faustinus and I went down to the lodge, near the garden wall, which was enshrouded by shrubbery, and there, aided by Myrrha, we put on our disguise, leaving her to watch for our return. We next hastened to the garden of Nero, buying the food on our way which we needed for Christ's poor. This ministry we were permitted to continue up to the fatal signal, when the flaming torches held by the guards were applied; and then, up and down the long vistas of the garden, flames arose, and martyrs, in chariots of fire, ascended to the throne of God. Oh, it was fearful! A cry of horror rose on all sides from the multitude of beholders, which, with the agony of the dying, broke upon the palace walls of Nero, while he, reposing in the arms of the lovely Poppæa, listened and smiled; his own sense of joy thus heightened by the wailing shrieks of his people.

"But I will hasten to the end of my narrative. The event so dreaded came. I had recovered my jewels, but at the cost of our lives. We were denounced by Felix. The Flamen of Jupiter, to whom so grave an accusation as this was conveyed, had been the friend of our fathers, and in full confidence that it was false, he came to us; and after a call of some length, with a smile, he told us of the charge brought against us by our freedman Felix, saying, 'So much for your unwise lenity.' Faustinus replied, 'It is true; we are Christians.' He lifted up his hands in amazement. That we should, without hesitancy, confess ourselves Christians, seemed to him madness; and his look told us that he doubted our sanity. Turning to me, he asked, if I was ready to enter the arena of the Amphitheatre. I replied, 'Faustinus and I do not seek martyrdom as some have done, but we will go to the lions rather than become apostates to the faith of Christ.' He conversed with us for an hour, and left us in deep dismay at the result of his long visit. He sought to have us banished to our estates in Sicily. But when the question was brought before Nero, the martyrdom of us two, belonging as we did to the old families of Rome, was just the event he wished for to signalize the birthday of his beloved Poppæa. It was therefore decided by him that on that day we should be destroyed by some magnificent lions recently brought to Rome, as a crowning glory of the gladiatorial shows he had been busily occupied in arranging for the celebration of the day.

"Our beloved friends now thronged around us. Every motive which could be urged by early friendships, a large retinue of devoted clients and the tears and cries of our household, was brought to bear upon us in the week which intervened. We were permitted to live in our palace under the guardianship of a centurion. The Flamen of Jupiter made a last call, and it was to me alone he came, hoping to induce me to sacrifice to the gods. He told me that he was sure of Faustinus if I would consent. I told him, 'It was certain I should share the fate of Faustinus, and that I knew my husband too well to doubt his integrity of soul to his Saviour and mine. If we were lifted above the common people, so much the greater glory would be gained to the cause of Christ;' and quoting Seneca, his friend and mine, I said, 'My leader hath not deserved ill of me; he hath judged me well.'

"The day came. All Rome thronged to the Amphi-theatre. By the order of Nero we were dressed in all the splendor of our rank, and led to our wonted seat in the gilded and cushioned balcony of senators. There we witnessed for the last time the horrid shows of gladiators killing each other to make a Roman holiday.

"The hour drew on apace. The senatorial seats near us were vacated. It was truly a fearful place of obser-vation. I glanced my eye up the ten benches, where I saw, pale and anxious, Christ's poor gazing down upon us, and I was comforted in the certainty that we had their prayers that our faith should not fail. The vic-tors were dragging the dead, by hooks, across the arena, and throwing them into the cells from which they had so recently issued in the vigor of life. When the arena was cleared, the Mayor of the Games, who sat below Nero's seat, called for us to come for-ward. There was a small altar upon which stood the statue of Jupiter, and the Flamen in his robes, bringing with him a cruse of oil, came and commanded us to make our libation in honor of the god. That was the crisis of our lives. The beautiful Poppæa, whom I had known as the wife of Rufius Crispinus, was roused to lean forward and see us make the sacrifice. And Nero, sympathizing with the feeling of anxious curiosity that pervaded the whole soul of that great multitude, rose in his seat. His was the fierce look of one expecting us to despoil him of an anticipated pleasure, and most unlike to the stare of the lovely woman at his side, who now for the first time waked up to the possibility of our contumacy. We made our obeisance to the Flamen of Jupiter, next to Nero and Poppæa, and then of declinature to the Flamen. Nero was roused. 'To the lions!' he cried in a loud voice; and as by one volition the cry came up on all sides, 'To the lions! to the lions!' Our centurion came forward and hurried us through the labyrinthian passages which led down to the level of the arena, and passing into one of the many vomitories, out of which in other days we had been wont to see gladiators and wild beasts ushered, we now came out hand in hand, and were led by the centurion into the centre, where he left us. We looked up blanched with terror, while the multitude welcomed us with shouts, as they were wont to cheer a coming spectacle. We stood close together, shuddering at the cries of the multitude, and looking anxiously at the iron doors of the arena, to see whence the lions would be let out upon us. Oh, it was a fearful hour! God willed it should be so, and the acme of agony of that moment of suspense was the fear, lest after all we should fail of the grace of God and be castaways. The interval of time we thus stood was brief, but it seemed to me a century. Every act of my life came up before me, and my sins flamed up into my face. My only cry was, 'Lord, save, or I perish!' What else could I do? The horrid din of the lifting up of the iron gates, under the seat of Nero, thrilled me through, and as the hungry lions with a roar rushed out, I was affrighted and about to fly, when Faustinus, whose arm was about me, held me to his side, saying, 'Courage, Calliste; 'tis but a pang and life is over.' Oh, it was fearful to see them leaping out of the darkness of night upon the arena, enraged by hunger and the scent of the blood of slaughtered gladiators. And as they came, their glaring eyes flashed flames which would have blazed across a desert. For an instant they cowered beneath the loud cries of thousands. But soon they discovered us, and stealthily circled round about the walls, stopping to lap up the puddles of blood they met with.

"This taste of blood roused them to frenzy, and they ran towards us with terrible roaring. We stood facing them, and they paused under the fiery glance of our eyes. It was but for an instant. Our glances could not arrest all three of the lions; and I know not how it was, but there was a leaping of the lions upon me, a crashing of my bones, and behold I stood up disembodied, arrayed in robes of light, and filled with unutterable amazement at the change. Shining ones stood by us, and welcomed us into the world unseen. Recovering ourselves, Faustinus embraced me, and then we gazed about us. Nero and Poppæa had risen, and were preparing to return home to their banquet. The crowd were already making their way out of the many passages, and the lions were fiercely feeding, with many growls, upon our

mangled bodies, tearing with their claws the rich garments which marred their feasting. We lingered, and
saw Christ's disciples stealing in behind the gladiators,
who now came to drive the lions back to their den.
These loving souls, with fond affection, sought to carry
away with them fragments of our clothing saturated
with blood, to be kept by them as mementoes of our
death. And when they turned up the faces of Faustinus and myself, with astonishment they recognized in
them the poor plebeians who were so constant in their
devotion to the martyrs of the gardens; for, my dear
madam, so many were the false brethren of that day, no
one but Myrrha shared our secret.

"'Are you not weary of such a sight of horror?'
asked our angel. 'I am filled with joy unspeakable,'
I replied; 'my soul clings to these dear ones whose
hearts are so sad for our martyrdom, and yet glad
that we have witnessed a good profession. I want
to speak words of comfort to them.' 'God, the Com-
forter, has them ever in his holy keeping,' replied our
angel. 'Now let us wing our way to the holy city, where
you will be welcome to your Saviour, Jesus Christ.'
This speech lifted us from earth; and with the delight
of birds freed from the cage, we soared away to the
open vision of our God and Redeemer."

CHAPTER V.

THE narrative of Calliste had ended, and Mrs. Jay, with profound sympathy and admiration, returned her thanks. Faustinus, addressing Mrs. Jay, said, "You come, madam, from a new world. Tell me, is it the new earth we read of in the Holy Scriptures, 'wherein dwelleth righteousness?'"

"O no! I wish it were. Our people have no claim to distinction on this score. They have made no progress in holiness that I know of in settling a new continent. Humanity is the same in all climes and all ages."

"But we hoped the Gospel would have renovated th world ere this," answered Faustinus.

"But it has *not*, sir, and I do not see that it will for centuries to come. Some pious and eminent divines of the present day have had their patience utterly exhausted, waiting for the triumphs of the Gospel; and have published sermons, and pamphlets, in favor of the world's being burned up. This summary mode of proceeding has been quite popular in certain quarters, but we have no knowledge whether this scheme of theirs will be entertained elsewhere. It seems to be the effect of petulance and a longing for a climax. I believe, St. Perpetua, there has been in every age an intense desire throughout Christendom to see the world destroyed by fire."

Perpetua, with a smile, replied, "My dear Mrs. Jay, you have your own way in saying things. In answer to your inquiry, Faustinus will tell you that in his day there was an earnest longing and looking for the day of the Lord, which was then believed to be near at hand. Toward the close of the tenth century, it was believed that the opening of the next would see the consummation of all things; an expectation spread by the great leaders of the Church who added vast domains to monasteries by compounding the sins of great barons in consideration of such grants;* and as you

---

* Hallam in his "History of the Middle Ages," chap. vii. says: "To die without allotting a portion of worldly wealth to pious uses, was accounted almost like suicide or a refusal of the last sacraments. . . . . . The church lands enjoyed an immunity from taxes. According to a calculation founded on a passage in Knyghton, the *revenue* of the English church in 1337, amounted to 780,000 marks

know, Mrs. Jay, since the days of Mede and Bishop Newton, every year has seen a new exegesis of the Revelations of St. John, of which the boldest and most specific has always paid best; nor has the skill of modern divines, in making 'taking books,' decreased in your day and generation."

"How much we have to learn!" exclaimed Faustinus, addressing Calliste. "Tell me, Mrs. Jay, the burden of the ministry in the present day. In ours, there was one absorbing theme—'God manifest in the flesh, justified in the Spirit, seen of angels, preached unto the Gentiles, believed on in the world, received up into glory.' 'Christ the Son of God, the Saviour of sinners,' was our cabalistic saying, by which we knew each other. That was the scope of the preaching then, and of our duty,—to confess Christ and lay down our lives for the brethren. His glory was the Alpha and Omega of all our exertions; the motive of all our sacrifices. Changes had come over the world in the third century, before we took our departure on the mission of love to the new world we have just now left. Alms-giving and celibacy began then to take the place of Christ, and faith in his complete righteousness, as the sinner's hope of justification before God. 'John, of

per annum. The clergy did enjoy nearly one-half of England, and I believe a greater portion in some countries of Europe."

Hallam says, chap. ix., part 1: "In the tenth century, an opinion prevailed everywhere that the end of the world was approaching."

the Golden Mouth,' as St. Chrysostom was called, with glowing eloquence was then leading away the Church of God from the true faith in Christ. And now, madam, after an absence of fifteen centuries, we come back to ask what are the themes of the Christian ministry in these latter days and in your new world. I cannot but hope that this virgin continent has been kept free from the pollutions of the old world."

"I wish it were so," said Mrs. Jay with great intensity of feeling. "Doubtless there are advantages resulting from the newness pervading our wide-spread country. The North American Republic consists of thirty-one Independent and Sovereign States. In the Northern States, the population is divided into a multitude of sects, called churches; some of these are very high, some very low; some extremely orthodox, some excessively heterodox, and those claiming to be most of all rationalistic, are of all others most irrational. Now among those known as Evangelical and Orthodox, the topics you speak of as being the burden of all the prophesyings of your day, are regarded as accepted truths, and the confessed stand-points of all subjects to be discussed. What is most needed now for a revival of primitive piety in our country, is a little of that of which you had too much—the lions of the Amphitheatre. Nor will you wonder at this when I tell you that our churches for more than two hundred years have possessed the largest freedom of religious liberty. We all sit under our own vines and fig-trees, having none to disturb or make us afraid. And yet, in despite of all the corrupting influences of such national prosperity as the world has never before seen possessed by any people, I hope and believe the kingdom of Christ is advancing and his glorious reign is extending over the wide world. But my judgment is like that of a man in the midst of opposing forces; he cannot tell on which side is the victory. What says Perpetua?"

"Oh, there is progress!" exclaimed Perpetua with a bright and beautiful confidence in her tone and manner. "It is, as our divine Redeemer has said it should be, the leaven is leavening the whole lump. The simplicity of life and manners existing two centuries since, and the principles which led the colonists of Plymouth to the rock-bound coast of New England, and which deep poverty enforced with stern rigor, has changed more and more as your country has become prosperous. And this is as true of Great Britain as of the States of North America. But while there has been a subsidence of some severe virtues, there is a wonderful development of the feeling of brotherhood. Since the days of the apostles, when the disciples, in the fire of their first love, tried the hopeless experiment of having all things common, never has the command of Christ to disciple all nations been so widely recognized and acted upon by the churches of Christ as now."

"I am glad to hear you say so, Perpetua," said Mrs. Jay; "and though I could never have had any desire to be killed by mad cows, or devoured by hungry lions, yet I have always felt that Christians of the early centuries had a confidence in their true-hearted discipleship that we never could attain unto in our days of peace and prosperity."

"Certainly, Mrs. Jay," replied Perpetua, "the cross of Christ was far more palpable in our day than in yours. To be a Christian in the lifetime of Faustinus and Calliste was to resist the current of public opinion; to commit treason to the state, and to bring down its terrible malediction. And yet, madam, the cross of Christ is ever one and the same. It demands of us the sacrifice of self, and the cross is a daily one; it meets us on the threshold of existence, and never leaves us till we sleep the sleep of death. And so obvious is this cross, that all can both see it and feel it at every step of life's progress, while, with an eye upon our Saviour's footsteps, we walk as he also walked, of whom it is said 'he pleased not himself.' Now, madam, the great truth which men are so slow to learn, and which millions have never guessed at, is this,—God has ordained in all worlds, that happiness shall consist, not in what is gained, but in what is given; and this being so, men ought to seek as their own highest happiness the gifts and powers to do the greatest good to the greatest number. You see in this world, so joyous and happy, what blessedness results from carrying out this course of action. As I have just said, few on earth have adopted the principle of *self-sacrifice* in very little things.   All ideas of taking up the cross of Christ daily, are vague and mystical.   In great exigencies Christians act well at all times, but in the 'sweet small charities of life,' upon which the happiness of a wife or a child chiefly depend, how often do men offend?   And yet, this willingness and power at once to sacrifice self in order to advance the well-being of others, is the philosopher's stone for which the world has so long sought."

"The adoption of such a principle, St. Perpetua, would indeed change the aspect of society, and the commerce of the world," said Mrs. Jay.   "I have had such dreams of a future of our world; but then I never believed it could be attained without some such purgation as a general conflagration. Why, Perpetua, who would sell us our silks and ribbons? and as for hucksters they would cease to be.*   No, no; while there is a necessity for buying and selling, there will always be more or less buying cheap and selling dear. And, Perpetua, I think the Saviour teaches us that in the last day, at the very instant when the pealing sound of the archangel's trumpet shall wake the dead, the ladies of our cities will be cheapening lace for their wedding dresses." †

Perpetua smiled at the illustration Mrs. Jay had used,

---

* Ecclesiasticus xxvi. 29,—"A huckster shall not be free from sin."
† Matthew, xxiv. 37.

while Faustinus and Calliste sat by with a look of incertitude as to what was meant.

"I think, Mrs. Jay, we all agree in believing," said
Perpetua in reply, "that the mission of Christ was for
the saving of the whole world. He has in his gospel
given as the law of love by which the world is to be
regenerated—'Thou shalt love thy neighbor as thyself.'
Now to recur to the subject of which we have been

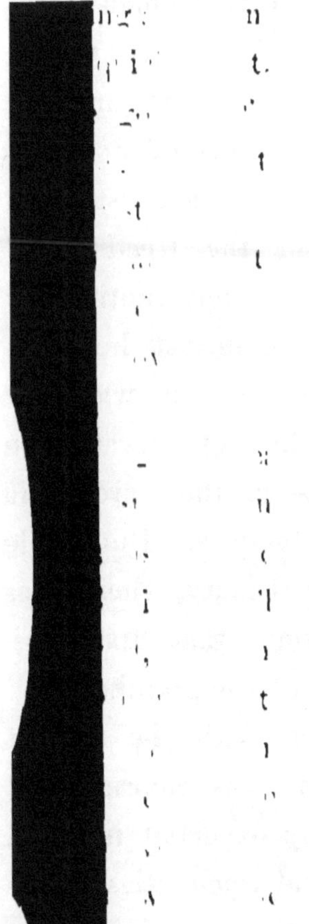

and Calliste, who listened with delight while Perpetua sketched the progress of society and the elevation of woman from the third century to the present day. This done, Mrs. Jay recalled Faustinus to the inquiry made by Perpetua.

"To recur to the past, then," said Faustinus, "and its days of darkness, sensuality and suffering, I will say to Mrs. Jay, that according to the testimony of Roman authors, and poets especially, women were never so abandoned as in the days of Augustus Cæsar. They describe the scenes then taking place, and say the framework of society and the bonds of domestic life were on the eve of disruption. Woman, distrusted by her husband, was deprived of the freedom of social intercourse, and being left without motive for the cultivation of her mind, she soon lost her delicacy of manners. Her form was all that was now left her for adornment, and this she saw elevated on a pedestal, the object of worship—in the porch, the vestibule and upon the altars of temples. But while there was all this reverence for beauty, there was none for Woman. It was Christianity that first attributed to woman a full participation of the godlike.

"To our rude Roman fathers, as with the ancient Greeks, there was nothing so grand as courage and strength. From timid women they expected nothing, and treated them accordingly. And when cities began to be built, women were confined to a certain section of the house, always the back part, and slept in the upper rooms well secured by bars and bolts; nor were they permitted, in the day-time even, to go from one part of the house to the other. Their keepers were old female slaves and eunuchs. If the golden fleece of Thessaly was not safe from the enterprise of Jason, the wives of the ancient Greeks and Romans were not safe from the men of their day. With wealth came refinement. Rome in the days of Augustus was enriched by the plunder of the world. She had laid a belt about the Mediterranean of a thousand miles in breadth; and within that zone she comprehended not only all the great cities of the ancient world, but so perfectly did she lay the garden of the world in every climate, and for every mode of natural wealth, within her own ring-fence, that since that era no land, no part and parcel of the Roman empire, has ever risen into strength and opulence, except where unusual artificial industry has availed to counteract the tendencies of nature. So entirely had Rome engrossed whatsoever was rich by the mere bounty of native endowment.* The city had become a nation in itself. It contained with its suburbs, in the days of Christ, not less than four millions; and by many it was believed to contain millions more;† for there were no accurate methods in use in those days of numbering all sorts of people.

* De Quincey—"The Cæsars," p. 16.   † De Quincey, p. 5.

"Women were made to share in the luxuries of the age. They were needed to grace the banquet; but their sphere was only to minister to the pleasures of men, and not to share their confidence. In the Pantheon woman was worshipped, but at home she was degraded; and though having the care of her children, and sharing in her husband's honors, she was the victim of a capricious jealousy, and could be repudiated by him at his pleasure; and more, she was at his sole disposal at his death."

Mrs. Jay, lifting up her hands, terrified at such a picture, exclaimed, "What would I have done to my husband had I lived in your day!"

"You would have submitted as the women of Rome did," replied Faustinus. "But listen awhile, for I have not told you the half of all that can be told of the degradation of women in the height of Roman glory. In the day-dawn of Christianity, a Roman mother was liable to see her most loved child torn from her bosom, if jealousy seized upon her husband, and thrown by him, or by some obedient slave, into the fish-pond of the house to become food for eels."

"Horrible!" cried Mrs. Jay. "This might be old Roman law; but could it consist with such civilization as was the glory of Rome in the days of Augustus."

"I could tell you tales of my own day," replied Faustinus, "but I would rather speak of those facts which are found imbedded in the pages of the great writers of the empire. You may think," continued Faustinus, addressing himself to Mrs. Jay, " that we Romans of the first century were monsters. We may have been, but we regarded ourselves as greatly in advance of the primitive laws and customs. Our civilization came to us from the people of Greece, who learned their lessons from Egypt. Xenophon, in one of his letters says :—'There are few of my friends with whom I converse so seldom as with my wife.' Nor were the domestic customs of Athens more mild and regardful of women than those of Rome. A Roman citizen could transfer his authority over his wife to his son; or, if he chose, could bequeath her to a friend as her future husband : and this, too, was Grecian law, of which we have a most notable instance in the father of Demosthenes, who chose Aphobus, his own slave, for his successor. And another example is supplied us by M. Porcius Cato, the great-grandson of Cato the Censor. This eminent man, amid the oriental voluptuousness of his age, retained a love of Samnite rusticity. He was proud of the name he bore, and the virtues which had made that name illustrious. And it was this Cato, who, failing to persuade Bibulus, who had married his daughter Portia (by whom Bibulus had two children), to give her up to his friend Hortensius, divorced his own wife Marcia, who was then married to Hortensius in the presence of Cato and her own father.' "*

* So Plutarch--"Cato the Younger."

"How wonderful!" cried Mrs. Jay. "I have now a new apprehension of the blessedness of the glorious gospel of the Son of God. Well might old Zacharias call Christ's coming the day-spring from on high, giving light to them that sat in darkness and the shadow of death, and of all, to woman. And our Redeemer might well say of his coming He was sent to bind up the broken-hearted, to proclaim liberty to the captives, and to open the prisons of them that were bound. But was there no protection for women? I have heard much about the famous Tables of Roman law, and did they contain no mention of us poor wives and mothers?"

"Oh, certainly," replied Faustinus. "They prescribe the form of divorce."

"A summary method no doubt, and what was it?"

"It was not more so than among the Jews, madam; and I think it was far more respectful. The law of the Twelve Tables prescribes as follows: 'When a man will put away his wife, the form of doing it shall be by taking the keys of her house from her and giving her what she brought.' Thus it was that Cicero dismissed Terentia, after a union of thirty years, because he said she was expensive and peevish;* and only eleven years before, while he was in exile, he addressed to her those beautiful letters, in which he says she had been cruelly robbed of her whole fortune on his account, calling her

* "Terentia denied all these charges, and Cicero afterwards made her a full apology."—PLUTARCH.

'*My Terentia*, thou most faithful and best of wives;' conjuring her to join him in his banishment, saying to her, 'I can never think myself ruined whilst I enjoy thy society.' "

"The wretch!" cried Mrs. Jay, "he well deserved to have his head cut off and a bodkin run through his tongue, for such baseness to his wife."

"My dear Faustinus," said Calliste, "you are making very slow progress in answering the inquiry made by Perpetua. You have been talking all this while about the condition of wives in order to enhance the triumph of Christ's gospel. But how much more strikingly is this shown in the condition of children under the law of the Twelve Tables. Wives have never had such hold upon the hearts of husbands as children upon the heartstrings of fathers; and I want you to tell Mrs. Jay, that by the authority of law, a father could kill his child, or sell him into slavery, and there was no appeal;* and as for the females born, it was a matter of incertitude whether to let the child live or die. The degradation of our sex came to us from Greece, and is shown by the quotation of one of their poets, who says: 'A man though poor will not expose his son, but if he is rich, he will scarcely save his daughter.' "

---

* The first law of the Twelve Tables enacts: " Let a father have the power of life and death over his legitimate children, and let him sell them when he pleases. But if a father has sold his son three times, let the son be out of the father's power. If a father has a son born which is monstrously deformed, let him kill him immediately."

"Well might St. Paul say of such men, 'without natural affection.'" said Mrs. Jay. "Was there ever such a catalogue of crimes as Paul has made in the first chapter of his Epistle to the Romans? It seems to me the Huns and Vandals were needed to crush such a race out of existence."

"How thankful should we be," said Perpetua, with her sweet smile, and taking Mrs. Jay's hand as she spoke, "that the long suffering of God leads men to repentance. Even James and John wished permission from Christ to command fire to come down from heaven to consume the inhabitants of a Samaritan village, for no other reason than that they refused to entertain Christ and his disciples on their way to Jerusalem; and we must pardon our new-come sister for her sentiments of abhorrence of Roman morals. And yet, dear Mrs. Jay, we three are native-born Romans, and love all that was noble in our country."

"I pray you forgive me, St. Perpetua, if I have in any degree pained you."

"It was not what you said, my sister, but there was in your tone and manner something which sounded like the prayer of the Pharisee—'Lord, I thank thee I am not as other men are.' I am not a Roman of the first century, but a Christian of the nineteenth."

"Yes, truly, St. Perpetua; for what but a Pagan should I have been had I been born in Rome in the times of Nero? or a Buddhist had I lived in my own day beneath the burning sun of Hindostan? Born as I was of Christian parents, listening to the preaching of the gospel every Lord's day, trained from my cradle to repeat the Divine Hymns of Dr. Watts for Infant Minds, initiated into the Christian church by baptism confirmed in childhood by a Christian bishop—I am here, a brand plucked from the burning; redeemed, while those who commenced life with me, under like auspices, have failed of the grace of God, and dying made no sign."

This little matter was soon settled, and the conversation was carried back by Faustinus to the condition of the children of Rome, in the higher walks, with which indeed he and Calliste alone were personally conversant. He cited these words from the great historian Tacitus, as illustrating this question—"The young infant is given in charge to some poor Grecian wench, and one or two serving men are perhaps joined in the commission; generally the meanest and ill-bred, and such as are unfit for any other business. With their tales and vagaries the tender mind, as yet a virgin soil, is saturated. Of all the inmates of the house not one regards what is said or done before the infant lord; while their very parents accustom their little ones, not to virtue and modesty, but to license of speech and behavior; thus, through this loop-hole made for impudence and contempt of obedience to their own parents, all vices find entrance. Nay," continues Tacitus, " the vices peculiar to Rome seem to be inborn, such as a fondness for the stage, and the arena, a passion for horses and the like."

Calliste now took up the topic. "Mrs. Jay, you want to know what were the stones of stumbling, and rocks of offence in the way of a Roman girl in becoming a Christian. Now I think I can tell you of some which would have been insuperable, had I been a Christian before I married Faustinus. And to begin at the beginning; the auspices were to be first consulted and found concurrent; for if an omen deemed unlucky appeared, the contract was forthwith dissolved as displeasing to the gods. It was rare for such omens to be discovered, when rich gifts rewarded the priest for successful ones. These in our case were declared to be auspicious in all respects; and forthwith our prayers were offered with sacrifices to the gods, and a lock of my hair was cut off and laid upon the altar as a consecrated gift. This fearful ordeal over, for such it had been to me, being ignorant of the persuasives Faustinus had made to the soothsayers to secure a favorable report, I with joy hastened to get ready for my espousals. It was a day forever to be remembered, when after much labor I stood arrayed in my long white robe with its purple fringe adorned with ribbons, called *tunica recta*, and had the girdle bound around me which Faustinus was to unloose. Then my maids having parted my hair with a spear in honor of Juno, the protectress of marriage, to whom the spear was sacred, put over me my bridal, orange-colored veil, called the *flammeum;* and last of all I put on my yellow shoes. Thus attired, I was led down into the hall where stood the priest at an altar placed there for the occasion. A sheep was then sacrificed to the gods, and the skin being rent off the victim (a most offensive sight it was to me), it was spread over two stools, upon which we sat with our heads covered. This done, our marriage was completed by pronouncing a solemn prayer, after which another sacrifice was made, and Faustinus then became my husband."

"And was that all?" cried Mrs. Jay. "I had supposed there was the greatest splendor attending the nuptials of the nobility of Rome."

"Oh, there was," replied Calliste; "but I wanted to show you how intimately the ritual of pagan worship was connected with the rites of marriage. Faustinus can best tell you what a retinue of nobility attended me on my way from my father's palace, to the one which was to be henceforth mine."

"By no means can I begin to tell of these ceremonies so well as you, Calliste. Pray finish your story," said Faustinus with a pleasant smile.

"Do you not see, Mrs. Jay, that this husband of mine slily suggests that this affair of marrying him was a matter of much more importance and interest to me than it was to him. But I assure you he was regarded as fortunate when he married me; and there were ladies of my rank who openly expressed their astonishment at my father's choice; but I believed then, as now, that it was only envy; for our love began in childhood, and was a union of hearts as well as of great families; and then, you know, matches are never entirely satisfactory but to those directly concerned in them. But I am not telling you of what I did and what was done to me on my nuptial day. It was a cloudless day, and I was dressed twenty times by my slaves before I could be entirely satisfied with my looks; so it was, when I ought to have been ready to descend, I had not as yet made a single step of progress. The second and third message hastened on the robes and completed this most momentous toilet. It was set down in the books that I was to be torn from the arms of my parents, as if reluctant to be separated from them. I believe I acted the part with more sincerity than is common on such occasions; for it was not only my parents from whom I was to be torn away, but from a troop of domestics whom I loved with all the ardent tenderness of a young girl.

"I was then conducted to my new home with music and dancing, escorted by young boys, friends of ours, whose parents were yet alive; one holding a flaming torch while the others carried my distaff and a spindle with woollen yarn—the only time I ever saw them. One boy, called *Camillus*, carried a vase containing certain bridal ornaments. Then followed a splendid train of persons who officiated on this occasion, composed of the friends of our respective families. When the procession reached the grand entrance, which was adorned with garlands and flowers, in compliance with ancient custom, I wound woollen yarn around the pillars and anointed them with lard. This done, I was taken up by Gellius and Plautus, two of my father's friends who had been married but once, by whom I was carried across the threshold; the utmost care being taken that I should not touch it with my foot, for this would have been a bad omen. On my entrance I was met by Faustinus, who presented me with fire and water, both which I was expected to touch."

"Pray, Calliste, can you tell me what all this symbolized?" asked Mrs. Jay. "Greasing the door-posts would not be regarded as a good beginning for a neat housewife in my day."

"I assure you," replied Calliste with a good-natured laugh, "I did not know then, nor did I ever make the inquiry.* In fact it never occurred to me. I was entirely absorbed in thinking of that gentleman "—bowing to Faustinus; "and as for the ritual, I was as reckless as most young ladies are on such occasions."

* Pliny says, the distaff and spindle were in memory of *Cata Cæcilia*, or *Tanaquil*, wife of Tarquinius Priscus, who, according to the venerable Doctor Kennett, " was a famous spinster." A bride called herself *Caia* because it was a fortunate name. The winding of the posts with woollen list or yarn, and covering them with tallow was regarded as the "sov'ranst thing," to keep out infection and sorcery. The bride was lifted over the threshold because it was sacred to Vesta—a chaste goddess.

Calliste continued: "Having touched fire and water as presented me by my Faustinus, I next saluted him with all the grace of manner I could command; and I will tell you privately"—and here Calliste leaned forward, and in a stage-aside, said: "it was the result of the steady practice of a month previous; this done, I addressed to him those sweet words: 'Ubi tu Caius, ego Caia.' *

"Thus I entered, distaff and spindle in hand, and being seated on a sheepskin, the keys of the house were placed in my hands. Then followed the banquet styled *cœna nuptialis*, given by Faustinus to my train of friends. At this feast I presided. The banquet over, I was conducted by matrons to the bridal chamber, which was magnificent as taste and wealth could contrive; the floor of which was strewed with flowers. On the day following, Faustinus gave another entertainment to his friends, after which I made certain sacrifices, according to prescribed customs, to the *Dii Penates*, and then assumed all the management of my new home. Such were the ceremonies of a Roman marriage among the Patrician order. As conducted by the citizens of Rome, it was made offensive to all delicacy and modesty. Now, Mrs. Jay, had I been a Christian, could I have poured out the libations required of me in honor of the gods? All these ceremonies were more or less intimately associated with the religion of Rome. Suppose

* "Where thou art Caius there am I Caia."

I had been one of the slaves of Faustinus, a poor kitchen drudge? There stood upon the hearth household deities to be sacrificed to daily; there was the sacred lamp to be kept burning, around which the *lares* * and *penates* were ranged. And sitting at the table with other servants, I must have eaten of meat offered to idols, and been expected to pour out of my wine-cup, my libation with those about me, in honor of the gods; and upon festival days to have joined in dances full of seductive blandishments. Every condition of life has its peculiar trials and tests of faith; and I think you will admire the grace of God our Saviour, manifested by multitudes of women, who in face of all these dangers, dared to embrace the religion of a despised and crucified Saviour—and he a Jew! The courage of a man was hardly equal to such horrors as awaited the confession of Christ; and yet,—with all the tenderness of a woman's heart, torn by contending passions, the love of life, the shrinking from suffering natural to all, and felt most by women; the rending of the ties of love to her parents, her husband, her children and her household, —there was no lack of martyred mothers, wives and daughters, in the three first centuries of the church of Christ."

* " The domestic Lares, like the Penates, formed the religious elements of a Roman household. When they took their meals some portion was offered to the Lares. When a young bride entered the house of her husband, her first duty was to offer a sacrifice to the Lares."—SMITH, vol. I. p. 722.

St. Chrysostom has an account of marriage rites in his day. In addition to

Mrs. Jay renewed her thanks to Calliste and Faustinus for all the pleasure she had derived from this conversation, so full of new and instructive thoughts as it had been to her, saying in conclusion: "The grace of our Lord and Saviour Jesus Christ, has been gloriously illustrated in the sight of angels and men by the triumphs of the cross over Pagan Rome. And there is yet another to be accomplished when the prophecies against Papal Rome shall all be fulfilled; when the angel of God shall come down from heaven endowed with great power, enlightening the face of the earth with the glory of his presence, and lifting up his voice shall cry mightily, "Babylon the Great, the mother of harlots and of mystery, is fallen, is fallen!"

"Can it be," cried Faustinus, looking at Perpetua, "that Rome has become the Anti-Christ of St. Paul, and the mystical Babylon of St. John?"

"Such is the faith of all Protestant churches," replied St. Perpetua.

"Come," said Faustinus rising, "let us change our places and our thoughts. I begin to feel the chill atmosphere of the Campagna of Rome about me. See! there

all that has been given—speaking of the trials to which a young bride was subjected, he says: "Not only in the day, but also in the evening, men are enlisted, who having been made drunk, besotted and inflamed with luxurious fare, are brought in to look upon the beauty of the damsel. Nor is this all; but they led her through the market-place in pomp, to made an exhibition of her, conducting her with torches late in the evening, so that she might be seen of all. And they do not stop here; but with shameful songs do they conduct her . . . . What can one say of these songs, crammed as they are with all uncleanness?"

are the young servitors of the palace gathering to keep
this festival day, under the shade trees; I am sure you
will all be glad of such a change as they will offer
us."

"With pleasure," said Mrs. Jay; and with a volition.
they landed on the shore, leaving Persis to ferry herself
over the lake alone.

CHAPTER VI.

The Party returns to the Palace Gardens—Scene—The Festivity of the Servitors—
Their Dances described—Mrs. Jay's Colloquy with St. Perpetua about Dancing
—Miss Mehitable Smith arrives—Her Horror at the Sight—Her Angel's contrast between the Dancing of Earth and the World of Beauty—Tibertius gives
a Recitation to Mrs. Jay and Perpetua of a Sermon Preached in the Metropolis
by St. John Chrysostom.

THE day had reached its meridian, and a throng of
young persons were clustered in happy groups in their
gala costumes, awaiting the coming of their *corypheus*
to begin their festive dances. His coming was told by
a sound of music, whereupon they all ran to meet him and
his band of some sixty orchestral performers. For these
a temporary platform had been already erected. So soon
as the performers were seated, the signal sounded for the
opening dance, when the confused groups became a
circle. The male and female *choreutae** sang as they
danced, and their gliding graceful movements were
inexpressibly beautiful. At times they were so mixed

* "The original of the *chorus*," says Dr. Kennett, "was at first nothing else
but a company of musicians singing and dancing in honor of Bacchus."—Ar'.
'The Comedy and Tragedy."

as to show only an undistinguishable mass, out of which these youth with ·magical celerity evolved the most graceful figures.

Mrs. Jay looked on with absorbed attention. Perpetua, as one dance was ended and another began, explained them, saying, "These bear a very close resemblance in their cadences and measure to those known in ancient Greece as the Lydian, Dorian and Phrygian dances."

"Pray explain! How could the ancient Greeks have obtained the knowledge of these dances?" asked Mrs. Jay.

"That is a very natural inquiry for Mrs. Jay to make," said Faustinus, "and I am curious to know what answer you have for it, Perpetua."

"I have a reply, which is satisfactory to myself, and if, Faustinus, you do not approve of it, I shall task your ingenuity to offer a better solution for the fact. My answer then to Mrs. Jay's inquiry is this: there is in all worlds a reaching forth of the soul for the ideal of grace and loveliness, which exists in its unattainable perfection in the mind of God. Now the Greeks had attained a higher and loftier conception of this ideal of the beautiful in nature and art than any other people that have lived on our earth. They, therefore, in their dances as well as in sculpture and architecture attained to a nearer conformity to this world of art and beauty than all others. And I will say further, that by the law of life, impressed by the Creator on all pure intelligences, this pursuit of the ideal in nature and art is an essential element in the unceasing happiness of all worlds."

Faustinus and Calliste bowed their approval, and then took leave of St. Perpetua and Mrs. Jay, and walked toward the palace.

"What do you think of dancing, St. Perpetua, for beings of the present day, upon our world, peopled by those whose very natures are, not to say totally depraved, but, as is stated more cautiously, and it may be with more wisdom, in the Book of Common Prayer, Article ix., 'Very far gone from original righteousness, and is of his own nature inclined to evil.' "

Perpetua replied: "Dancing, in its simplest forms, is the natural expression of youthful joy and gladness. See! how lovely is this sight. There is no movement, no look but is the sign of innocence out of the very soul of purity."

"Oh yes, it is beautiful, but the young men of the present age are not angels, if our young ladies are."

"It is a vexed question I know," replied Perpetua, "and one hard to be decided. There are no two villages even, much less towns and cities, where the conditions of morals and culture are alike, and consequently no rule can be prescribed which it would be safe to follow. Only this is forever true, piety ought to make home the centre of all happiness; and this is done by guiding, and not damming up, all natural expressions of youthful gaiety."

Persis coming up, Perpetua requested her to keep Mrs. Jay company, and promising to see her in the evening, took leave.

Persis was delighted to explain all the dances to Mrs. Jay, and to point out those who excelled, telling her their names and occupations in and about the palace. While they stood conversing, a female and her angel descended, and alighted near Mrs. Jay and Persis. The new-comer lifted up her hands with amazement as she looked on the dancers, and turning to Mrs. Jay, she exclaimed: "Dancing in heaven! who would have thought it!" *

Mrs. Jay, with that delightful perversity which adds so much to the attractiveness of all brilliant women, replied: "And why not dancing, madam? What do you see in this but new manifestations of God's love of beauty? Is not this the perfection of grace?"

"Dear me!" exclaimed the lady, taking a long breath, and looking around after her angel, as if suffocating, for relief. "I did not expect to hear this nonsense about the poetry of motion repeated here. The high priest of

* Milton thus describes dancing in heaven:

   "That day, as other solemn days, they spent
    In song and dance about the sacred hill;
    Mystical dance . . . mazes intricate
    Eccentric, intervolved, yet regular,
    Then most, when most irregular they seem;
    And in their motions harmony divine
    So soothes her charming tones, that God's own ear
    Listens delighted."— *Paradise Lost*, book v., line 617.

modern Pantheism might well say to his lady friend, while sitting in the Boston theatre gazing, while Fanny Ellsler was making a pirouette, with a steadiness that would have looked an eagle blind, 'Maria, *this* is religion!' but I must say this sight takes me all aback!"

"How long have you been here?" asked Mrs. Jay.

"I have this instant alighted, direct from the Holy City, and here I am in the midst of a mixed multitude of dancing men and women!"

"You have doubtless come then from some town settled by a primitive people, far removed from the centres of social life?"

"No, madam, I came from town of Newbury-port, and have been for fifty years a member in good standing in the orthodox church—a church which has thus far escaped the march of modern refinement."

"Indeed! and will you tell me if you have allowed the introduction of a pitch-pipe into your singing seats?"

The lady was a little embarrassed, and replied, that she had heard that old Dr. Spring had publicly reproved so much as the use of a pitch-pipe; but since his day, in regard to music, there had been a great change in public opinion, and now they had not only one pitch-pipe but many, for they had the most costly organ that was in the town.

"Ah well," said Mrs. Jay, as she bowed to leave her

with Persis, "when you have been here a year or less, you will look on such a scene as this divested of all associations of earth, and will thank God that he has conferred on pure natures such sweet pastimes; and it may be you will join them in their dance, as I would do now, if I knew how."

The angel of the new-comer, who had left her for a moment to greet his friends among the servitors, now returned to the lady, who stood gazing with a look of painful intensity upon the gay scene. She recovered herself on his addressing her, and in a hesitating way asked how his mind was affected by the sight of such sports as these. He, who had been her guardian angel from the day of her conversion,—had studied all her moods, knew every sentiment she had entertained, and almost her thoughts from her looks, at once comprehended her feelings and motive in making this inquiry.

"Wait awhile, Miss Mehitable, and you will look at things as they are, and not through the medium of the —atmosphere of your native town."

·"It may be so," she replied, "but it upsets all I have ever conceived of as belonging to the life of worlds of light. It is beautiful! I never saw dancing before; and if this be the aspect of one of our fashionable assemblies, I do not wonder it should be so fascinating to the young."

"Earth has no such scene as this, my sister. Here you see heavenly grace, unfeigned gentleness and the most complete unconsciousness of self. Goodness and purity glows in every feature and beams from every eye. But had you visited those grand saloons of earth, you would have seen the floor of the hall covered with extremely well-dressed persons, distressingly anxious to be perfectly proper, languidly walking through quadrilles, paired but not matched, whose features, schooled into marble, wake only to show some token of being excessively *ennuyed*, but at a later hour, polking — rushing from one end of the hall to the other, or circling round and round in the seductive and bewildering waltz."

"I am glad you do not sanction the dancing of the lower world, if you find this commendable," replied Miss Mehitable. "You must not leave me until I have become familiar with the scenes about me, for though they are pleasing to me, they are as yet strange."

"Let me now introduce you to the Mayor of the Palace, who will make you welcome, and do not doubt I shall be equally devoted to you as ever, until my Creator shall send me on some other mission to earth. Let us go to the palace."

———

The singing and dancing continued, one set following another, until the chimes of the temple were heard, when they dispersed without delay, equally happy in the discharge of duties as in their festive dances and song-singing.

Mrs. Jay, accompanied by Persis, went to the palace. She found the porticos, great saloons thronged with the Redeemed who had returned from hearing an oration in the new "Academy of Music," at the Metropolitan City; delivered by no less a person than St. John Chrysostom. They were in raptures over it; and the scene was described to her by a young artist, who was one of the saint's stars of glory. It was a pleasure all unexpected to them; for the saint was on a mission to a distant world and could stay but a day. The messenger with the news had reached the palace after Mrs. Jay had left in the morning with Persis. Whereupon, all who could be notified, sped away to the metropolis in order to listen to this eminent and eloquent preacher.

"Oh, that you could have heard him!" said this artist to Mrs. Jay. "He was always 'golden-mouthed;' but by no words of mine can you conceive of the dignity of his form; the grace of his action; the light which beams from his eye; and then the richness of his tones, their various inflections, from a gentle whisper to the rolling thunder. Ah! he has not been in vain all this while a hard student in the schools of eloquence. So much, madam, for his manner; but his theme—'The glory of Christ.' It was one he loved to dwell upon fourteen centuries ago, while I with multitudes of other converts to the faith, sat at his feet in Antioch. After having proceeded for an hour or more, for I cannot now recover the time, he became rapt away with his subject, when the audience by one impulse rose and stood, every eye fixed, every soul absorbed by his kindling eloquence; and when·he had climbed to a vast height, taking us up into the heaven of heavens, he closed abruptly, as if his conceptions outran all language to express. Whereupon the vast audience found relief for their burdened breasts by bursting forth and singing 'The Hymn to the Trinity.' This over, we dispersed; and here we are, every one filled to overflowing with the theme so grandly upheld by my beloved father into the kingdom of God."

St. Perpetua coming up, Mrs. Jay expressed her regret that she should have been the cause of her losing this splendid oration. Perpetua assured Mrs. Jay, that she was well content to have spent the day as she had done with her; and that Calliste and herself had agreed to call upon her, at her parlor, the next morning; and with her permission she would bring Faustinus; to which Mrs. Jay acceded with her thanks, for their intended kindness.

"I have not seen Mr. Laurens and your friend Peter," said Perpetua; "do you know where they have gone?"

"I am sure I do not; and now, for the first time, have I missed them," replied Mrs. Jay.

Perpetua said: "I learn there are several arrivals to-day from our world; and I want to find them out. Have you seen any one of these new people?"

"I met with a lady from Newbury Old Town, in

New England somewhere, who seemed to me, consider-
ing the maturity of her years, quite fresh. We met in
the gardens where she had just alighted; and while her
angel ran to greet some of his friends, we entered into
a discourse about the propriety of dancing in heaven."

"Of which you no doubt disapproved," replied Perpetua, smiling.

"Oh, you do not know me, St. Perpetua. I did no
such thing. I found this lady so full of virtuous indig-
nation, that I took up the defence of dancing."

"And did she think that these dances of ours were
copied from out the ball-rooms of the present day? If
so, I should like to know in what part of the world they
are practised. I know of nothing in vogue in the courts
of Europe, or the republican homes of the New World,
which can be compared with them."

"Oh, this lady, in all likelihood, never was present in
a ball-room in her life."

"You are no doubt right in your guess, Mrs. Jay.
Our new-come sister will be able to discern the difference which exists between words and things after she
has been at home here with us for a little while."

Tibertius, a sculptor, who was a martyr of the third
century, and who was a beloved friend of St. Perpetua,
and had already been presented to Mrs. Jay, now came
up and conversed awhile concerning the oration of
St. Chrysostom.

"Come, Tibertius," said Perpetua, "go to my rooms with me and Mrs. Jay, and give us a recitation of this famous sermon." To this invitation he at once assented, and when they were seated in Perpetua's parlor, Tibertius recited the oration, word for word, with every inflection of voice, and every gesture used by Chrysostom. Such memories have the Redeemed!

"How wonderful are your memory and powers of imition!" exclaimed Mrs. Jay to Tibertius when he closed. "I have never seen anything like it before.'

"Oh, do not think my recitation gives any true idea of St. Chrysostom's manner. And then, too, there is wanting that wave of sympathy which rose and swept over that vast audience, helping every soul to a higher point of rapture. I could keep you longer, but the chimes are striking twelve, and I bid you good-night."

Tibertius gone, the ladies separated soon after, promising to meet again early in the morning.

Note. Doctor Isaac Watts, in his sermon "*On the Happiness of Separate Spirits,*" asks, "Are we sure that there are no such entertainments" as here described? And further, "May not Christ himself be the everlasting Teacher of the church? May He not at solemn seasons summon all heaven to hear him publish some new discoveries of nature or of grace?"

CHAPTER VII.

Mrs. Jay rises at an early Hour—Her Recollections of her Infancy—She ascends into the Air and seats herself on a Cloud—Her Thoughts of God—Returns to the Palace to receive a Morning Call from Perpetua and Calliste in her own Room—Their Colloquy—Of the School of Eloquence—Why there are no "Strong-minded Women " in Heaven—Perpetua's Opinion of Woman's Rights—Of Modern Fashions—Influence of the Science of Phrenology on Beauty—Variety of dresses now worn—Paint not now used—Of Diamonds—Modern Invention of making Money out of Paper—Of the Fashions at Carthage—Advantage of an Auto-da-Fé—Satirical sayings of Tertullian—Of Celibacy—Asceticism—Monasticism—Rise of Nunneries—Character of Girls educated in Convents—Of the Convents of the United States—Of escaped Nuns—Of political Parties in the United States—The Admiration of certain Mothers for Nunneries as Seminaries of Education—Perpetua and Mrs. Jay discuss how these Prisons of the Unhappy can be made subject to Law.

Mrs. Jay was wakened by the song of birds, and rising—having renewed her thanksgivings to God for life and redemption—she walked out upon the piazza, listening to the melodies of the garden, and watching the dawning of the day. Her mind, full of the activities of immortality, recalled her earliest recollections of childhood, the emotions of her soul when she heard for the first time a bird carol his morning song; and with this reminiscence came thronging up the memories of her child's life; and

these came not dim and misty, but with the entirety of
first impressions.   Her childish aspirations, her little sorrows, her blind kitten, her china doll with its defaced
nose—all were recalled and renewed, as vividly as the
reality had been, with all the inconceivable rapidity of
which the soul is endowed; of which drowning men,
and men in great peril, are fearfully conscious, who live
over a long life in a few seconds of time.   This was to
Mrs. Jay, as it is to all happy beings, a blissful exercise
of the soul; for such is the constitution of the mind of
the Redeemed, that those inkspots of memory * which
once rose unbidden, are all washed out, and events the

---

* The Holy Scriptures teach us as follows :—Ps. ciii. 12 : "As far as the east is
from the west, so far hath he removed our transgressions from us." Isaiah xliv. 22 :
"I have blotted out as a thick cloud thy transgressions; and, as a cloud thy
sins ;" and in the 43d chapter, 25th verse : "I, even I, am he that blotteth out
thy transgressions for my own sake and will not remember thy sins."

Babbage, in his Chapter on Future Punishments, says : "To the major part of
our race oblivion would be the greatest boon," and that the misery of the wicked
may be, with exalted moral feelings, to survey their past existence.   But oblivion
is impossible ; for thought is eternal.   Goethe goes so far as to say :

> "They are not shadows which produce a dream :
> I know they are eternal, for they are."

Babbage, in the same chapter, asks : "Who has not felt the painful memory of
departed folly ?   Who has not at times found crowding on his recollection,
thoughts, feelings, scenes, by all perhaps but himself forgotten, which force themselves involuntarily on his attention ?   Who has not reproached himself with the
bitterest regret at the follies he has thought, or said, or acted ?   Time brings no
alleviation to these periods of morbid memory : the weaknesses of youthful days,
as well as those of later life, come equally unbidden and unarranged, to mock our
attention and claim their condemnation from our severer judgment."

most painful to them in life, are now seen in all their
bearings as heightening the glorious grace and mercy
of Christ in their salvation; and no more offensive to
the soul than are shadows in a picture by which the
bright points are relieved and made resplendently beautiful by strong contrasts.

Seeing a little islet cloud bathed in the golden rays of
the ascending sun, Mrs. Jay, by a gentle volition, rose
gracefully like a filmy vapor into the atmosphere; and
having reached the gorgeous couch, there reclined, lost
in transcendent thoughts of God and his beneficence as
manifested in his works of creation. She wished to be
alone with Him, whose immanence pervaded the immen-
sities of space, and of which only the Redeemed are conscious—akin to waves of light, forever flowing forth
from the throne of God.

She had remained there for hours, floating far away
upon the cloud, when she awoke to the recollection of
her morning engagement with her friends. With the
rapidity of an angel she flew back to the palace and hastened to her room, just as Persis was about to enter
with a message from St. Perpetua, announcing her coming accompanied by Calliste.

Mrs. Jay, aided by Persis, arranged her seats for
her guests who soon entered, and after their morning
congratulations, Mrs. Jay asked after Faustinus.

Calliste replied: "He and Tibertius have gone on a
visit to the metropolis, to see a work on which Tibertius

is now engaged, and to walk through the galleries of Art, and see what has been done these last fourteen centuries; and do you know, Mrs. Jay, he dared to say that he would be one too many, for we should wish to talk over matters of our own; and I told him in reply, that he was very thoughtful for us, and that he was right; for I do love, sometimes, to be alone. Is not that wife-like?"

"Oh yes!" said Mrs. Jay, "and I dearly love to hear you say so, Calliste; and that you have not yet become a perfect saint."

"Such as is Perpetua?" said Perpetua, smiling.

"No, my dear saint," cried Mrs. Jay. "I never had such a thought. Every sentiment inspired by you in my heart has been full of satisfied affection. What I meant was this—and I said it under certain impressions long since made upon my mind—that I was glad to hear Calliste speak as she did, out of the naturalness of her womanly heart. Now what could be more wearisome than our being forever all alike perfect, seeing everything in the same light, impressed in the same way and to the same extent. Should we not long for a change of any sort to break up the distressing monotony of such an existence? Therefore it is I am glad Calliste retains her womanly likings, to be sometimes away from her dearest Faustinus, and in grand conclave with her own sex. This is all delightful; and now then what shall we talk about? Calliste, were you not sorry to have

missed the oration of St. John Chrysostom, yesterday?"

"I was sorry we were not all there to listen to him.
Tibertius says it was the grandest effort he has yet
heard. He hopes to go into the school of eloquence so
soon as he has completed the group he is now at work
upon. I tell him his eloquent thoughts will live in marble, informing and elevating the minds of all coming
ages, and that he is as much an evangelist as St. Chrysostom."

"Doubtless," replied Mrs. Jay. "The aim and end
of oratory is to mould the minds of men and angels, and
sculpture reaches the soul through the eye as oratory
does through the ear; and yet, Calliste, I sympathize
with Tibertius in his longing for the power of swaying
a living multitude, whose very life hangs upon the lips
of the orator. But I suppose, Perpetua, we have here
neither women orators nor 'strong-minded women.'
How is it, my dear sister?"

"There are no 'strong-minded women' here, Mrs.
Jay, only because we have no woman's wrongs to be
righted," said Perpetua; and turning to Calliste, she
went on, "'strong-minded women' is a popular cant
phrase of the present day, my Calliste, ironically applied
to those of our sex who have dared to stand forth in
defence of the rights of women; to their just and equal
claims to the control of their children; the rewards of
their own labor, and possession of their own property."

"Ah! if they had rested in these demands, Perpetua, there would have been no grounds for the ridicule of the world; but they claim to be senators, judges and chieftains; and in a word to do whatever men perform in all the departments of civil, religious and military service. Now that is the madness of monomania intensified."

"Pardon me, Mrs. Jay," replied Perpetua, in a quiet, even tone, which was in sweet contrast with the earnestness of Mrs. Jay. "Do not injustice to a great cause by charging upon it the extravagant and impracticable claims of women, in whose minds the rebound transcends the conditions of human society. God has not created man and woman ever to be antagonistic in their social or domestic relations; but to be forever the complement of each other."

"It is very sweet to hear such words as these, Perpetua; but there is one little obstacle to be surmounted to make these new views of society work harmoniously, and that is this: women as now constituted are not, *all of them*, angels of peace and gladness."

"It seems to me," said Calliste, "that Christianity has not done all for woman that was hoped for, if a mother has not an equal right to her children's affections, and the sole right of her own property. Why, Perpetua, though our husbands could drive us away from their homes, they were not allowed to retain a single drachma of our property."

"Indeed!" exclaimed Mrs. Jay. "Was it so? Then

that was one bright spot in the life of a Roman wife which has been lost to us in the subversion of the empire. Now, a woman, except in a few of our North American States, gives up everything she calls her own, for the *doubtful advantage* of having a husband."

"Then I shall be on the side of 'strong-minded women,' Mrs. Jay; and I wonder how there can be two sides to such a question as this, among the wives and mothers of the day."

"Oh, but there is! and Calliste, you would not be found with these strong-minded women, for the reason that, for the most part, they are all free-thinkers, and hold the teachings of the Word of God in great contempt."

"Is that so? Alas! how hard it is to find the exact mean in any of the great reforms of our world. Everything goes on by conflict of some sort; and God only, from antagonistic forces, can work out perfect ellipses in worlds above and worlds below."

Calliste now addressed Mrs. Jay:. "In all ages of the world, my sister, dress has exerted an important influence upon the position and destiny of woman. Luxury had reached a wonderful height when I left Italy last, in the middle of the fourth century. How is it now? Are women the slaves of dress now as they were then? I hope not, and beg you will tell me what are the customs and fashions now prevailing."

Mrs. Jay replied: "The dress of a modern lady is

vastly different from what it must have been in your day, if we are to judge of your costumes by the statues that have come down to us. To begin with the hair; this is now worn parted and brushed plain, sometimes in puffs, sometimes it is plaited, and fastened low down in the neck. This fashion prevails, because of the form of the bonnet; which, just now, is a pretty creation of lace and artificial flowers, and so placed as to cover the organs of inhabitiveness and philoprogenitiveness; leaving the face and head uncovered as far up as the organ of firmness."

"Pray pause one minute, Mrs. Jay," cried Calliste, "and tell me what all these words mean. What kind of organs are you speaking of?"

"Certainly," said Mrs. Jay, laughing. "I had forgotten, Calliste, that you know nothing of the new science of Phrenology. It supplies a most convenient map of the head, and is universally adopted both by believers and skeptics. The brain is not now regarded as a unit, but is believed to be congeries of organs which 'crop out,' as geologists say, upon the surface of the brain; and make certain bumps on the skull, which are designated by names, such as those I have mentioned; so that now-a-days one does not need any other index of character than the curves of the cranium, which tell all that is sedulously concealed by men and women, under a courteous mien of their passional tendencies."

" And do you confide in it implicitly ?" asked Calliste, with a look of amazement at such a " discerning of spirits " having been attained since her day."

Mrs. Jay answered with a smile, " Sometimes I do, and sometimes not."

" You are as dark as an oracle, my sister. In my day we sought to know the character of those about us by the expression of their eyes, their manners, and above all, their voice ; but this reading the inmost secrets of the soul by the contour of the skull is to me inconceivable."

" My dear Calliste," said Perpetua, " when you have visited our earth once more, you will find this science among others a mere matter of fashion. It was the rage in and about the city of Boston, in North America, some years since, and was regarded as an auxiliary to the skepticism which obtains in the fashionable and liter ary circles of that vicinity. It has had its day, and, as Mrs. Jay says, has afforded a convenient nomenclature when speaking of the outside of the head ; in which she has shown some skill in discoursing of the modern headgear."

" Such a science, whether true or false, must have given great significance to the form of the head. Do lovers sigh and sing sonnets in praise of dark eyes and low brows, as they did from the days of Homer down to those of Nero ?" asked Calliste.

" Dark eyes are always in good repute, if they be full

and lustrous," said Mrs. Jay; "but blue eyes are now preferred, as light hair is regarded more beautiful than black hair; but when low brows are bestowed upon a fair girl, she regards it a calamity thus to have her intellectual organs hid from sight; and some extirpate these gifts of nature, once so much admired, in order to show their grand intellectual developments."

"And do they look any the wiser for so doing? I should think such folly would be obvious to the eye as their eyebrows. And now to proceed, let me ask, what is the form and texture of ladies' robes in these days?"

"They change with every season, and are made of every variety of material. There is a dress for the morning, a dress for dinner, a dress for walking out, and a dress for the evening. The fashion of all these change with the season. There is a new style for spring, for summer, for autumn, and for winter. These are got up by a class of men in the pay of great manufacturers of France and England, usually residing in Paris, whose aim is to bring out those fashions most favorable to the interests of the men who pay them best. These costumers seek to get as much material into a dress as may be possible. The latest invention of theirs has been to revive the wearing of hoops, under the new name of *crinoline*—thus enabling a lady to consume some sixteen to twenty yards of silk in a single dress."

"How strangely they must look! In our day the

great art in making our toilette was to dress our hair and paint our faces. Do modern ladies paint?"

"No, or very rarely: a fair skin is regarded as the greatest beauty attainable. White paint and small spots of black, called beauty-spots, made of court-plaster, was the style with our great-grandmothers, a century since, but now a little rouge is allowable."

"Jewels are doubtless worn now as in my day?" said Calliste.

"They are worn by the few who possess them; but in my country wealth is not absorbed by the few at the cost of the many; and gold ornaments have to supply the place of diamonds and pearls, except in our cities, where they manufacture money out of paper, and in such quantities and with such success, that the wives and daughters of bank directors are illuminated on gala nights with pure diamonds."

"Let me ask, Mrs. Jay, before you go further, if there are in these latter days, magicians who make money out of paper? I mean such money as will buy diamonds and pearls. I have no capacity to understand what you can mean—making gold out of paper! How wonderful!" said Calliste, turning to St. Perpetua, who was sitting quietly by, greatly amused with Mrs. Jay's mystification of her friend.

"It is indeed, wonderful," said Mrs. Jay with emphasis. "This grand discovery was made centuries since, by Jews of Lombardy; but they required as much gold to be paid into their hands as they made into paper-money, and so the art and mystery continued for centuries; but the great convenience of carrying paper-money from place to place made it so necessary, that after a while, the common people came to regard a paper bill as an equivalent to gold. In the United States of America, where everything goes with railroad speed, certain bankers and rich men combined to create a multitude of shops for the manufacture of paper-money, by which the labor of the poor and the industry of the farmer has been upset. All this while these honest, hard-working men are made to believe themselves the richer for this paper-money, until a great crisis comes, which overwhelms the country in ruin. Only those bankers and bank-directors, and bank-stockholders, retain uninjured their real estate, purchased out of the dividends paid on their bank stocks; and *their* wives continue to wear diamonds. The working men, who are made to pay the piper, are led to believe that the cause of the last convulsion is all owing to something else than paper-money. Just before I left the world, one of these great earthquakes commenced in my own native city; and like a wave, has circled round the globe; and now can you guess to what cause paper-money making men have attributed all these monetary disasters? I know you never could guess, and so I will tell you; it is all owing to wives an l daughters wearing what is now called ' Crinoline.' " *

* Appendix B.

Calliste caught the frolicsome mood of Mrs. Jay, and entered into the mirthfulness of such a description of a great revolution in the commercial world. In this, Perpetua joined with the greatest zest and heartiness.

"Now I have told you of modern fashions, Calliste, will you not tell me of the fashionable manners of your day? I have read Juvenal, and he certainly does not flatter the ladies of Nero's court."

"He does not, Mrs. Jay; but satirists are never safe guides. Human society could not have been held together, had such vices as he has portrayed, pervaded all circles of Roman life. What do you say, Perpetua?"

"Perpetua replied: "I cannot say what would have been the condition of Rome, if Christ had not come down from heaven to save the world. Certain it is, my adopted city of Carthage presented in strongest contrast the power of faith to overcome the world, and the power of fashion to enslave it."

"Dear Perpetua, will you not give us some illustrations of this remark?" asked Mrs. Jay.

"Before Perpetua complies with your request, Mrs. Jay, will you not tell me what you meant when you spoke just now of 'railroad speed?' In my day we likened speed to the flight of eagles and of falling stars; but what is now the superlative of speed?"

"Sure enough, Calliste, this is all new to you. Well then, the speed I spoke of is not quite 'up to time,' when compared with falling stars, or even the eagle's flight. It is a very simple matter, as you will see. Instead of your old Roman roads, which have been revived in our great cities and are called 'Russ pavements,' railroads are made by levelling the surface of the land, and then iron rails are laid upon wooden logs. Upon these rails long trains of cars are placed; and at the head of each train, instead of horses, we have now a single iron-horse, propelled by water heated into steam. This iron-horse drags hundreds of travellers and tons of baggage, at the rate of thirty miles an hour, for days and weeks together, stopping only for a drink of cold water, once in a while."

"Iron horses and paper money! O Perpetua, how can you sit by and smile at my incredulity. What next?"

"What next? why this; the genius of Franklin and Morse, countrymen of mine, born within striking distance of each other, has brought down the lightning from the clouds; and what was once the symbol of the power of Jove, now runs with messages of all sorts, from one end of the continent to the other, and at the bidding of everybody."

"Is it possible! what mysteries, hid from the creation of the world, has the genius of men eliminated! After all you have told me, Mrs. Jay, there is nothing quite so wonderful to me, as that men can make money out of paper: money, which lapidaries and jewellers will receive, as of equivalent value, for pearls and diamonds."

" That is, Calliste, *par excellence*, the invention of the present age; suggested by Lombard Jews, and improved upon by the Bank of Amsterdam, and subsequently by the Bank of England; but brought to its perfection in my own day, by the clever men of North America. Those old banking institutions of Europe required nearly as much gold to be paid to them as they made into paper; but the last perfection of American banking is, to make paper money to any amount without the smallest outlay of gold. You think *that* wonderful, Calliste; but to my mind the wonder is, that men of labor, those who compose the millions of these sovereign States, consent to give to a few astute rich men, by charter, the right to plunder them of the rewards of their patient industry."

Mrs. Jay, now addressing Perpetua, begged her to go on.

" What I had to say, my dear Mrs. Jay, was this: that at the very time when the disciples of Christ in the higher walks of life in Carthage were ready to lay down their lives rather than deny the faith of Christ, they would not deny themselves the luxuries of that luxurious age. And to show you the temper of those times, when Scapula, the Roman governor, in order to extirpate the Church, threatened a renewal of tortures and death, Tertullian addressed him a letter in these words: ' Bethink thyself, Scapula! What wilt thou do with so many thousand men and women, of every age and dignity, as will freely offer themselves? What swords wilt thou stand in need of? What is Carthage likely to suffer, if decimated by thee; when every one shall find there his kindred and neighbors; and if you shall see matrons and men, perhaps of thine own rank and order?' What words are these! they show the highest enthusiasm prevailing among the Christians of that day; and would you not, as a consequence, believe these matrons above the love of dress and ornament; whose hearts were so full of glorious anticipations of a life with Christ, that to them the crowns of earth would have become baubles?"

"Certainly I should," said Mrs. Jay. "I have always thought that the great want of the present day was an occasional *auto-da-fé*, for the special benefit of Christians of all Protestant denominations; at which some of our most eminent pietists, clothed in ' the blessed yellow vest of penitence,' with a cross on their breasts and backs, painted all over with devils, could be burned up, in proof of the perpetuity of the martyr spirit on earth, and for the edification of the Church universal; which I beg Calliste to understand, is the antipodes of ' *the* Holy Catholic Church,' as the Church of Rome calls herself.

"If you want me to comprehend you, Mrs. Jay," said Calliste, "you must tell me something by way of explanation of these *auto-da-fés*." *

----

* *Auto-da-fé*, which being interpreted means an *Act of Faith*, was invented by the Inquisition at Valladolid, in Spain, and was first celebrated on 21st of May, 1559, in the presence of the royal family. This procedure was made necessary

"Do you tell Calliste, St. Perpetua; for Calliste, I see, begins to distrust my entire fidelity in my replies to her inquiries."

"*Auto-da-Fé*, my Calliste, is the name of the martyrdom of heretics by the papal Church of Rome. Heresy and heretics have a different signification now than in the days of Hippolytus and Origen. These words, at Rome, now embrace all Christians out of the pale of the Romish church."

"And has the Church of Rome been guilty of persecution, and to what extent?"

says Llorente, Secretary of the Inquisition, in his famous history, in consequence of the arrest and trial of so great a number of Spaniards. This bonfire of the disciples of Luther, was made of eminent men and women, and became quite the fashion all over the world. It was first introduced on this continent in Mexico, in 1574. Llorente says, "this first *auto-da-fé* was celebrated with so much pomp and splendor, that eye-witnesses have declared it could only be compared to that at Valladolid, in 1559, at which Philip II. and the royal family attended." The following is from Washington Irving's "Student of Salamanca," describing an *auto-da-fé*, as given by Gonsalvius:

"The sound of bells gave notice that the dismal procession was advancing. It passed slowly through the principal streets of the city, bearing in advance the awful banner of the holy office. The prisoners walked singly, attended by their confessors, and guarded by familiars of the Inquisition. They were clad in different garments, according to the nature of their punishments; those who were to suffer death, wore the hideous *samarra* painted with flames and demons. The procession was swelled by choirs of boys, different religious orders, aud public dignitaries, and above all, by the Fathers of the faith, 'moving,' says Gonsalvius, 'with a slow pace and profound gravity, truly such as becomes the principal generals of that great victory.'"

Llorente says, "the number of those who perished cannot be determined." He makes an approximate estimate, excluding Mexico, Lima, Carthagena, Sicily, and Sardinia, and says the number of those burnt and condemned to severe penances amounted to 323,362 men and women.

"It is hard to tell," said Perpetua.   "The lives lost in persecutions and religious wars carried on at the instigation of the papacy, extend through centuries and cover the globe. The number has been estimated by many millions of men, women and children."

"And you, Mrs. Jay, want these times of trial restored!"

"Not exactly that; but when I have seen the little faith there was in the world about me, I have thought if I was in danger of being burned up some day, it would have a wonderful effect upon my character as a Christian; but here is Perpetua about to tell us that all my speculations on this head are vain."

"I only wish to show you what I have before said is true; that the present age is in advance of all that has preceded it, from the days of the apostles down; and although you have told us that the last great financial convulsion has had its origin in the expensive fashions of the women of the present age, I doubt if their luxury begins to compare in costliness with the luxuries of the second and third centuries. Tertullian, who has just been cited, boasting of the devotedness of the saints, reproves the excessive love of finery in his day. He tells us (I quote his words), 'A great estate is drawn out of a little pocket. It is nothing to expend many thousand pounds upon a string of pearls,' and continuing in this strain, with fine satire he says: 'a weak, slender neck can make a shift to carry about whole forests and lordships.'

And then the way our lady-folks managed their money matters, was very much after that of modern times. He says, ' Vast sums borrowed of the banker, and noted in his account-book to be repaïd every month with interest, are weighed at the beam of a thin slender ear ;' and with undiminished keenness of irony, he continues thus, ' So great is the strength of their pride and ambition, that even the feeble body of one woman shall be able to carry the weight and substance of so many pounds taken up at usury.' He tells us of a single row of pearls which was valued at upwards of two hundred talents.* In his work ' *De Disciplina et Habitu Virginum,*' he gives us his views of abstaining from sumptuous apparel and vain ornaments, from the use of paint and frequent public baths; and moderns may guess at the manners of that day by his warnings and entreaties. There is no circle of society now existing in England or the United States where such exhortations as are here found would not be regarded as offensive and excessively out of place ; and, for a modern illustration of the same sort, I might add, the sermon which that eminent man of God, Jonathan Edwards, preached at Northampton, in Massachusetts, on fast day, about a century since."

" I am much more interested, Perpetua, in the fashions and manners of the ladies in the martyr days of the church, than I am of those in the wildernesses of New

---

* In the currency of the present day this sum is upwards of two hundred thousand dollars. A vast sum to be represented by a necklace.

England a hundred years ago; and now I want you to tell me something more of these ornaments. What was then the style, and how were jewels worn?"

"They were of diamonds, beryls and all manner of precious stones. These were made into bracelets set in gold; and bandeaux for the hair consisting of gold, and jewels and pearls; and our costly suits of apparel were wrought of golden tissues, embroidered with pearls."

"How superb must a splendid woman have looked in her grand gala dress! And then your drapery all hung in graceful folds, and not as is the fashion of the present day, when these are almost obliterated by crinoline and flounces. I have often thought how odd it would be to have a statue of Queen Victoria perpetuated in marble in the court dress of the present day. There is one thing to be said in favor of the ladies of Rome and Carthage; if their dresses were costly, they were not, like those of the ladies of my day, forever changing —three dresses a day, made up in different styles, trimmed with different ribbons and laces; so that a lady with a small family of daughters is nothing more than a family costumer; to say nothing of the wearisomeness of shopping, buying a ribbon here, a pair of gloves there, and gaiter boots at another place, and a bonnet at still another, in order to have all the colors of a dress in perfect trim. Our costumes cannot be so splendid as yours were, but I can see why they cost nearly as much money."

"Your ladies must be weary of a dress before they put it on," said Calliste, who had been a good listener. "I think, Perpetua, if I had made my dresses, or had even the task of selecting them out of the variety of fabrics of our day, I should have been content with few changes of raiment."

"Was there not in those days, St. Perpetua, a large number of nuns, as they are called now, who had taken vows renouncing the pomps, pride and vanities of this life; and were they like all the rest of the world?"

St. Perpetua replied rather demurely: "And let me ask, if there are not any number of young ladies of the present day who take the same vows; and further, if they too are not like all the rest of the world?"

"You hit very close, St. Perpetua; but then the young ladies who take these vows now-a-days, have husbands to win; and I don't think it hardly fair for you to put our vestals alongside of your virgins."

"You are right, Mrs. Jay," said Calliste. "Perpetua has not taken into account the vast difference made by the vow of celibacy. Now St. Paul himself, my Perpetua, in his first epistle to Corinth, tells us that 'those who are married care for the things of the world, how they may please their husbands,' as if it was their bounden duty so to do; and if so, how much more will a young girl care for those things, which are the means of gaining one. Certainly then, Mrs. Jay has good ground for her reply. For what had those women of

Rome and Carthage, your contemporaries, who had taken the vows of celibacy, with wearing costly apparel; whose slippers and sandals even, as St. Clement tells us—and which we, Perpetua, very well know to be true from our own observation—were adorned with gold and precious stones.   And besides, their chambers were the very centres of luxury; containing couches with silver feet, bedsteads inlaid with ivory and gold, surrounded with gold and purple hangings; and indeed, crowded with rich furniture, and statuettes and pictures of immense value; to say nothing, Mrs. Jay, of their love of pearls, peacocks, parrots and Maltese lap-dogs; and more, and what was far more unchristian, though not so regarded in our day, their use of costly perfumes, and the expenditure of large sums in the purchase of beautiful boys." *

* This enumeration of luxuries is found in the Epistles of Clement. St. Clement was very unlike the fashionable preachers of our day. His address would be regarded as out-Spurgeon-ing Spurgeon. Exeter Hall would refuse to listen to such home-thrusts as St. Clement gave his hearers. Speaking of this love of perfumes, he says: "Christians should smell not of ointments, but virtue. As dogs trace wild beasts by their scent, so may we trace the luxurious by their perfumes." Another of these old ministers of the fourth century, thus describes the scene presented in one of the then fashionable churches: "I went into one of the churches and I heard Paul say to the women, that they should ' not adorn themselves with gold and pearls' (1st Epistle to Timothy, xi. 9); but I saw everything contrary in their practice. When one sees the women adorned in the galleries above, and hears Paul thus speaking below; will he not be able to say, our religion is a mere show and fable?"

It may interest some of my readers to know of the modes then practised by

"I am surprised," cried Mrs. Jay, "to be told your fine ladies were so very like those of these latter days. Lap-dogs! why, these are now regarded as 'the superfluity of naughtiness,' and as for beautiful boys, that is something we know nothing of. My wonder is, dear saints, that with such luxury, there could have existed the eminent piety which supplied martyrs for the ten persecutions of the Cæsars."

Perpetua replied, "This corrupt condition of social life gave rise to a sentiment of utter despair of meeting the demands of a life of holiness, and made Christians anxious for the martyr's crown. It led, also, to the rapid development of asceticism in the church. The first of Christian hermits was Anthony, the Egyptian, born 251. His example was made famous by Athanasius, and followed by multitudes. It spread like wild-

ladies to heighten their beauty. St. Cyprian tells us that the fallen angels taught women to paint their cheeks, and draw circles of red round their eyes. His language is very earnest. He says to the fine ladies of his church: "Are you not afraid that when you rise from the dead your Maker will not know you; and that he will shut you out of heaven with this strong rebuke: 'You are none of my work; you have not my image; *you have stained your skin with drugs; your hair is adulterated with dye;* your face is disguised with falsehood; *your figure is transformed;* your look is strange; you cannot see God, when your eyes are not such as God made them, but are infected by the devil. You have followed him; you have imitated the red-colored eyes of the old serpent; and having been decked out by your enemy, you shall burn with him.'"

There is some pertinency in the reproduction of this testimony of so eminent a saint, which certainly has some points of resemblance to our present fashions; and inasmuch as the mode of coloring the eyes, so severely stigmatized by this venerable saint, is said to be coming into vogue.

fire from Egypt to Palestine and Syria, and before the close of the fourth century, there was scarcely a mountain in the eastern part of the Roman empire between Armenia and Arabia without its Laura, or colony of monks." *

" When Faustinus and I last visited Carthage, it was near the close of the fourth century. We were horrified by the condition of morals consequent on making celibacy and not Christ the way to heaven ; and were disgusted with the disgraceful methods by which questions of extreme delicacy were concluded ; and now, then, what has followed since our day ?"

Perpetua replied : " Separate communities of monks and nuns became a necessity. The dogma of celibacy once enunciated must be maintained. Men give up everything sooner than their idols. The cry now is, as when Micah followed in pursuit of the children of Dan, ' Ye have taken away the gods which I have made, and what have I more ?' The history of Monachism, which you ask me to relate, would be painful even here ;" and pausing a moment, Perpetua continued : " Woman has ever been the victim of cruelty and crime. Girls of the

* The Fathers of the latter half of the fourth century, considered these arid deserts as a heaven upon earth. " Go, now," says Chrysostom, " to the desert of Egypt, and you will find it more delightful than paradise, for there are ten thousand choirs of angels in human form." Epiphanius said of them : " The monasteries are like tabernacles, full of heavenly choirs, singing psalms, reading and praying.'> 'Fathers of the Desert,' vol. II. p. 128. St. Augustine describes some of the monks of the desert as hideous for their ugliness and nastiness. Saints in that age, even, saw the same things in very different lights.

present day, who have the misfortune to be educated by nuns, are taught to look upon married life as degrading; and certain it is, that such girls, educated in convents, are utterly worthless as wives and mothers. Indeed, so deeply has this truth been burnt into the souls of men in Catholic countries, that it is a Roman proverb—'Do you want a faithless wife? Marry a girl brought up at a nunnery.' " *

"Alas! to what a wretched condition has the world come! Rome, no more the mistress of the world, and the Church of Christ a prey to wolves in sheep's clothing! What a contrast to our hopes fourteen centuries since, Perpetua!"

"Do not despair of the Church of Christ, my Calliste," said Perpetua. "That lives, and will live, while thrones and empires are passing away."

"What a worthless sacrifice of human happiness," said Mrs. Jay, "have these great fathers of the church inflicted upon the world, and what untold and unappreciable misery have they inflicted upon our sex, by the institution of these convents. But what astonishes me most of all is, that in the United States of North America, a land peopled by men who left their homes because of oppression, and to secure to their children freedom of conscience, that Romish convents are built

* See a work entitled, "Nuns and Nunneries: Sketches compiled entirely from Romish authorities, pp. 242-273. London, 1852." Will no American publisher bring out this book?

in every State, and schools maintained in them for the education of *Protestant* girls, and are patronized by men who claim to be Protestants. Such is the enmity of the hearts of these fathers and mothers to the religion of Christ, that they hazard the happiness of their children for this world and the world to come, 'to show their superiority to prejudices of education!' The history of Europe, and the condition of Catholic Italy and Spain, and of sensual, infidel and Catholic France, at the present day, reads them no lessons; nor even the sad history of many homes of our own land, robbed of their children, who have been beguiled to become nuns. Nothing can reach the hearts and consciences of such, so-called Protestants. The most astounding developments are met with indifference. And all the while, they are so jealous of forcible and illegal confinement, that lunatics even are visited in their asylums once a year by the governors of States and the council of state, to see if any one sane person is unjustly deprived of liberty. And yet convents are allowed to exist, and no one doubts that great cruelty is exercised to poor nuns, heavy chastisements inflicted, and death itself; but these poor, weak, pious women, who have been lured into these Bastiles of religious despotism, hoping to escape from cruel parents, or the misery of unrequited love, are left without the faintest hope of escape, to die of their unspoken sorrows and unredressed wrongs."

"My dear lady!" cried Calliste, interrupting Mrs. Jay; "why does not the Christian church cry out in a voice of thunder against such unspeakable cruelty?"

"Cry out, indeed!" replied Mrs. Jay. "Why one half of the Christian church is democratic, and the other half is republican—these being the two great political parties of our country. Now all the Romanists side with the democracy, and if a case occurs of a nun who has escaped from her prison-house, and she dares to tell the story of her wrongs and wretchedness, she is defamed by half the presses in the country, and the other half so feebly defend her, that she is treated as a castaway, and her last state is often worse than her first. The priests are powerful; they have money, and they use it on all such occasions, with great sagacity and success. This treatment of nuns who have escaped from their convents and sought to return to society, and who have been hunted down by calumny, and thus left without sympathy and countenance of those who call themselves protestants, has silenced others, who in a happy hour have achieved their liberty. These escaped nuns have won an immunity from persecution, by the most entire silence of the secrets of their convents."

"And your country is a free republic!" said Calliste. "What strange contrasts and contradictions continue to exist, my Perpetua! Here is a land of freedom, where the greatest jealousy exists as to personal liberty, as is shown in the treatment of the insane, and yet convents exist which no magistrate can enter! I am greatly mystified by such contradictions."

"It is in all respects as Mrs. Jay has told us," replied Perpetua. "The strangest anomalies exist in that country on this subject. The fashionable mothers, those especially whose fortunes have been speedily created, are greatly taken by such romantic names as the Romanists adopt for their seminaries. The building is of wood, or brick, or stone, and like all academies, but then it is styled—'*Ladies of the Sacred Heart*,' '*The Academy of the Visitation of the Blessed Virgin*,' '*Carmelite Sisters' Academy*, '*Sœurs Notre Dame*,' and the like. These mothers, who are conscious of their incompetency for training their children for the fashionable circles to which they themselves aspire, and which they hope to reach on bringing out their lovely daughters, send these dear ones to have their manners formed by nuns who have no knowledge of either life or manners. It is very odd, but so it is."

"Yes, indeed, Perpetua," said Mrs. Jay. "How is it you are so well-informed, Perpetua? Have you been recently in the United States?"

"No, I have not; but one of my descendants, who was with me some years since, was educated at Emmittsburg, and from her I derived a full account of what is passing in American convents and in American society."

"What can be done, Perpetua, and who is to do it?

I mean to ask, How shall the mind of my countrymen be reached to induce them by law to open these dark habitations of cruelty?"

"It is a question of vast interest, and one upon which I have speculated with the deepest anxiety. I had hopes that a wise, cautious and courteous movement was about to be made in the Legislature of Massachusetts some little while since; but how happened it? A committee of vulgar, sensual and corrupt men was appointed to make an examination of certain Romanist seminaries, and they disgraced themselves and the State, and postponed the action of the public mind in this matter for a century perhaps."

"Oh, it was horribly disgraceful!" exclaimed Mrs. Jay, "and it was a great triumph for the Roman party. Politics pollute everything in our country, and it is this that makes the difficulty. Massachusetts owes it to the world to recommence the effort, and if there are any men of high moral standing in the legislature, to place them in the position to act."

Perpetua shook her head. "Such men are rare everywhere; and men of high moral courage, willing to become martyrs for the cause of humanity, are not likely to be found in the halls of modern legislatures. The cause of woman must be advocated by Christian women. They must petition the legislatures of the several States, with a paper carefully prepared, and which shall prescribe all the steps to be taken, and all the course to be pursued; not leaving a single point to be decided by political hucksters, who will not fail to mar by their amendments the work to be done, and so defeat the movement."

"And, Perpetua, what ought women to do? pray, be more specific," said Mrs. Jay.

"With pleasure. I would have a bill carefully drawn in the form of a petition, praying that the governor and his council shall, once a year, or oftener at his option, and without previous notice, visit every convent and monastery in the State. Their position would insure society that such investigations would be made with all refinement compatible with the end to be attained. Each recluse, male and female, should be had alone before the governor and council, in a room where they should be examined without any possibility of being overheard, and the replies should be made in writing. These nuns and monks should be assured of protection from all harm. It should be a provision of law that a register of the inmates should be kept. All penances inflicted and the offences thus punished should be registered; and this record should be placed before the governor and his council, to aid them in their scrutiny. In case of the death of a recluse, an inquest should be held by the coroner, aided by one or more of the leading medical faculty as jurymen, whose report should be registered in the convent and then sent to the governor. In case of cruelty or unjust imprisonment, the Superior

and all of her accessories, should be punishable as other
criminals, by due process of law. Now, my dear Mrs.
Jay, who can doubt, if this shield of protection were
thrown over women in convents, much misery would be
prevented. And why is not this shield interposed ? only
because the hearts of American women have not been
roused to the condition of their suffering sisters in bondage."

"You speak, Perpetua, with a tone of rebuke, as if
this was a triumph that could be achieved by a single
impulse of the womanhood of my country. Who is to
give the impulse ?"

"God knows ! I cannot tell. It may commence with
any one woman competent to place this matter in proper
form. That is the great matter. This done, then let
all the women agitate. Let every church send its petition. Let every circle of friends send a petition, and
every neighborhood—not once, but for a series of
sessions of their several State legislatures—and let such
an act be passed, and one of the results will be the sudden removal of these convents from State to State, and
when such laws are created and enforced in every
State, finally they will remove across the Canada line on
the north, and that of Mexico on the south."

" 'That is a consummation devoutly to be wished,' and
I think if those who have so much to say about the dangers of the Roman priesthood in controlling the elections
of our country would take this view of this question, it

might at once enlist the attention of the presses of " The American Party,' so-called."

" I hope it never may, then," said Perpetua, " for if ever this movement can be successful, it must come from the pure well of woman's sympathy for woman, and not out of the miserable motives which defile American statesmanship of the present day."

————

Calliste rose and exclaimed, " What dismal topics we have had for our first call upon Mrs. Jay! Come, now, suppose we ascend into the clouds and take a survey of the world below us ?"

CHAPTER VIII.

St. Perpetua, Calliste and Mrs. Jay rise into the Air and sweep over the Country, alighting to visit attractive Pleasure Grounds—Perpetua's Remarks on English Manners—The Villa of Anastasius—Frankie Guilford and her Music Lesson— Her Account of Herself and Studies—Emerentia welcomes our Party to her Villa—The Music Hall—New Music by Beethoven—Mrs. Jay sings some Airs, "Native" to good Society in New York—Their Visit to the Studio—Perpetua and her Party remain to Supper—Conversation at the Table—They take Leave of the Family of Anastasius—Evening Scenes at the Palace—Mrs. Jay contrasts the Appearance of the Saloons with a Grand Party of her own—Mrs. Jay's Difference between Ancient and Modern Martyrdom—They join Sulpicius Severus and St. Hedwiges—St. Chrysostom's Opinion of Modern Monkery—Of the Origin of Asceticism.

WITH the graceful movement of angels on the wing, Perpetua, Calliste and Mrs. Jay rose into the air from off the balcony of the palace, and sweeping over the surface of the country, engaged in happy converse, they enjoyed the ever-varying landscape. Sometimes they alighted to admire a classic miniature Temple of the Winds which adorned an extensive lawn, or to examine a nicely-trimmed and well-kept garden, ornamented with groups of statuary. Wherever they alighted they were welcomed with smiles of courtesy. There were no dismal signs of civilization—"Man-traps set here," warning them to keep out of harm's way. No fierce bull-dogs with their hideous faces and crooked legs, chained at the gates of entrance into parks and pleasure-grounds, a terror to all visitors, and a warning to all vagrants.

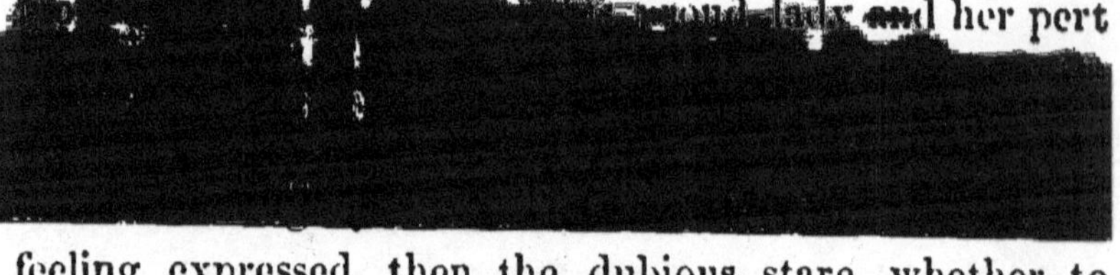

feeling expressed, then the dubious stare, whether to cringe in base servility, or to wear a frowning hauteur.

A manor-house, as it would be called in England, hid amid a grove of splendid shade-trees, lay beneath them. It wore such an air of elegance and comfort, as well as of opulence, that Perpetua proposed they should descend and make the acquaintance of the family. To this, Calliste and Mrs. Jay gladly assented. As they entered within the open gates, Perpetua, with a smile, said to Mrs. Jay: "How happy it is for us that we are not thus straying into the park of some proud English gentleman. I have known a well-dressed party to be warned to quit premises of this sort, with as little courtesy as if they had been gipsies."

As they drew near the house, they discovered a group of lovely girls sitting on couches beneath the pillared portico, with music-books in their hands, in the height of merriment. The party consisted of three girls, of about twelve, fifteen and sixteen years, dressed with the grace and beauty which characterizes the higher walks of social life upon this globe; and a young lady of twenty, wearing the robes and halo of immortality, whose lovely face and bright eyes beamed with gladness. The children were clustered around this young lady, and their merry laugh made the sweetest music. So soon as our party were discovered coming up the shaded walk leading to the main entrance, they all rose; and advancing with a grace and buoyancy of manner, which in itself created in the mind of Mrs. Jay a sense of exquisite pleasure, they hastened to welcome their approach.

The young lady first presented herself to Perpetua, as one who had been known on earth as Miss Frankie Guilford; and then Perpetua, having introduced Calliste and Mrs. Jay, was herself presented by Calliste. This done, the young girls were in like manner introduced.

After they had entered the grand saloon and were seated, the young ladies nestled around the shining one with the sweet solicitude of those whose love made nearness essential to happiness. Perpetua began the conversation by apologizing for interrupting their mirth. Frankie, with her bright laughing eyes, replied, "I must explain to you the cause for such an explosive laugh as we were all enjoying at the moment. I am one of the few of earth who are born without a love for melody. I might have had the germ of music developed in me, but my attempts to sing were so odd as to provoke the laughter of those about me, until I ceased to make the effort, and grew up into the belief that because 'I had no ear for music,' I had no soul for music, and thus I lived on till my short life ended.

"On reaching the celestial city, I soon discovered my great want of all knowledge of the science of music; for though my soul was on fire while the songs of the Redeemed arose in the vast congregation, yet I could not sing. It was my happiness to be sent here under conduct of my angel, who placed me in this beloved family to be instructed by these dear children, and so be made fit for the circles of the Redeemed. Now I can read the notes with the facility of printed letters, and the science of music is rapidly opening itself to me, so that I am becoming quite at home in the exercises of the grammar of music, but this matter of singing is not so easily attained. And my singing-lessons are an unfailing source of mirthfulness. I practice the scales, and when I make a slide they slide into smiles, and just now I had made my first burst into a *bravura*, whereupon my teachers, taken all by surprise, found relief in inextinguishable laughter; and I joined in the laugh. I do not get on very rapidly, but I do not know how I could be happier."

"Sister Frankie does herself great injustice," said the eldest girl, who was seated with her arm around her waist. "Her progress in the science of music, so full as it is of occult laws of sound and the sublimities of mathematical science, she has made almost at a bound, so that her teacher has often expressed his pleasure and surprise at her skill and success. It is only with regard to the discipline of the voice to which she has not yet attained."

"I am sure, Miss Frankie, that you have made good progress," said Perpetua.

"Yes, I do succeed surprisingly well. This is my own consciousness; and then my patience is only surpassed by the loving persistency of these sweet sisters of mine. I tell them that by and by I shall enjoy my new-found capacities far more than I could have done had I too been born to the full appreciation of harmony."

"Certainly, Miss Frankie," replied Perpetua, "the law of compensation is universal. Let me ask, are you doing nothing more than studying music?"

"Oh yes! I have various masters who come to give me lessons in art, science, literature and languages. I have no idle hours here. But then there is such a joy in study in this life of ours. All we have attained in our past life is at our command, and my past acquirements aid me immensely in my present studies. Then, too, the perfection of our mental power, in seizing a new idea; its widest generalizations come into the mind with such rapidity as to seem an intuitive perception of truth. Then we have here such happy changes of intellectual labor. I go from mathematics to painting in the studio, and thence to the garden to study botany, thence to the gorges and mountains for pebbles to aid me in my lessons in mineralogy, and last of all, come my lessons in singing, when these dear girls assume the very responsible task of teachers."

"Have you no sense of weariness?" asked Mrs. Jay.

"Far from it," replied Frankie, with flashing eyes of joy; "delightful as are our visions of the night, I wake with eager delight to reach some far distant point in the illimitable range of mathematics which had just made its appearance in the mind's horizon on yesterday, or it may be of some other of the various branches of knowledge which fill the soul with ever growing consciousness of the wisdom and love of God—the source of all life, all beauty, and all wisdom; and I, saved by the death of Christ!" *

"I congratulate you, Miss Frankie," said Mrs. Jay, "that you have been led to begin at the beginning from the very day-dawn of immortal life. But in my own case, I felt the trammels of society so great, that when I

---

* Babbage, in his Ninth Bridgewater Treatise, says, "If, in a future state, we could turn from the contemplation of our own imperfections, and with increased powers apply our minds to the discovery of nature's laws, and to the invention of new methods by which our faculties might be aided in that research, pleasure the most unalloyed would await us at every stage of our progress. Unclogged by the dull corporeal load which tyrannizes even over our most intellectual moments, and chains the ardent spirit to its unkindred clay, we should advance in the pursuit, stimulated instead of wearied by our past exertions, and encountering each new difficulty in the inquiry, with the accumulated power derived from the experience of the past, and with the irresistible energy resulting from the confidence of ultimate success."—Chapter xiv.

found myself free of earth, I was possessed of a wish to enjoy the widest range of my new-found liberty. Sweeping from sphere to sphere, I have been coasting along the shores of creation, glad to be alone with God. I have not lost all my time in so doing; for I have gained grand conceptions of the power of my heavenly Father, who has impressed his Almightiness upon all his works. But I may have made a mistake, Miss Frankie, in not following your example."

"I do not know whether I have done wisely or not," replied Frankie; "but I have been perfectly contented here, and have not now a single wish ungratified."

"Is it possible that you have not been tempted to ascend to these bright spheres above us?" asked Mrs. Jay.

"I have thought, at times, that I would do so, but then these sweet friends of mine have looked sad when I have talked of leaving them; and as I have but little time to spend with them, I never have put forth the exercise of my will to leave this villa for a single hour. Sometimes when we are walking, and a flower is seen growing at a height not approachable on foot, I rise to gather it; and this done, I return to the ground and have almost forgotten my powers of will."

"From what part of the earth do you come?" asked Mrs. Jay.

"I was born and brought up in the State of Connecticut, within sight of Long Island Sound, the lullaby of whose waves, in my childhood, sang me to rest."

"You have a lovely home," said Perpetua, bowing to Frankie. "And what are the names of the proprietors of this villa and the parents of these dear children?"

Frankie replied, "They are known as Anastasius and Erementia, whose domains are quite extensive, as you may have seen. Anastasius holds these lands from his forefathers through many centuries, and is sedu'ous to leave them in a more perfect state than when he received them. His only son is now with him overlooking the labors of the peasantry, whose lovely cottages, covered with climbing flowers, must have attracted your attention."

While Frankie was thus speaking, a lady of forty, in the full maturity of woman's beauty, in a splendid toilet, swept into the room, and was presented by Frankie to her guests. The amenity of this lady's address was so beautiful as to arrest and absorb the attention of Mrs. Jay. She had never witnessed any thing to compare with it. Seating herself beside St. Perpetua, Erementia made her acknowledgments for the distinguished honor of her visit, and continued the conversation by asking after certain eminent persons resident at the palace, known to St. Perpetua. And this ended, she spoke of the oration of St. Chrysostom, which she had had the happiness of hearing. And being requested by Perpetua, she gave a most skillful analysis of the argument, repeating with entire accuracy, and perfect elocution, certain passages of striking eloquence which had sunk into her heart, Mrs. Jay all the while gazing and listening as one charmed. She had seen the graceful manners of the Redeemed, and of the people at the great oratorio, and of the servitors of the palace, but here was her ideal of womanly grace and intellectual culture. Having finished her remarks about St. Chrysostom, Erementia expressed her satisfaction that her family had been so highly distinguished as to be selected for the residence of one of the Redeemed, and of the unceasing interest she and her husband and children took in Frankie, and in the cultivation of her intellect.

"I have all reason to believe it is so," said Frankie; "and it is so strange that beings so vastly superior to me in all that I am now constituted to love, should see in me anything to move them to admiration; but it is not me they admire, but the grace of God that has clothed me in the robes of Christ's righteousness. And this it is that makes me happy to be so loved as I am by these gifted friends and their loved children."

One of the girls, standing at the side of the chair occupied by Frankie, leaned forward, and placing her arm round Frankie's neck, kissed her on the forehead, and said in a low tone, "Why need you ask, dearest Frankie, what prompts us to love you, so you are loved? We do not seek to know what impels us, but are unceasingly happy in loving you."

"Yes, sweet one," said Frankie, returning her embrace, "but such thoughts in my heart increase my apprehension of the love of God and Christ towards me, thus enhancing, inexpressibly, my joy in your love."

"Oh, then it shall be so forever!" cried the dear girl, again kissing Frankie, her hand still resting upon Frankie's shoulder, from the simple love of having it there.

The father and his son, a youth of twenty, entered the saloon, and were welcomed by his lady with charming courtesy. She then presented them to our party with all her characteristic grace of manner, to the admiration of Mrs. Jay, who was busy thinking how much the happiness of life may be enhanced by a careful attention to the sweet charities of courtesy and kindly tones of voice; and of the negligence of husbands and wives and children to each other on earth, and how much of heart-felt happiness was thus lost.

Anastasius at once entered into easy conversation with his guests. His son seated himself by Mrs. Jay, and was soon absorbed, listening to all she had to tell him of her impressions of the world of art. While they were thus occupied, the circle broke up; Perpetua and Erementia going into a long gallery of paintings and statuary, and Calliste and Anastasius into a conservatory filled with rare plants; not only of this world, but various plants raised from seeds sent to him by his father and mother in the far-off world, where they now resided, and which had been brought by angels returning to this world. The girls with Frankie returned soon to the saloon, and gathered around Mrs. Jay. Frankie felt a great interest in one so recently from her native land, and from a city so well known to her, and which she had often visited. Then, too, there was something attractive in Mrs. Jay to Frankie, which made all she said a source of amusement and interest to herself and the children. Returning with his lady, Perpetua, and Caliste to the mansion, Anastasius invited our friends to go with him and his family up into his music hall, and listen to some new compositions of the illustrious Beethoven, which they had recently brought home with them from the metropolitan city. This proposal was gladly assented to by Mrs. Jay, who at once rose, greatly to the regret of her happy auditors, who were all absorbed by the tale she was telling of her early days. This was broken off most inopportunely, but it could not be helped. She had already so won the hearts of the youngest girls that they accompanied her up the grand staircase with their hands held in hers, making many fond entreaties for her to stay with them and Frankie.

Anastasius called to his children to take their places, which they did with alacrity, while he led Erementia to a magnificent harp. The beauty of the performance was forgotten in the exquisite tones of their united voices. Mrs. Jay thought she caught something of *Adelaide* in this composition. It was full of the genius of the great master, and held our party absorbed and delighted. When this was ended, the girls and brother sang a quartette, Erementia playing for her children an accompaniment. Perpetua said, "That must be Haydn's;" when the youngest girl, running to her mother and throwing her arms around her neck, as she sat at the harp, exclaimed, "Oh no! it is mother's." Erementia left her instrument, and begged Perpetua to sing for them some of the songs of Carthage; which she did, accompanying herself on the harp. Calliste was then called upon for a song; and without rising she sang some sweet melodies which she said were native to the world from whence she had so recently returned. Anastasius next begged Mrs. Jay to sing some of her native songs.

"My native songs!" exclaimed Mrs. Jay. "I came from a land as yet without music. I was next neighbor to Frankie. She lived in Connecticut, and I in New York. We import all our music from abroad, as we do our silks and satins. We have some negro melodies which may be called native airs, sung by the slaves of the south, in the corn-fields, with little other effect than to scare away the crows. But that I may not seem unwilling to contribute my share to our musical entertainment, I will accompany myself on the harp and do my best to sing airs *native* now to the circles of good society 'up-town.'"

And with a degree of skill which outside the world of art would have been regarded admirable, Mrs. Jay sang "Ah non guinge," from *Somnambula*, and "Qui la voce," from *Puritani*. She then was about to rise, when the young ladies begged so earnestly, that she reseated herself, and sang "Salut à la France," "Quando il destino," from the *Child of the Regiment*, and "Robert, toi que j'aime," from *Robert le Diable*.

"These are some of the popular airs from the operas of the day when I left," said Mrs. Jay as she rose from the harp.

Anastasius was very kind in his acknowledgments, and Erementia expressed her thanks in her accustomed graceful manner; as for the young folks, they were evidently greatly taken with this lady so fresh from earth.

Perpetua now proposed that they should return to the Palace, and invited Frankie to return with them for the night. "We have a reception of our near neighbors this evening, and are promised visits from some very distinguished persons from the Metropolis. I think as you have never been to this one of our 'many mansions,' you will see it now under very happy auspices."

Perpetua's movement was met by entreaties to prolong their visit so far as to share the family repast. Now it is fitting to say here, that eating and drinking with the Redeemed is no longer a necessity, but, as with those angels who dined with Abraham, it is optional. And these repasts are now a bond of union, enlivened by wit and anecdote, and enriched by the various knowledge of the circle.

Frankie united her earnest entreaties, and it was agreed by Perpetua and her friends to stay, with the understanding that they should leave immediately after the feast was over. This done, the girls took possession of Mrs. Jay and Frankie, whom they led to their studio, where it was their custom to work two hours every day with their masters at their several studies. One had a picture begun, another was moulding a flower girl, and the eldest had a statue of Frankie in marble, blocked out by her master, which she was now bringing into its perfect shape by her mallet and chisels, and various files. They all expressed their delight in their labors, and having shown Mrs. Jay their works, they drew aside a curtain, very much against the will of Frankie, who sought to prevent them, and there was revealed Frankie's first attempt with the pencil. It would have been regarded in any studio on earth a very clever picture; but after the eye had been satiated with splendors of design and color in the gallery of Anastasius, it certainly did wear the marks of the brush of the sign-post painter rather than the pencil of an artist. Mrs. Jay honest y expressed her full faith that Frankie would, in due time, become quite as eminent an artist in painting as in music. This doubtful compliment drew forth a burst of laughter, in which Frankie led the way with the highest satisfaction.

They were called by a servant to return to the house, and found the host and hostess awaiting them with their guests to go to the supper-room, where the banquet was all prepared. It was a room of rare magnificence, and the vases for fruit and grapes were of singular beauty, wrought of gold and of porcelain—a pottery which would have astonished and delighted even Bernard Palissy. The repast was purely ante-diluvian, and the delicious fruit might well be called "angel's food." The entertainment of the palate, however, was not comparable to the pleasures of their social converse. Erementia told some very pretty tales of her birds. This led Calliste to tell of the splendor of the birds of her new world, and their habits, which were full of wonders. Anastasius made many inquiries as to the electrical changes of atmosphere in that globe, but Calliste confessed she did not know the meaning of the word. This was explained, and she gave a description, glowing and graphic, of the sun-sets, and the skies both by day and night in that world, and next, of the gradual development of that new race of beings; and thus it was that the hours flew until the stars began to glitter, when they rose from the table and passing through the hall stepped out upon the portico. The girls clung to Frankie as Perpetua renewed her invitation for her to spend the night with her at the palace.

"I think we must leave," said Mrs. Jay, "for I have an intuition that my friend Peter Schlemihl has returned, and is now searching for me."

"Peter Schlemihl!" cried Frankie, breaking away

from the young ladies and laying her hand upon Mrs. Jay's arm; "which Peter do you speak of—the German Peter Schlemihl, or ' *Peter Schlemihl* in America?' "

"Peter Schlemihl in America," replied Mrs. Jay. "Pray, tell me, do you know him?"

"Know him! why he is my dear friend Peter," replied Frankie, her bright eyes beaming with joy.

"Is it so? Now you will go home with us and meet him there. How glad he will be to see you and receive your congratulations, that he who was shadowless, bootless and homeless is now at home with every wish of his soul satisfied."

Frankie stood in doubt. The children begged her to send word to her friend Peter to come to see her; and the eldest girl, with a modest, roguish air, in a low tone of voice, suggested that it was not ladylike for Frankie to go in search of her gentlemen friends. This provoked a general mirthfulness, and Frankie declared it was due to the gallantry of all worlds that a lady should be sought. She, however, obtained a promise from Mrs. Jay, that she would certainly bring him with her at no distant day.

Anastasius and his lady, with that beautiful air of entire sincerity which is so winning when it is felt to spring from the depths of the soul, begged St. Perpetua, Calliste and Mrs. Jay to bring Frankie's friend, and to confer upon them the high gratification of their society; not for so short a time as now, but for days and months,

It was wi.h many loving courtesies they left, rising rapidly into the upper regions of the air, until they saw with the space-penetrating glance of angelic vision, the distant, illuminated domes of the palace, for which they sped their way, reaching the grand entrance as the chimes of the great temple sounded the hour of ten.

Their first purpose was to find their friends; Calliste went in search of Faustinus, and Perpetua kept Mrs. Jay company in looking after Laurens and Schlemihl. In so doing, they promenaded the halls, saloons and porticos of the palace, which were filled with guests and residents; some walking, others stood in groups conversing. Within the saloons, were companies of the Redeemed and their visitors, occupied in various ways. In one saloon they were singing some glorious quartettes. In another they were all listening to an eminent elocutionist repeating a new Epic by Milton, a poem recently brought out by him, and which was already winging its flight across the wide plains of space, borne by angels and the Redeemed, to be recited by them, as now, to beings fitted to appreciate its sublimity.

They thus strolled along the halls and upon the balconies, looking into the rooms for their truant friends, until they were satisfied they were not to be found. Mrs. Jay could not but remark to Perpetua, the contrast of which she was conscious, between the crowded parties of good society in New York and what she saw before her. "Here," she said, "all are alike occupied, and with such earnestness, as if they were compressing all that was possible into the passing moment. Look at that happy group! Listen to the gaiety of their laugh, see the sparkling of eyes, as the ready reply follows the brilliant sally. And if we look into other rooms where grave subjects are under review, there is no wandering eye, nor one who is not wholly absorbed in the discourse. But, my dear Perpetua, had you looked in at one of our grand parties, you would have seen the hostess all anxiety to save young ladies from *ennui* at being left alone to gaze at her pictures; or if in the dancing hall, from becoming fixtures against the wall for want of proper partners in the dance. And one-half of all present, weary of the stupidities of a party, which nothing could have induced them to meet, but the fear of losing caste, and so dropping out of the world of fashion. I never willingly ventured upon such a fiery ordeal of my patience; but somehow the demands of society—such as a wedding party for a cousin, or a niece; or when my Augusta had been elected bridesmaid to a school-girl friend, she must give a party to the bride in acknowledgment of the distinction thus conferred—in some such way I was made a martyr to good society about once a year."

"And you demeaned yourself with the patience of a saint," replied Perpetua, with a smile.

"A saint 'all of the modern time,' Perpetua. There is some difference in the martyrdoms of the present day,

and those sixteen centuries since. Then you were consumed to ashes by those who hated you; but now we
are only *done brown* by our 'dear five hundred friends.'"

Passing a room in which there were but two persons
seated on a sofa in earnest colloquy—

"Come," said Perpetua, "let us join Sulpicius Severus
and St. Hedwiges, both dear friends of mine." So saying, she led Mrs. Jay into the room and presented her.
"Do not let us interrupt your conversation, which we
come to share," said Perpetua.

"With pleasure, Perpetua," said Severus. "I was
telling St. Hedwiges of my interview with St. John
Chrysostom; and was about to tell her what he said,
speaking of my life of St. Martin, and of his own works
and mine in favor of Christian asceticism and celibacy.
The remark I was about to repeat to St. Hedwiges as
you came up was this—that Chrysostom in reviewing
all that had followed his own labors in this direction, and
which were to follow for centuries to come, unless God
should interpose and consume the world by the brightness of his coming; with intense feeling said: 'I feel,
Severus, as if I could adopt the language of Paul, and
wish myself accursed from Christ, rather than have
inflicted all this weight of misery which has rested and
will rest upon misguided youthful hearts.' He added:
'God's infinitude of mercy is alone equal to the forgive-
ness of such as have corrupted the simplicity of the
Gospel of Christ, and whose lives and labors are to be

regarded as a curse rather than a blessing to the world. Ministers of the grace and mercy of God we have fastened heavy chains of a cruel bondage upon those whom Christ has made free. What height and depth of wretchedness has followed your labors and mine!' exclaimed Chrysostom."

These remarks at once interested Mrs. Jay, who could not but express her astonishment that the great men of the early church could so soon forget the Saviour, and substitute for his righteousness the idols of celibacy and alms-giving. In reply to this, Severus showed by what slow steps the great doctrine of salvation by faith became corrupted and changed. He traced the rise of asceticism to Hindostan, far into the depths of antiquity. He spoke as follows: "Monachism did not take its rise in *the* church. It is not a Christian institution. In the laws of Menu, written fifteen centuries before the Christian era, the following directions are given how to become a saint. The words of Menu are: 'Let a man seclude himself from the world, and gain the favor of the gods, by fasting, subduing the lusts and mortifying the senses. Let him crawl backwards and forwards on his belly ; or let him stand all day on his toes. Let him remain always sitting or always standing : only at sunrise, noon and sunset, let him go to the water and bathe.'* In this last direction the Fakirs of India far surpassed our early monks; for the Hindoos associated holiness

* Cited by Ruffin, in his " Fathers of the Desert," vol. i. p. 24.

with personal cleanliness, but not so the saints of our age. St. Athanasius, in his Life of St. Anthony the Monk, speaking of his mortification of the flesh, in a tone of high commendation, says: 'St. Anthony wore inside a hair shirt; outside a skin. These he kept on to the end of his days. He never washed the dirt from his body. He would not even wash his feet, nor let them touch water when he could help it.' " *

This subject thus introduced was made the topic of an hour's talk, in which St. Hedwiges shared largely. It was to Mrs. Jay a novelty to listen to a discussion of this sort, by those who could say with Æneas, " All which I saw, and part of which I was."

As it was getting late, Perpetua and Mrs. Jay rose, and thanking Sulpicius and St. Hedwiges for their kind courtesy, they took leave.

* Ruffin, vol. L p. 277.

CHAPTER IX.

EARLY the next morning the palace was all astir, eagerly crowding into the great temple to listen to the new oratorio composed by Mozart, called "The Crucifixion." It was performed at sunrise, in order that the intense sadness it inspired might be dispersed during the day of sunshine.

At the feast of fruits and flowers which followed, and which was not unworthy Raphael's entertainment, Perpetua and Mrs. Jay had taken their seats together, when two of the Redeemed, a lady and gentleman, whose air

... attention of Mrs. Jay, took seats
... Perpetua, and addressing her,
... Mozart's music. They had
... time, greatly to Mrs. Jay's
... recollecting herself, turning
... dear Mrs. Jay, I have
... persons with whom I am
... dy. This is——

have written the Psalms and Hymns of Dr. Watts than all the epics the world has ever seen."

While this lady was so fluent, in speaking to Dante, Mrs. Jay felt awed in such presence. There was an atmosphere which surrounded these personages, something beyond and above anything she had before experienced; inspiring in her heart emotions of homage and profound interest, so deep as gave force to their every action and word.

Perpetua remarked this awe impressed by Dante upon her friend, who had never before manifested any remarkable development of the organ of veneration; for now Mrs. Jay sat perfectly quiet, contented to be an observer, and replied briefly and explicitly to all Dante's inquiries, as if she regretted every second of time thus absorbed by herself. It was evident she had in some sort the terror of the ancient Florentines for the man who had descended into the abodes of the damned.

Rising from the banquet-table, in company with all the guests, Perpetua and Mrs. Jay walked out upon the lawn, when Laurens and Peter alighted from the clouds and joined them.

"Where have you been playing truant, Peter?" asked Mrs. Jay. "You would not have left me a stranger in a strange city ten years since."

"It is all my fault, Mrs. Jay," said Laurens. "I will tell you how it has happened. Let us go into this summer-house where we can sit down."

This proposal was at once acceded to, and they entered a sweet arbor of flowers not far distant, where they took seats.

"To begin at the beginning," said Laurens. "On the day we left the palace, my friend Peter and I rose up into the air, to enjoy the scenery below us. While thus engaged in taking a bird's-eye view of the country around, we were joined by an angel and two gentlemen who were on their way to a great Convocation for the Advancement of Knowledge, to be held in a distant world, at which they told us the great minds of the ages would be present, and urged us to go with them. Now I was earnest to go, and Peter out of kindness consented to keep me company.

"It was a long flight, and we did not come within the atmosphere of the world of science till it was high noon. We reached the city where the savans were assembled, and found the sitting for the day had already commenced."

At this point of time, Faustinus and Calliste, who were in search of Perpetua and Mrs. Jay, discovered them, and hastened to enter the arbor. They were joyously welcomed, and at once presented to Laurens and Peter. This done, Perpetua told them of what Mr. Laurens was about to communicate; whereupon they both expressed their great satisfaction, and the pleasure it would give them to listen.

Laurens, having rehearsed all he had said, went on

thus: "The Academy we found in a central square. It was a stately pile, whose high and burnished dome reflected the rays of the meridian sun, as if it had been a great beacon fire. We alighted in front of the grand entrance, and were instantly approached by citizens who acted as marshals. They received us with kind courtesy, and inquired to which of the several sections or departments of the Academy they should lead us. The angel and his friends requested to be led to the section or sitting of the chemists, and Peter having no choice, I asked them to lead us to the sitting of metaphysicians. On reaching the platform of the pillared portico, we walked into a magnificent rotunda, whose dome rose five hundred feet, and was adorned with suitable frescos and bass-reliefs, illustrative of the arts and sciences. It was here we separated from our travelling companions, they being conducted to one wing of the building and we to the other. On entering the apartment, we were led to raised seats appropriated to the spectators. The hall was circular and lighted from the dome. It was as plain as marble could make it. There was the absence of all ornament. No bass-reliefs ran around the cornice, no statues stood along the wall, no angels in fresco hovered over the assembly high up in the dome; nothing could be more massive and severe than this spacious hall of science. When we entered, our attendant, at our request, took a seat beside us, to point out the chief personages below us. It was awe-inspiring thus to look down upon the great minds of the Christian world."

"How many were present?" asked Perpetua.

"There must have been over five hundred," replied Laurens, looking towards Peter, who bowed his assent. "We were told the person presiding was none other than Blaise Pascal."

"A glorious soul!" exclaimed Perpetua. "Was not Jacqueline present?"

"She was," replied Laurens, "and sat next Arnauld, of Port Royal, in company with Madame Dufargis d'Augennes, Prioress of Port Royal des Champs."

"I had the pleasure of meeting both those eminent and saintly ladies, soon after they were liberated from earth, in company with Pascal, Arnauld, Singlin and others of Port Royal. A noble company of confessors! I believe Blaise and his sister have never been separated for a day since they met in the world of spirits. Pardon me for my interruption, Mr. Laurens. Pray go on, and tell us all that interested you."

Mr. Laurens proceeded: "Sir William Hamilton having that day been duly elected a member of the Academy, was for the first time introduced to the assembly, and was seated on the right of Pascal, in the seat of honor."

"I have heard of him before," said Mrs. Jay, with delight to think she had reached so high up into this world of science, as to be familiar with the name of a great philosopher. "Perhaps, Mr. Laurens, you may have seen some other notabilities whose names at least I have before heard of?"

"Doubtless," said Mr. Laurens. "I confess most of the names were quite new to me. They may have been eminent in the dark ages; but they have not come down on the stream of time, which hides beneath its surface all that is weighty and solid in philosophy, while that which is light, swims." *

"How do you know this, my dear Mr. Laurens? Have you any diving-bell to make this grand discovery?" asked Mrs. Jay, thinking to make a hit upon her friend.

Laurens replied with a smile full of good humor: "I was taught to believe so by one to whom the world is, and will be forever indebted; who said, that 'the greatest geniuses in all ages have suffered the greatest violence'—and it is his image and not mine that I have just made use of; and which his translator instances in a note as exemplified in the philosophies of Plato and Aristotle, in contrast with that of the lost philosophy of Democritus. But Mrs. Jay, I can tell you of some whose names you have certainly heard of before: There sat the Angelical doctor, † Thomas of *Aquine*, and Duns Scotus,

____

* Lord Bacon.

† In the Lives of the Saints (for the 7th of March), published three centuries since in English, this title is thus explained: "This holy Doctour is called the

the Subtle; and other divine and irrefragable doctors of the Latin church, who, if they failed to discover the *matter* of knowledge, have been unsurpassed in inventing the *forms* by which it is conveyed to the minds of men. And besides these, there was pointed out to me, Lord Bacon, Doctor Chalmers, Doctor Samuel Clark, Jacob Böhme, Leibnitz, Fenelon, Sir Isaac Newton, John Locke, Bishops Barrow, Butler and Berkeley, Doctor Thomas Brown, Doctor Arnold of Rugby; Dugald Stewart, and Doctor Beattie and Coleridge, and many more whose names I need not repeat; and last not least, certainly not in my eyes, sat the eminent Jonathan Edwards side by side with the genial and lovely Bishop Berkeley. Doctor Clark and Doctor Chalmers appeared to be on most intimate terms, and Coleridge sat dreaming, ever dreaming, during the session; every new phase of the discussion giving a new impulse to his reverie. I was pleased to see Newton and Leibnitz whispering together every now and then, as the discussions went on; as I guessed, comparing notes."

"Pray, tell us, what was the matter in hand?" asked Mrs. Jay. "I am curious to know what they find to talk about this side of the grave; are not you, Faustinus?" she said, turning to Faustinus for a reply.

Angelical Doctour for three respects; *first*, for the ingeniousness wherewith he handled his questions; *secondly*, for that he wrote of the angels like an angel; the *third*, for that he was a Virgin; for that which an Angel is in heaven, a Virgin is on earth."

"I left off with Plato," replied Faustinus. "I know nothing of modern methods of philosophy. Doubtless they have made important discoveries; and these philosophers of whom Mr. Laurens has been speaking, may have made as great advance upon Plato, as Plato upon Heraclitus and Pythagoras."

"Let me reply to you, my Faustinus," said Perpetua. "'Speculation has advanced not one step farther than when he left it. Plato stands confessedly at the head of the speculative genius of the world.' But I beg Mr. Laurens will answer Mrs. Jay's inquiry, and tell us what was the subject under consideration."

"You must pardon my inability to do justice to these great minds," replied Mr. Laurens; "and I will do what I may to comply with your request. The subject-matter was the *Absolute*, and our cognitions of the Absolute. The point made was the occult question, whether it was possible to bridge the abyss from the *subjective* to the *objective*—from the apparent to the real.* Lord Bacon was speaking when we took our seats. He remarked, that 'as navigation was imperfect before the use of the

---

* This seems to have been the aim of Plato. A writer in the London Quarterly, *Article :* "Institutes of Metaphysics," etc., says : "Plato's dialectic (which seems to answer to what we call *self-examination*) had clearly this one object : it was an attempt to bridge over the gulf between man and the ideal world. . . . Was there not an ideal world, the region of real being, whether or not in the mind of the Deity, in which the soul of the votary might be lost forever in the mystic contemplation of the True, the Beautiful and the Good? Was there not as surely some pathway by which the soul could ascend to this its native region, and by searching find out its truest heaven? Plato gave a long answer to this inquiry."

compass, so will many secrets of nature and art remain undiscovered without a more perfect knowledge of the understanding, its uses and ways of working.' * He was followed by Duns Scotus and Thomas Aquinas; but such was the strangeness of their terminology, so numerous their subdivisions, that I was unable to comprehend anything of their line of argument. Next, Locke spoke in his clear, simple style; and though the speeches that followed were brief, they were so entirely satisfactory to my mind, that it seemed to me the last speech settled the vexed question; but I soon grew diffident, and before they concluded, I listened without any attempt to form a judgment as to the dark oracles which were opened."

Mrs. Jay, turning to Peter, who sat quietly listening to all that was said, looking as if his mind had wandered leagues away from the subject on hand, said: "Well, Peter, I suppose you heard so much about the *me* and the *not me*, until you did not know whether you stood on your head or your heels?"

"Precisely so, Mrs. Jay. Of course I made out so much as this, that all the knowledge of a world outside ourselves came to us through our senses, and I came to the wise conclusion that if our wise men of modern times will not believe their seven senses, there is then no hope for them." †

* "De Augmentis Scientiarum," translated by Shaw.
† The able President of Rochester University, New York, M. B. Anderson,

"Seven senses!" exclaimed Calliste. "And has the area of the senses been enlarged as well as the land on our globe since we last visited it?"

"Did I say seven senses?" asked Peter demurely.

"Yes, sir, you did; and I would like to have you tell me what these are."

"If I said seven senses, seven it shall be. Well then, madam, there is the sense of seeing, of feeling, of hearing, of smelling, of tasting," and he paused.

"Yes, Mr. Peter, I had all these myself; what next?"

"Common sense! Did you have that?" asked Peter.

"And what is common sense?" asked Calliste.

LL.D., in a brief review of "Lewes' History of Philosophy." thus speaks of the latest of all philosophical systems, known as "Comte's Positive Philosophy:" "It follows, from Mr. Lewes' own showing, the external world is only a matter of inference, and this inference is not *necessary*, but contingent. He is placed, in reference to the external world, in a relation precisely similar to that which led Berkeley and Collier to deny that matter had any existence out of the perceiving mind." And further on, President Anderson says: "In view of the deductions which we have made from the principles which Mr. Lewes holds, in common with his master, Comte, one cannot but be amused at his extravagant claims for Positive Science. On his own showing, this boasted method is conversant only with shadows. So far from having anything to do with the real, the solid and the certain only, it stands before us a philosophy of matter, which cannot even certify us, by any legitimate method, of the real existence of the earth on which we tread; as a philosophy of the real, which is founded on a denial of all knowledge of reality at the very outset. It comes to us as a philosophy of law, while it denies the existence of all necessary convictions. It comes to us as a philosophy of effects, while it affirms the knowledge of causes to be impossible, and their pursuit absurd."

"Do you not know what common sense is? and did you never hear of this in *your* lifetime?"

Calliste shook her head.

"How could you get on without it?" continued Peter.

"Peter Schlemihl!" cried Mrs. Jay, "how can you be so rude? Common sense, dear Calliste, in the parlance of the present day, means the instinctive decision of the mind unperverted by passion or ignorance; or, in other words, sound practical judgment. Now then, Peter, please explain yourself."

"With all pleasure, so I do not weary my audience," said Peter. "Doctor Reid told us this morning that common sense was 'the mathematical affections of matter;* a part of human nature which,' he said, 'had never been explained.'† In answer, Doctor Beattie rose and declared common sense was, 'that power of the mind which perceives truth or commands belief, not by progressive augmentation, but by an instantaneous and instinctive impulse;' ‡ and further, 'it is instinct and not reason.' § Doctor Stewart declared it to be 'the *common reason* of mankind.' This did not quite satisfy Doctor Reid, who would have it far above all this, for he said expressly, 'that common sense was the direct inspiration of God, leading us, where our reasoning faculties leave us in the dark.' " ‖

---

* Reid's Essays, vol. i. p. 95.   † Inquiry, ch. vii. p. 480, sec. iii. p. 115.

‡ Beattie on Truth, part i. ch. i. p. 2.   § Ibid. part ii. ch. i.

‖ Reid, ch. vii. p. 482.

"Ah! well, Mr. Peter," said Calliste, smiling, " if that is all your wise scholars have discovered for a sixth sense, I do not think much of their long labor. We Romans were not wanting in it, though we never perplexed ourselves about it. But what for your seventh sense?"

"Oh, that is a modern discovery," .replied Peter, "and some good folks call it 'a realizing sense.'"

" Calliste, this dear friend of mine has shown a sad lack of his sixth sense, and the entire want of his seventh," said Mrs. Jay. "I insist on it, Mr. Schlemihl, that you shall give such a description of what you have seen and heard as we shall all comprehend."

"I wish it were in my power to comply with your request; but comprehending but little of what I heard much, how can I do so?"

"Try, Peter; there is nothing like an honest effort," said Mrs. Jay.

Calliste, who had entered into the humor of Mrs. Jay, united her entreaties that Peter Schlemihl should do his best in meeting her wishes.

Peter bowing, commenced: "You must all have in your mind's eye, this conclave of philosophers, with a sprinkling of philosophic ladies, every one of whom looked the impersonation of wisdom. On taking my seat there was, to my apprehension, a hideous gabble about words. The Scholastics had a great deal to say in praise of their logic and method; of the distinctions to be made in causation between what is *formal, material* and *final*—that logic must be as a lighted lamp, in the hand of scientific investigation, in finding our way along the labyrinth of the soul. Others claimed that the method so long followed was nothing better than the attempt to dip up moonshine; and that a review of all that had been done since the Christian era, as Perpetua just now remarked, was not a step in advance of Plato. It was said, that 'modern philosophy had lost its way for three centuries, and was like the traveller on western prairies, who galloped all day long in terror upon his own track, until he returned to the place from which he started, and the sun was going down.' *

"As for myself, I was soon at sea without compass, sail or rudder. Realism and Idealism, the Absolute and the Apparent, were terms bandied about from one to another, as if they had been a shuttle-cock, which all sought to keep up in the air. One gave it a hit, and, to use the terms of Louis Philippe's Chamber of Deputies, away it flew to the 'extreme left,' and when it was hit again, it bounded to the 'centre-right,' and so it flew about, till at last it went directly into the face of Sir William Hamilton, who gave it a fillip, when it rose high into the dome, and falling, lit upon the nose of John Locke, who gave a puff and away it went into the lap of Mr. Jonathan Edwards; who, having examined it a moment. put it into his breeches-pocket; whereupon

* London Quarterly.

the Bureau of Metaphysics rose and reported progress
(but what progress they had made I cannot so much as
guess), and asked leave to sit again. Now, ladies, having given you my experience, I refer you to my friend
Laurens for the *rationale* of all I have told you."

The ladies complimented Mr. Schlemihl on his admirable sketch of what he had seen and heard; and then
begged Mr. Laurens to interpret his parables.

"I fear I am unequal to such a task," replied Mr.
Laurens, "because of my inability to follow all that was
said. You are all aware that the Absolute, as a funda-
mental notion and as the chief constituent of all intel-
lection, has been of all subjects the most difficult to·
manage. If Truth, as has been said, lies at the bottom
of a well, no finite mind has been able to touch bottom,
and drag her up by her locks. Sir William Hamilton,
in his speech on the Absolute or 'unconditioned,' advocated his ideas as published in his works."

"Cannot you give us a brief of his ideas," asked
Faustinus; "for I am ignorant of all that has been done
on earth for many centuries; and this I can see is a matter of instant moment in all the circles of heaven as well
as on earth."

"Is it possible?" exclaimed Mrs. Jay. "I had supposed all such discussions, which necessarily surpass the
comprehension of creatures, whether angels or men,
would have been, on this side of existence, confined to
the Paradise of Fools. The use of these famous sound

ing words reminds me of one of the Eastern magi of modern times. She was called upon in a court of some sort, to give her testimony in a case of misplaced affection. In giving a narrative of her acquaintance with the deserter, she told the judges, that while he talked to her of the ontology of Locke and his theory of ideas, of Condillac, of Baron d'Holbach and the French Encyclopædists, and then of the Scotch school, of Adam Smith, Reid, Stewart and Thomas Brown—she listened with cold indifference, and could not have told the color of his eyes. He never enlisted her attention, and her heart was untouched; but when in lapse of months he came to speak of the school of Hegel, of Fichte and Schelling, then it was her bosom heaved its first sigh; and when at last he spoke of our Cognitions *à priori*, and of categorical Imparatives synthetically understood, the flood-gates of her heart were broken open, and all the gushing tides of her pent-up affections burst forth. What do you think of that, Faustinus and Calliste? Did you ever hear of anything like this in your times?"

Calliste and Faustinus both confessed themselves ignorant of any such method of reaching a lady's heart. This matter was made the theme of some playful remarks, when Faustinus begged to be permitted to go back to the subject of their colloquy, and asked Mr. Laurens to give him some idea of Sir William Hamilton's method of reaching the Absolute, which he had supposed must

can be gazed upon by a higher facul... intellectual intuition; and when so grasped by reason, can be brought within the compass of our real consciousness."*

"Is it not too much of earth to bring such discussions into the worlds of light?" said Peter Schlemihl. "How strange it is! God's people, the Jews, had no philosophy, and it was their highest wisdom.† God said, 'Let there be light and light was.' That was all sufficient for

* Sir William Hamilton tells us, that "Philosophy is wholly dependent upon consciousness: the possibility of the former, supposing the trustworthiness of the latter." Again he says, "How the will can possibly be free, must remain to us, under the present limitation of our faculties, wholly incomprehensible." How true it is what Paul says:—"The world by wisdom knew not God"—and the last result of modern times has reached this abysm.—If there be truth in philosophy it cannot be demonstrated by the mind of man.

† "Before the Babylonish Captivity the Jews had no philosophy of their own, and were too little acquainted with foreign nations to learn the philosophy of others. They had no speculative opinions; they formed no theories concerning the origin and nature of things, that is, they did not philosophize; they did not reason on things in heaven or things on the earth . . . the only question that divided their religious sentiments was, whether they should serve God according to the precepts of Moses, or Baal, according to the custom of the Canaanites."— *Fathers of the Desert*, by Ruffin, vol. i. p. 157.

them. They did not seek to chain the Almighty to 'Laws of Nature.' *That* was a phrase not as yet forged out by philosophy, falsely so-called—a mere phrase, like gravitation, which when examined is a nullity, means nothing and explains nothing.* And here, where it is our highest happiness to have our wills one with God, what need have we thus to seek to find out God to perfection. It is a vain search, beyond question, for mortal mind, whether on earth or in heaven." †

"Not so, Mr. Schlemihl," said Faustinus. "To say, 'Thy will be done,' is the joy of earth and heaven; but

---

* " The attraction of *gravitation*, the weight of bodies, these are but forms of words, in which either our materialism or else our reverence, leads us to speak of the modes of action in the Divine Will. It is no figure of speech, but the literal truth, to speak of Him that formed the Seven Stars and Orion, as guiding them on their way. Their circling orbits, by their figure, and the golden orbs themselves by their motion, continually manifest His guiding hand."--*Geometry and Faith,* by Thomas Hill, p. 27.

Babbage, " *On the great law which regulates matter,*" says: " Ever since the period when Newton established the great law of gravity, philosophers have occasionally speculated on the existence of some more comprehensive law, of which gravity is a consequence. Although some have considered it in vain to search for a more general law, the great philosopher himself left encouragement to future inquirers; and the time, perhaps, has even now arrived, when such a discovery may be near its maturity. . . . Many of the discoveries of the present day point towards some more general law; and many philosophers of the present time anticipate its near approach."—P. 160.

† In an article entitled " Philosophy, Old and New," in the *Eclectic* for November, 1857, the writer says: "Speculation has advanced no jot since Plato. The most bold, sustained and daring thinkers of the world have soared to these heights, and found an infinite beyond them; their fall has proved that to us the absolute, the unconditioned, the infinite, must ever remain the unknown."

neither in earth nor heaven has the Almighty set limit. to our desire for knowledge. We know, and we rejoice it is so, that all the streams of knowledge and art find their confluence in God—in the Absolute. These are mysteries ' the angels desire to look into,' and just so far as the Redeemed of earth grow in knowledge they become more and more like God—Whose sons we are by adoption, made one with God, even as Christ and God are one !"

When Faustinus had spoken these words, they all rose as by one impulse, and sang "Gloria in excelsis." After the glow of love and enthusiasm, induced by these unspeakable ideas of the love of God, had subsided and they had taken their seats, Perpetua resumed the discourse, by saying: " It is as Faustinus has just now told us, ' Divine Philosophy ' is the highest of all sciences, and those minds devoted to the study of the Absolute in God will see most of his glory—just as the traveller who climbs the highest peaks of earth has the widest landscape beneath him."

" I am sure it must be so," replied Laurens, "and Sir Isaac Newton, millions of cycles of ages hence, may repeat with a pregnant meaning unknown to him before, his last words on earth: 'I have but picked up on the shores of time, a prettier pebble than others, while the great ocean of truth lies before me untraversed and unknown.' "

" Yes," said Perpetua, "an ocean whose depths are

never to be sounded, but whose precious pearls enrich all who search for them."

"I see I am all in the wrong," said Peter, "and it is my misery that I never could see into the obscurities of metaphysical science."

"And I say 'ditto' to Peter Schlemihl," said Mrs. Jay.

"I believe, ladies, *women*, I beg your pardon, Mrs. Jay," said Laurens, correcting himself, "women then, are pleased to consider this science above their reach; but my belief is, that they will never hold their proper places in the world until they shall regard this as the first of all studies to be attained by those who assume the vast responsibility of mothers."

"It may be so, Mr. Laurens," replied Mrs. Jay. "All I can say is, I am glad I have done with earth. This world of art is much more to my taste than that inhabited by metaphysicians, and so I will stay here."

"Let us bring this colloquy to a close," said Perpetua; "and now, Mr. Laurens, please tell us how did the discussion end. Was it confined to the objectivity of the Absolute?"

Mr. Laurens replied: "No, it was not. Toward the close of the session the question slid away into the possibility of laying down a *theoretic* basis for the history of religion, in the necessary mo e of the Divine Being and Manifestation—God, Man and Humanity—th Triad of the Infinite in the process of realization in time.* Such

* Ed. Rev. May, 1853, art. *Hippolytus.*

a basis was regarded impossible while as yet the drama of human life was in process of elimination. It was held as an unquestioned verity that there was such a philosophy of religion, but to assume a *basis* now, would degrade history from its scientific position. It was to be regarded in time as a collection of facts, out of which in a future age the divine science imbedded in history would be made plain to the admiring gaze of the Church of God; when every individual would see for himself his relations to the world's history, and a solution for every complication of his life."

Mrs. Jay drew a long breath, and with a puff of expiration, said: "For one I can say 'I will wait.' I certainly shall not now, nor ever, seek to arrange all that has happened to me and mine into a perfect circle. When on earth I quieted myself as a weaned child while under discipline, by saying, 'It is all as God wills it, and let his will be mine;' and now I am here, redeemed and disenthralled, I would as soon dive down into the ocean for pearls as sink into such an abyss as this. That is what I have to say, Perpetua."

Perpetua replied with a sweet smile, "You are but a child in the divine life. Eternity is all before you, and *you* will not lack of docility in this life when you succeeded so well in your life on earth."

"I was all wrong in saying I was docile in the pilgrimage of earth. No, I was restless and unhappy to be the subject of trials of any sort; and I am disappointed now, that there is no king's highway to geometry and all science. But I see we have here to creep before we go. Facts are to be collected and laid together like pieces of a dissected map, and when all is done, then we are to set our wits at work to come to a proper conclusion of all that lies before us. Instead of this, I had hoped we should have reached certainties by infallible intuitions, and by a volition have attained the ultimates of truth."

Perpetua rose and the company followed.

" Before we leave this arbor," said Perpetua, addressing Mrs. Jay, "I wish to say to you, my sister, that you have made a mistake common to most minds, who make the goal of their philosophy the spot where they become weary of thinking. The science of the soul lies at the base of all knowledge. All religion reposes upon the idea of God. Without this idea, revelation itself has no weight. The idea of a God must first be attained. But who is God? and where are the evidences of his existence? This must be settled before the Scriptures can be received as authority; and when once this inquiry is started, it cannot be settled without deep inward reflection upon nature, and upon man as its interpreter." *

" That being so, dear Perpetua," replied Mrs. Jay

* Morell's " Modern Philosophy," p. 33.

10*

smiling, "I am glad I never started upon the search. I was content with the open Bible, and my own consciousness that it was the Word of God."

"The chimes are calling us to the great temple," said Perpetua, as the silver tones came floating on the air. "Let us all go and hear Beethoven's new composition. The words selected by him form the anthem of the Redeemed in the Apocalypse, 'Blessing and honor, and glory and power unto him that sitteth upon the throne, and unto the Lamb forever and ever, Amen.' The theme is worthy the capacities of an archangel, and I am sure we shall soar as on eagle's wings, uplifted by the noble and sanctified genius of Beethoven—

> 'Untwisting all the chains that tie,
> The hidden soul of harmony.'"

With one consent they now hastened to the temple, and soon joined the moving masses coming up from all directions to the first performance of this new labor of love by a great master. It was one of the inducements offered to those residing at a distance to make a visit to the palace at this time. The great temple was soon filled to overflowing, and as the performers came in, the score of the new anthem was handed to them. It was a lovely sight to see an orchestra crowded with talent, who sung and played at sight with true and entire appreciation of the genius of the author. As they took their several seats, they ran over the sheets in eager delight, pointing out to each other some beautiful surprise of a master mind which had met the eye.

"Look at St. Cecilia!" said Laurens to his party. "Was ever such beauty and sweetness combined in one person before?"

This lovely saint on entering had taken her violoncello, and with her arm lovingly embracing her instrument, leaning forward, she turned over the leaves of the *libretto* placed on the music-stand, her eyes beaming with delight.

Beethoven now entered, baton in hand, to lead the performance. He made his way slowly through the crowd of the orchestra and choir, for all sought to detain him, and congratulate him on his splendid success. And when passing St. Cecilia, she, too, detained him awhile; and turning over the leaves, she was evidently telling him of her approval and admiration of his work.

All was hushed expectation when Beethoven ascended the pedestal. Every eye was fixed upon him, the lips of those who sang were half unclosed, and their chests swollen with a deep inspiration earnest for the signal. It was given, and a volume of harmony rose which took with it all souls to heaven. The attention of both performers and audience was so absorbed, that when the last note died away, they woke as as from a blissful dream.

——————————————————————"The song
Of heaven is ever new ; for daily, thus,
And nightly, new discoveries are made
Of God's unbounded wisdom, power and love,
Which give the understanding larger room,
And swell the hymn with ever-growing praise."*

* POLLOK.

CHAPTER X.

The Story of Angela, the Nun—Mishael, the Guardian of Angela, leads her to the Temple of the Winds, where Perpetua and our Friends were seated—Her Appearance described—While Perpetua takes her on a Walk in the Gardens, Mishael, at the request of Calliste, tells the Story of her Life—Angela having completed her Education at Home, is taken by her Mother to Paris, where she returns the Love of a young Nobleman—Her Mother gives her Approval; and while Count Gratz is on a Visit to Vienna, she breaks up her Home in Paris, and returns with Angela—The Count, in his Despair, takes the Vow of Celibacy and becomes a Priest—He writes her a Letter, which she receives at Home, praying her to become a Nun—Angela takes the Veil—Her Decline and Death.

LEAVING the temple in company, Perpetua, Faustinus, Calliste and our friends, walked together till they reached Perpetua's favorite place of resort, a miniature Temple of the Winds, where they took seats and enjoyed the wide landscape; for the view opened on the lake, and in the distance glittering glaciers rose high into the air. It was a scene of singular beauty. In the grounds around them, the highest forms of art were seen, and far-off temples covered every island and every headland of the lake shore.

Seating themselves, Calliste chanced to make a remark

as to the sources of the sublime and beautiful, which was replied to by St. Perpetua. It was something wonderful, thus to hear Perpetua, who had lived so long in the world of Art, give an analysis of the laws which make one object more lovely than another. They were all absorbed as Perpetua proceeded to show that while Beauty, like its Author, was infinite, yet there were fixed laws of its manifestation. These laws were revealed to those great minds, who in sublime intercourse caught the inspiration of God and realized such lofty conceptions, imperfectly and partially, in their productions of the chisel and the pencil. And thus it was, that Art was forever revealing more and more of God to created intelligences of all worlds.

They had closed this topic, when an angel approached leading a lovely girl, whose timid downcast look bespoke her a newcomer from earth. Perpetua, recognizing the angel, rose hastily; and in glad tones welcomed him as Mishael, once her own guardian angel, and begged to be introduced to his last charge.* The young girl stood at the foot of the steps, her hands folded across her bosom and with her eyes downcast as Perpetua approached her with hands extended. On hearing Mishael say, "This, Angela, is your own St. Perpetua," she sank at her feet and made a profound obeisance, while in a whispering tone she sought her blessing. Perpetua gently lifted

* St. Jerome says: "Nothing gives us a greater idea of our soul, than that God has given us, at the moment of our birth, an angel to take care of it."

her up and kissing her on her forehead, drew her close to her side; thus assuring this timid child of heaven of her love and sympathy.

"You have, doubtless, just reached our world," said Perpetua.

In a tone of voice just audible, the girl answered: "I have this moment alighted with my angel."

The young lady was next led up into the temple and duly presented by Perpetua to her circle, as was also Mishael. There was something in the air and manner of this young saint, so much like that worn by recluses, that Mrs. Jay asked her if she had been a nun?

To this, Angela answered, much to the surprise of that lady, decisively: "*I am* a nun!"

Perpetua said to Mishael: "I am about to take charge of your friend for a little while, and I leave you to supply my place. Come, Angela, and walk with me in the gardens."

The nun rose with that air of submissiveness which is so strongly marked upon the religious orders of the Roman church; and Perpetua, with her arm around the waist of the nun, led her away.

"Will you, good Mishael, tell us the history of this sweet saint? She has evidently come to us through the gratings of a convent," said Peter.

"Pray, Mishael, first tell us, how could it be that she should have made such a worshipping obeisance to Perpetua in this world of perfect equality among the Redeemed?" asked Mrs. Jay.

"I will explain," replied the angel. "St. Perpetua was selected by Angela for her patron saint. And on reaching the Holy City, I made inquiry for Perpetua; and learning she was here, I sent her word of my coming, and that I needed her aid to induce my Angela, without violence, to give up her idols of the mind, the results of her education, and thus to introduce her into the glorious liberty of the children of God. The soul grows into use of its powers; like the eyes of the blind, when cleared of a cataract, it must become accustomed to the open vision of worlds of light."

Calliste now spoke and begged Mishael, while Perpetua was away with Angela, to tell them her story.

"With all pleasure," he replied. "Angela is the eldest of three daughters. Her father, Mr. S. W. Jones, is a man of large fortune and eminent for his professional skill. He married a young lady whose misfortune it was to be a belle and an heiress; one whose education was all of the head and nothing of the heart. It was a union of fortunes and not of affections. Their children were brought up by nurses in infancy, and by teachers of fashionable schools during the important years of childhood. The father was necessarily occupied by important pursuits, and the mother thus rid herself of her children, whom she regarded as dead weights upon her pleasures, and whom she cared not to see about her until they were ready to take their places in society, and add to the attractions of her parlors. The season was approaching when Angela would be ready to make her *début*, when her mother became suddenly deeply impressed with the necessity of taking her daughter to Paris; for she was shocked to find Angela was wanting in a perfect pronunciation of French. The secret of all her solicitude was an earnest desire to reside awhile in Paris. Her husband was made to see that this absence from home was a first necessity, and he at last consented to be left behind.

"On reaching Paris, Mr. Jones's banker soon placed Mrs. Jones in a hotel of her own, with all the splendid appliances which money can buy in that great city. Masters were called in, of course, for the young ladies, who really had little to learn as to the true pronunciation of the French language; for they had had in their school, as one of their teachers, a Parisian lady of eminent attainments in her native language and literature.

"Angela now became her mother's companion in her rides, her morning visits; and her evening parties. The lavish expenditures of Mrs. Jones made her saloons attractive. Among the crowd of elegant society into which she was introduced, and who made one of her visiting acquaintance, was Count Gratz, an *attaché* of the Austrian embassy in Paris, who in due time became the familiar friend of *Madame* and the shadow of my charge.

"Count Gratz was a young man of twenty-three. His family was as ancient as that of the Pucklers to whom he was allied, and which for eight centuries had preserved the purity of its blood free from all admixture. The count was a younger son of slender means, for the family had, with many others, been impoverished by the armies of Napoleon. He was a Catholic, or to speak strictly, a Romanist, and earnestly attached to his church. When first introduced to Angela, he was attracted by her beautiful truthfulness and simplicity, so strikingly in contrast with the artificial and brilliant manners of French society. He made the discovery, and a painful one it was, that she was no Catholic. Without design he undertook to labor for her conversion. That was all. It was so pitiful to see one so lovely, so good and pure, out of the pale of the only true church! Had the idea been presented to him then, that he would have been tempted to ally his name with that of Angela's, he would have left Paris and its fascinations the next morning. It did not. Unconsciously to himself his own affections were enlisted, and he had enlisted the affections of Angela. At balls, or at the opera, or at parties, the count and Angela would fall into long talks, and become oblivious of all about them. Madame Jones did not see it; for she was herself too entirely occupied by the whispering attentions of Baron Grimme, the friend of Count Gratz, a man of high rank and devoted to the admiration of women, who gave good dinners, and hot suppers after returning from the opera. The young friends of the count gave him credit for the same high appreciation of the elegances of the mother's hotel. Now, I know that the chief topic of all these long conversations was all about the mysteries of the Romish church. It was delightful to Angela to be told by the count that she had a soul to be saved. She had a vague idea of this sort, as most young ladies have, but it never was realized by her before, and she became anxious that his wishes should be gratified. It was not long before the count expressed a wish that she should go to confession as a first step towards obtaining the grace of a true faith. Changing her religion was to Angela no great gulf to be crossed on the edge of a sword. The count made no such a request as that she should become a Catholic, but simply expressed a wish that she should see an eminent minister whose church was near their hotel. To this confessor Angela was duly presented, and while the count was saying his prayers before the high altar for the conversion of Angela she was making her first confession. Thus it was that these young hearts were being united in the bonds of love, by a sweet and tender union of their sympathies in the great matter of the soul's salvation. The count now became solicitous that Angela should receive the sacrament of communion from her confessor, Father Joseph, in the Catholic church. To this she deferred compliance unless the count would allow her to ask the consent of her mother.

"The count, who perfectly understood the character of the mother, entreated Angela to take counsel of her own conscience. It was always sweet to Angela thus to hear the count's earnest persuasions for her to become a true Catholic; for with a woman's intuitions she saw in this the depth of his love. She could not be made to see that there was no salvation out of the pale of the Roman church; but then she was sure of being saved in it, especially when she had one so pious as her confessor, and more than all, the count to aid her in her faith.

"There was something clandestine to Angela in joining the church without the consent of her mother, and she told the count that she must tell her mother of her purpose. Seeing the mind of Angela resolute, he asked her permission to see her mother, and having declared his wishes to obtain her sanction to his love for her daughter. This had been for weeks the purpose of Count Gratz. He had long since made the discovery of his love to Angela, and his heart had been brought to look upon an alliance at first as a matter possible, next, as probable, and last of all, desirable; but he felt a deep repugnance to this interview.

"During this tête-à-tête with Angela, the count was greatly moved. Asking all she did of a lover, Angela was for the first time content. The depths of the count's soul were broken up. There was now no longer a withholding, a reserve which she had felt in former interviews with him.   She was sure that her love to him was what his love was to her—dearer than life itself.   His soul was full of forebodings of the consequences which would follow his avowal to the mother, but Angela delighted herself in dispelling these doubts; assuring him that her mother would do everything to promote

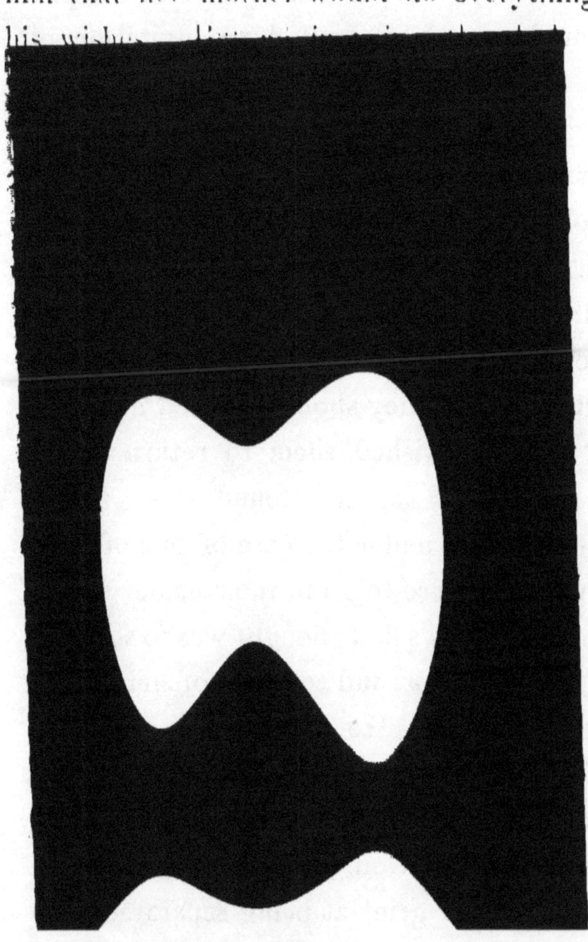

painful surmises that his fears on the last evening would become living realities.

"The week that followed was marked by no change in the manners of Mrs. Jones towards the count. No change was made in the social life of the family, and yet Mrs. Jones was all the while making arrangements for her departure. In order to relieve herself from the presence of her daughters, she accepted an invitation of some friends to take them on a visit to the ancient city of Tours. Angela was glad to go, for the count had gone at his own request with important dispatches to Vienna. He told Angela privately that his object was to communicate his plans to his family.

"Angela and her sisters were recalled after a week's absence by a letter from their mother, saying it was of the first importance that they should be in Paris on a given day, and that she wished them to return on the day previous. They did so, and found their trunks packed and sent to Havre under the care of one of their servants, and that they were to go in the steamer sailing the day following. Angela's first thought was to seek out Father Joseph, her confessor, and tell him of her griefs. This she did without stint. He sought to discover the motive for the sudden departure of her mother; but Angela could tell him nothing. He exhorted her to continue true to the Church of God, and she entreated him to tell the count of all her grief at being separated from him.

" On returning to the hotel she sat up till near day·break writing a letter to the count. It was often begun and often destroyed, until at last she grew desperate, and wrote out of the fullness of her soul all her love and all her wretchedness. This letter she carefully sealed, and then lay down to weep herself asleep. The next day her mother was early with her, and when Angela gave her letter to a servant to give it to Count Gratz on his return, she was not inattentive. Sending Angela up stairs on an errand, she sent for the man and told him her daughter had requested the letter to be given to her. On receiving the letter she read it attentively, and then destroyed it, and thought she had acted both wisely and well.

" The count, on returning to Paris, hastened to call on Mrs. Jones, and found the hotel already occupied by new tenants. His proud soul told him he was the cause of this sudden return to America. A letter from Mrs. Jones was placed in his hands the day following, by her banker, in which she said, having reviewed all the embarrassments attending the union of Angela with a foreign nobleman, whose fortunes were to be made, and whose home must be in Europe, thus separating Angela from her father and family, she had concluded it best for both parties to take Angela home. She believed the count would be grateful to her for saving him from an alliance which could not but mar his fortunes. This letter wounded him to the quick, for he had communicated his plans to his father and mother, and they had with the greatest reluctance consented to such an alliance; for they had said to him that they felt it to be the first blot on the family records. And now to be discarded by such a woman as Mrs. Jones, made his blood hot with rage. In such a state of mind, Father Joseph called upon him, and told him all he had to say of the grief and love of Angela. It was pleasant to know that this sweet girl, was true in her devotion to him. He did not doubt it, and it was oil upon his troubled spirits to receive this assurance from Father Joseph, who bore with exemplary patience his oft repeated cross-examinations, until every look had been recalled and described.

"And now was instantly developed a desire long repressed, to devote his life to God by becoming a monk. To this he had been devoted by his mother at his birth; but the boy was ambitious of honors, and his father having secured him a place at court, she was compelled to sacrifice her hopes. These had been fostered by splendid promises made to her by a brother who stood high at Rome, as one of the cardinals and ministers of the pope. The count determined never to cross the Atlantic in search of Angela. He believed the husband and the wife must be alike incapable of appreciating the honor he had, by the force of love, been made willing to confer upon them by an alliance with their child. There was the end of all hopes of happiness on earth, and now he would devote himself to God and the church.   Resigning his position in the embassy, he hastened to Rome and was received with open arms by his uncle, the cardinal. He told him of his purpose to be a priest, and of his desire to be a missionary among the Indians of Paraguay. The cardinal was delighted. He was content that his nephew should devote some years as a missionary. It would give him reputation at Rome. He would be able to put him in proper training, and to recall him at the proper time, to succeed him in his honors and office at Rome. He saw that some great disappointment had come over his handsome relative, doubtless a love affair; but as the count was silent, he made no inquiries. Indeed, he needed no such aid; for sending to one of his friends in Paris, at the end of a month, he knew all that Father Joseph could tell, concerning his love for and loss of Angela.

"The cardinal delayed the consecration of the count, so that he should become acquainted with the pope and the conclave. He was much admired by the ladies of Rome, who thought it a great loss to society that so young and handsome a person as the count, should go on a mission to the miserable Indians of South America. It added greatly to the sensation produced by the count, that he could not be persuaded to give up his purpose of devoting his whole life to the conversion of naked Indians.

"Count Gratz was much caressed by his holiness the

11

pope and his cardinals, and by the gay circles of Rome. Had he been permitted to do so, he would probably have given up his mission to St. Ignacio, on the Rio de la Plata. But this was not the wish of the cardinal. The count, therefore, laid aside his title and became Father Ernest; and with every possible care of his future wants, and in company with a learned monk, belonging to the cardinal's own household, whom he detailed to be the companion of his nephew—but who was in fact to become his instructor in theology—the count left home for Paris. While in Paris, he gave in charge to Father Joseph, a packet for Angela which he had prepared and sealed the day previous to his consecration as a priest. After a short stay, he left for Havre, and sailed for Buenos Ayres.

"On reaching St. Ignacio, Father Ernest found himself among an ignorant race of mixed breeds, whose language he could not speak, and which it was his first business to learn; and there he is now at work, nominally laboring for the conversion of the Indians of Paraguay; but really reading the great Latin fathers, and writing sermons under the guidance of Father Ambrose."

"And how are the plans of the cardinal to be accomplished?" asked Calliste.

"I was once in the cabinet of the cardinal when he was talking over his plans with Father Ambrose, whom he had enlisted by promises of preferment in the church.

He expressed the hope that Father Ambrose would make his nephew a respectable theologian in three to five years; and so soon as the young father could do himself honor, of which Ambrose was to advise him, he would procure an autograph letter from the pope to Ernest, requesting him to prepare a series of sermons for Lent, to be preached in the church of St. Giovanni, in Rome. The composition of these discourses would require him to call up the audience to whom his sermons were to be read, and Father Ambrose was to tell him, that should they be approved, he would be sent for to preach them. This exercise the cardinal believed would naturally revive in his nephew all his love of elegant society; and his zeal in the conversion of Indians having long since been obliterated by the hopelessness of doing any good, he would rejoice to be once more in Rome. As his recall would be by command of the pope, Ernest would find himself regarded as a martyr missionary; and as such would hold a high rank among the pietists of the church everywhere, and by the time he was forty he would certainly be a bishop. All which seems to me probable."

"What wonderful skill these wily cardinals have of making men automatons!" exclaimed Mrs. Jay.

"They certainly have," replied Mishael. "Some of their great works, showing all the ways of operation upon the minds of men and women, and which are studied by the students of Jesuit seminaries, are never to be printed, but are multiplied in manuscripts. It would produce a world-wide sensation should they ever be made public." *

"Will you please continue your narrative of dear Angela," said Calliste.

"Oh, do not leave off with the count until you tell us whether he still loves Angela," said Mrs. Jay.

Mishael bowed to Mrs. Jay, and went on thus: "As a priest he has taken the vow of celibacy, though he hourly thinks of Angela, in his prayers for her conversion. Surrounded as he is with miserable native women, Angela shines in his memory with the brilliancy of the evening star. How it will be when he shall return to Italy, and is again surrounded with lovely ladies, and treated with all that charming confidence bestowed by them upon *monsignori* of Rome, I cannot say; but I have many fears he will forget his first love, and, it may be, make shipwreck of his soul."

"And will she be living on in this bright world hoping for a reunion of souls?" asked Mrs. Jay. "Please inform me and these friends of mine," pointing to

* Will the reader ponder and weigh well the testimony of the great French historian, Michelet, who says: "The manuscript books which form the course of a student of theology, contain matter the boldest have never dared publish." Speaking of those that are printed, he says: "They furnish a set of questions by which a confessor can search a woman's inmost thoughts, compel her to sift her own secrets, to give them up entire, to open her heart fibre by fibre, thread by thread, so to speak, unravel before him, the whole skein, which he, thenceforward, holds in his own hands "—MICHELET: *Priest, Women and Families*, chap. ii.

Mr. Laurens and Peter, "for we are all new arrivals here."

Mishael replied: "Angela will find her love for the count fading from out her soul should her lover fail of the grace of salvation, and she will be happy in the love of God—glorying that she is forever and ever ' complete in him.' "

"And now," continued Mishael, "I will return to the story of my dear Angela," to which all bowed assent.

" Angela, on reaching home, told her father all that was in her heart. He listened with profound sympathy, and while he felt sad that his child's affections were placed upon one whose home must be on the other side of the Atlantic, yet he assured Angela he would sacrifice every wish of his heart for the promotion of her happiness. He made many inquiries, and so ascertained that his wife had neglected all the precautions he had urged upon her, to save Angela from any attachment which would separate her from her family and country. When he communicated to his wife all he had heard, with severe reproaches of her utter neglect of her children's and his own happiness while abroad, she replied, defiantly, that she had not the eyes of Argus, and if she had it was impossible for her to be but in one place at a time. It was a most unsatisfactory colloquy to Mr. Jones. He saw more and more from all that his wife said in defence of her ignorance of what was transpiring under her own eye, that she had been regardful only of her own pleasures.

"Mr. Jones was silent for awhile, meditating on what he had heard and what it was his duty to do. He saw that his dear child had been innocently beguiled into an attachment which would separate her from her family But Angela had said her happiness was at stake, and at all sacrifice of his own wishes, she should be upheld by him with all the love, sympathy and support he had to bestow. When he had reached this result, he made known his purposes should Count Gratz seek his Angela. This brought forth the loudest complaints from Mrs. Jones. She, who was proud of her superiority of rank among the democracy around her, tracing her line to a signer of the Declaration of Independence, saw nothing to commend a young man without fortune, though of one of the noblest families of Germany.

"The fashionable season was about to open, and Mrs. Jones was desirous of making a grand display of the millinery she had brought from Paris, and this she could best do by bringing out Angela. In this she was utterly disappointed. Angela was sick at heart, waiting for letters from Paris, and would not go out into society, nor consent to have any parties made for her, either by her mother or her relatives. This was the first resistance to her will this lady had met with in the management of her family affairs. Her husband she had always made to bend to her decrees, but not so now. Mr. Jones took

part with Angela, and severe was the punishment inflicted upon his lady when she found her plans frustrated.
Mr. Jones' love for Angela, and his sympathy in her
silent sorrow of heart, made him a lion in her defence;
and for the first time in her life did Mrs. Jones quail
before her incensed husband.

"One Sunday morning, as Angela was about to leave
the confessional in the church of St. Thomas, the priest
placed in her hands a packet sealed in black, bearing the
arms of Count Gratz. She hastened home and ran up
into her chamber, laying the packet upon her dressing-
table while she divested herself of her bonnet and furs.
She looked at these seals, and hesitated—'what could
they mean?' but whoever was dead her dear Ernest was
alive, and had addressed this package to her. Seating
herself on a sofa, she broke the seals, and there was a
letter from the count, which she opened with joyful
haste. The first sentence drove the color from her
cheek and she fainted. I read the letter. It was brief.
The count told her of his love and deep despair. That
he had determined to devote his life as a missionary to
the Indians of Paraguay, and would take the vows of
celibacy on the morrow. He sent her a set of beads
which he had received from the pope in person, and he
concluded by beseeching her to become a *religieuse* and
to 'meet him in heaven.' The beads had attached a
diamond cross. This last gift of her lover lay at the feet
of Angela, and was the first object which attracted her

attention as she wakened out of her state of insensibility. Rousing herself she took up the letter and read it and re-read it. Then she kissed the beads which had been blessed by the pope himself, for so had the count written in his letter. She sat meditating; living ages in a single hour, until her soul was all aroused, and kneeling down she consecrated herself to God; in which act of devotion her spirit was lifted far above all the sorrows and wretchedness which had shrouded her for months past. This state of exaltation lasted for days. 'She had lost her lover on earth but she would meet him in heaven!' Life now appeared but as a dream, and she felt that she stood on the threshold of eternity.

"Angela concealed her beads and cross, and the count's letter, and made instant arrangements for becoming a nun. She visited all her relatives with a smiling countenance. They were delighted to see the rosy hue once more upon her pale cheek; and such was the sweet flow of affection expressed by Angela, that there was a general rejoicing for her restoration to society. Such it appeared to her family and their near relatives and friends.

"A month had elapsed since the packet of Count Gratz had been received, when Easter Sunday came, and the family as usual drove down town to attend church, leaving Angela at home; for she had been to morning mass and had returned before they left. She permitted her mother and sisters to leave the house without any sign of emotion; but when handing her father his hat, she could restrain herself no longer; throwing her arms around his neck and kissing him, she burst into tears. She ran up stairs on the instant, and Mr. Jones stood in doubt what to do; when the servant came in from the carriage, with a message from his wife that she was waiting for him. 'Poor Angela!' sighed the father as he put on his hat and buttoned up his coat to go.

"At dinner, Angela did not appear; but as she rarely dined with the family on Sundays—-it being her custom to go to church in the afternoon, no notice was taken of her absence. Mr. Jones left the house for his usual walk, Mrs. Jones took her siesta, and the sisters, not knowing what else to do, went up to their chamber. After remaining there awhile, they strolled into their sister's chamber; and seeing her drawers all open, they looked in, and saw slips of paper pinned to her dresses and collars, with their names and those of their cousins, indicating for whom they were designed, with a note to each requesting their acceptance of these gifts. Filled with wonder, they went down to their mother's room; and wakening her, told her what they had seen. The mother roused herself in alarm; and when she had reached the chamber of Angela, and had examined her drawers and opened her wardrobe, and saw slips pinned to every article of dress, and had read these farewell notes of love from Angela, the idea of a suicide came like a flash of lightning into her mind, and she swooned. The children's cries brought up the servants, and thus the departure of Angela became known to the household; and before night it was a matter of speculation on both sides of the square.

"Mr. Jones, on his return home, was met at the door by his daughters in tears. Leading them into the parlor he sought to quiet them of their grief, so as to enable them to tell him what had happened. They told him all they knew; and that their mother had said Angela had drowned herself. This idea Mr. Jones resented. He knew his child had done nothing unworthy of herself. On entering his wife's chamber, he found her in a highly excited state of mind; she declared her belief that Angela had made away with herself. Mr. Jones ordered his wife to be silent; he would not hear such words from her; and told her, that the public would hold her to a severe account for whatever might have taken place—a singular remark for him to make at such a time as this, but that he knew this to be the only tribunal before whom his wife feared to be arraigned; for, odd as it may seem to you, Mrs. Jones claimed to be a pattern woman, and was ambitious of being so regarded in the circles of good society, in which she was a shining light.

"Night came on apace, and Mr. Jones waited in silence for the return of his child till long past midnight, when he reluctantly retired to rest; and though when awake he chased away the surmises of his wife, asleep his dreams were full of horrors. With the dawn of day the entire family were up and dressed. Mrs. Jones was for employing the police, and even suggested the street-crier being sent about to cry her lost child ; for she was restive under this state of incertitude. Mr. Jones would do nothing of the sort. He sent a message to all the family relatives to come to his house as early as nine o'clock, on important business. These missives were promptly complied with, and at that hour the parlor was full of uncles, aunts and cousins, all whispering to each other concerning the disappearance of Angela, when Mr. Jones and his brother entered ; as for Mrs. Jones, as the easiest way of avoiding the mortification of such a meeting, she sent an apology that she was too much indisposed to see any one. Mr. Jones told them what had happened, and asked if they could aid him to discover what had become of his child. After a little hesitancy, they gave their guesses, and the reasons for such guesses; and it was wonderful how much they had gathered up of the story of Count Gratz and his love of Angela, from their friends who were residents in Paris at the same time, and on familiar intercourse with Mrs. Jones in that city.

"While they were thus conversing and comparing observations, a man came to the door with a letter addressed to Mr. Jones. This was brought in by a servant woman who had received it. As soon as his eye caught the direction of the letter, Mr. Jones rose and exclaimed, 'Thank God, she is safe!' The servant hearing this, ran up to her mistress with the glad news.   Mr. Jones was reading the letter with eagerness, and that he was troubled by what he read was seen in his features, and the tears which rose to his eyes, when Mrs. Jones rushed into the room and almost rudely seizing her husband's arms in her impatience, cried, 'Where is she?' Mr. Jones having glanced over the remaining portion of the letter, folded it up, and with cutting coldness, addressing his wife, said: 'Angela has gone from us never to return. This, madam, is the last sad result of your life in Paris.' Then turning to his relatives, he said: 'My sweet child, as you all know, while in Paris became attached to a younger son of a noble family of Austria. His avowals were listened to by Mrs. Jones with courtesy, and he received her assurances that she would lay his proposals before me, and that they had her entire approval. This done, the count having gone to Vienna to see his family, Angela was hurried home; but not before she had, poor girl! seen her confessor, and communicated all she knew. On returning to Paris, this gentleman was told of the departure of Angela, and received a note from Mrs. Jones, saying she never would consent to her daughter making a love match, and what else I do not know; for that such a note had been written was unknown to me till this morning. Outraged and deeply mortified, Count Gratz resigned his position in Paris, and hastened to Rome, where he has an uncle, a cardinal and a minister of state, in order to take the orders of the priesthood. This he has done, and is now on his way to Paraguay as a missionary. In a letter recently received by Angela, so she writes in this letter, he exhorted her to become a nun, that in heaven their union might be made perfect. Angela has become a nun. She took the veil yesterday, and is thus lost to us forever.'

"No sooner had Mrs. Jones heard this than her tongue found a theme on which to discourse with fluency and energy. She urged her husband to take legal steps to recover Angela; and if these should fail, then to rouse a mob and tear down the walls of this prison-house, with its bars and bolts. As Mrs. Jones found relief in this outburst of passion, she was indulged in it to the full; after which Mr. Jones again addressed his relatives in these words: 'My dear friends, no one can more deeply deplore the step taken by Angela than myself. She is of age, and has acted in accordance with the pleadings of a hopeless love, and I must submit. Let who will indulge in reproaches, Angela will hear none from me. May God bless her sorrowing heart with the light of his countenance and the joy of his salvation!' So saying, he took his brother's arm, and bowing to all, left the room. Mrs. Jones then again endeavored to get up a party for tearing down the convent, but without success. The relatives retiring left her alone to her own thoughts; and though these were not pleasant, they were not reproachful of herself.

"And now I must return to my charge. Angela in making her arrangements had secured the aid of a catholic lady, belonging to the circle of her mother's friends, who had her carriage in readiness at 12 o'clock; and when Angela came to her house, went with her to the convent of the Sacred Heart, where her confessor had made all the arrangements for her reception. The lady abbess felt that this was a case demanding instant compliance; and Angela, at the evening service, was invested with the white veil. This done, she gave to her lady-friend the letter she had prepared for her father, which was forwarded by one of her servants, as I have already told you.

"Angela, in Paris, was in the bloom of beauty; joyous and happy; the playfulness of her wit, and the lovableness of her character, constituted her the central attraction of her mother's circle. Everybody loved Angela, and Angela loved everybody. But on her return home, all her buoyancy was gone. Her rosy complexion became pale and sallow, and signs of a hectic were seen by her father whose sympathies were all enlisted in the fortunes of his lovely daughter. He only was acquainted with all that Angela had to tell. He desired to write to Count Gratz, and to express his approval of his union with Angela; but she felt the count owed it to her, to reply to the letter she had left for him—the letter her mother had destroyed. And thus the months rolled on till Count Gratz's packet came. Her soul rose to a

height of heavenly repose, so soon as she had consecrated herself to God. The mystery of life to her was now
solved; and her enthusiasm gave a lustre to her eye and
a flush to her cheek, which filled the heart of her father
with gladness. But when the vow was taken, and the
newness of a nun's life had worn away, the signs of decline became more and more apparent. Her father and
sisters came every week to see her; and she listened
with a grieved heart to their entreaties to return home
and make them happy once more. She longed for the
months to roll on, when the black veil would save her
from these sad importunities. She was zealous of her
duties, and met the pains and penalties of a nun's life
with cheerful submission. It was evident to all that she
could not maintain the rigor she had assumed; and her
mental conflicts increased with her diminished bodily
strength. Her soul was often in darkness; at times,
repining against the providence of God; as when the
recollections of the count and their happy life in Paris
came up before her so vividly, that it was all but reality.
These day-dreams she repelled as the instigations of the
devil. Poor child! she did not know that these were
the necessary results of her debility. But it was my
privilege to call up before her mind, sweet visions of the
heavenly world; and when she awoke, she wept that she
was yet alive. And thus the months rolled on; and disease with stealthy steps advanced. Angela was looking
forward to Easter Sunday, when her novitiate would be

ended and she should take the black veil; as if that **vow** would shut out of her heart all its loves and memories of the past. Passion Sunday came, and Angela was unable to rise from her pallet. Her eyes shone brightly with the fever which was consuming her life. She was very happy in her meditations of the love and death of Christ. Her mind had been enlightened by the Holy Spirit; and when the lady superior came to her bedside with her kind inquiries, the eloquence of the novice, as she spoke of her joy of faith, filled this lady with admiring wonder. But I linger in my tale—let me hasten to a close.

"It was but a week that she was confined to her bed. The nuns who waited around her, saw with awe the light of immortality shining from out her eyes. She loved to lie in silent reverie, looking up with such a fixedness of gaze, that the nuns who gathered around her bed were sure she had a vision of angels. And when once they whispered to her, 'Sister Angela, are the heavens opened to you?' She replied, 'There is a pencil of light streaming down from the throne of God, filling my soul with joy unspeakable and full of glory.' * It was a sweet, trance-like state of repose.

"Although this was all beautiful and saint-like, yet it became a matter of painful regret to the lady superior and her nuns, that Angela had as yet no vision of the

---

* This was the happy experience of that eminent saint, Mrs. Edwards, the wife of Jonathan Edwards, the great divine.

Blessed Virgin and her child. They, therefore, consulted the priests of the monastery near by; who, after mature deliberation, believed that if the relics of St. Bridget, of famous memory, of which the convent had the veritable cross-bones, were, with fitting ceremonies, taken from beneath the altar, and should be laid upon the breast of Angela, they would purge the films from her eyes. This was accordingly done, and Angela thanked them for this singular expression of their love and sympathy.

"'Do you not now see the Blessed Virgin, Angela?' asked Father Bonner.

"Angela, who lay feeble as an infant, smiled, but did not answer.

"'You do see the Mother of God!' cried Father Bonner, exultingly.

"'I see Jesus!' whispered Angela.

"And so it was, after waiting till patience was exhausted, Father Bonner took the relics from the breast of Angela, and with a sad heart returned them to their shrine.*

"On the Monday following Angela's father came out

* Robert Fortune, Esq, in his recent work, published in London, 1857, entitled "A Residence among the Chinese," chap. ii., gives an account of the idols worshipped by the Buddhists of China, he says: "The Queen of Heaven (Kwan-yin) with her child in her arms, was the only idol that did not seem to frown. . . . Some have supposed that this image represents the Virgin Mary and Infant Saviour, and argue from this that Buddhism and Christianity have been mixed up in the formation of the Buddhist religion; or that the earlier Buddhists in Thibet and India have had some slight glimmerings of the Christian faith."—P. 89. From a remote period, anterior to the Christian era, these people have had their

unaccompanied to see her. He was grieved to see his child had reached this closing stage of her decline. He was convinced she would never leave her couch alive; and when he spoke to her of his fears, she replied, that she had long since given up the expectation of taking the black veil.

"'Alas! dear child, you are about to be enshrouded with the veil of the tomb, and will be forever hid from our eyes.'

"'Not forever, my dear father,' said Angela; 'Oh, no, not forever!'

"Angela now requested the nuns, some of whom were ever present, to raise her head so that she might sit up awhile. When this was done, laying her hands in her father's, she said, 'I wish, my father, you could realize what a dream is life. I wonder that I have been so grieved by the loss of my hopes of happiness on earth. I see now that this great grief has brought me to the cross of Christ. Dying! what is it, dear father? I have in my soul the highest exercise of consciousness that my life is hid with Christ in God, and when he who is my life shall appear, then shall I also appear with him in glory."

"Angela earnestly entreated her father to devote him-

monasteries, and monks who wear a rosary, and use them in their devotions in the same way as in Catholic countries, to the great astonishment of St. Francis Xavier and the early Jesuit missionaries. See account of Cochin China, in Pinkerton's Collection, vol. ix., p. 762. After describing the monks and the nuns and their customs and modes of worship, the missionary says, naively, "*So near has the devil endeavored to imitate us.*"

self to the service of God. There had been until now an insurmountable barrier which prevented her pouring out all that was in her heart to her father. This was all removed. With the utmost fluency and ease she sought to enlist her father to make the salvation of his soul and of those dear to them both, the chief concern of his life. And when, fearing to exhaust her strength, he proposed to leave her, she said, 'Not yet, father, I have one last request to make. This diamond cross,' holding it up as she spoke from her bosom, 'and this rosary were sent to me by Count Gratz in the letter he addressed to me the day before he assumed the habit. I have a letter which I wrote the week before I made my profession, which I wish you to send him, accompanied by this cross and these beads. The cross you will take from my neck, and the rosary will be found at my side. My letter I will now place in your hands, and I shall sleep all the sweeter, dearest father, knowing that you have received this my last request.'

"The letter was taken from a bureau by a nun, at the request of Angela, and handed to her. After having looked at the superscription, she gave it to her father. Many memories of the past rushed into the mind of Angela as she held this letter in her hand, and imagined the circumstances which would attend its delivery; the emotions it would induce in the mind of Count Gratz, and the sad satisfaction he would receive in knowing that his wishes had been met.

"The following days Angela was regarded as in a dying state, but she revived again, and was able to receive the last visit of her mother and sisters. To her mother she said everything which could comfort her and relieve her mind from all remorse concerning her conduct towards Count Gratz and herself; but such was the condition of that lady's mind, that she had little consciousness of what was said to her by her child. Not so her sisters; they were alive to every look and every word, and all the sweet expressions of Angela for their conduct in life was written deeply upon their hearts: and I am confident the death of Angela will be the day-dawn of a spiritual life to her family.

"Death came, and the last offices of the church were administered to Angela in the presence of her father and the lady superior. She was radiant with joy and peace. The morning star visibly shone over her lovely face. Her eyes, full of love, were turned upon her father. She wanted to speak, and all hovered around her to catch her last words. Finding she was unable to do so, with a sweet smile she offered her lips to her father for his last kiss. With the utmost self-control, Mr. Jones kissed his Angela again and again, and then hastened out into the hall where he could vent his cries and tears.

"Angela's eye followed her father as he left the room. She then closed them, and crossing her hands over her breast, without a sigh her soul was released. Waking into life, she found herself clothed upon with the vesture of immortality."

Calliste and Mrs. Jay thanked Mishael for his interesting narrative.

"You have said nothing, Mishael, about Angela's becoming a nun, and not one word against convents," said Mrs. Jay.

" Guardian angels are not called upon to discuss such questions. Wherever Angela went, by God's permissive will, it was my duty to follow."

"Granted, Mishael; but you have seen the interiors of convents, and what do you think of them?"

"I *know* them, madam, to be prison-houses of both body and soul. Of this Angela was saved all knowledge; for the dark chambers of mystery are kept closed until the black veil, like a pall, has shut up novices in their living tombs."

CHAPTER XI.

Life at the Palace described—An Evening Entertainment at the Temple—A Sunset described—The Sabbath—The Ritual Service of the Temple—A Sermon is preached by John Howe, once Chaplain to Oliver Cromwell—Mrs. Jay and Peter meet Mr. Howe in the Gardens—Their Colloquy—The Necessity of a Creed—Mr. Howe on Conversion—Mrs. Jay's Account of the State of the Churches of Christ in the United States—Her Notion of the Work of the Ministry.

THE stars began to glitter in the clear skies of twilight, when our friends, Peter, Laurens and Mrs. Jay, met St. Perpetua, Angela and Miss Mehitable Smith upon the terrace. Perpetua apologized for not rejoining them in the morning, but she had been happily absorbed by Angela; whereupon Angela gratefully expressed her high sense of the honor thus conferred by St. Perpetua. The step of Angela was elastic, and her eyes, which had been so downcast, were now radiant with joy and freedom. Miss Smith next spoke; alluding to her first meeting with Mrs. Jay, she said with a smile, "You must have been amused with my remarks, Mrs. Jay. It was all so new to me!" Mrs. Jay replied, " Nothing could be more natural to a new comer, for she had herself said the same things to St. Perpetua on seeing for the first time this doubtful recreation of fashionable life in such good repute here." St. Perpetua gave Mrs. Jay a knowing look, and smiled.

While they were promenading the terrace, Faustinus and Calliste, accompanied by Tibertius, joined them. Calliste presented Angela to him, and Perpetua, in like manner, Miss Smith. This done, they broke up into pairs, Tibertius attending Angela; and it was sweet music in the ears of Mrs. Jay to listen to the bright joyous tones of Angela's voice, who walked immediately behind her, conversing with Tibertius. Mishael joined them, and told them that an eminent scholar who had been for eight centuries studying in the school of eloquence would recite certain rhapsodies of the Homerides, some portions of which were found woven into the Iliad. This was equally delightful to our group, and they all agreed to attend.

When the chimes told the hour for these recitations, the entire company in the palace began to move toward the temple.

As they descended the steps, they saw the dome of the temple, high above the trees, glowing with light; and when our friends entered the building, they paused to admire the splendor of the illumination. This was in itself a miracle of art. Beads of light, of different hues, revealed every ornament, while a noon-day radiance came down from above, as sunshine through the foliage of an over-hanging forest.

The audience were all in their seats, gaily conversing, when some one unseen began to play on the great organ. The tones were far off, but gradually drew nearer, until there was a grand opening of the full organ. Then it gradually diminished, now swelling as if the music of military bands was heard ascending some far mountain; then it was lost, as if descending into a valley; then a strain was caught, as if reflected by the face of some steep hill, till it was heard no more. Just as the ear was straining to catch another echo, the orator came forward and was received with bursts of applause. Never before had Mrs. Jay or Peter realized the power of the voice. These ancient poems were delivered with such exquisite skill, that when the recitations were over, Laurens said he believed he should have known what was the burden of the poem, if he had not understood a word, merely by listening to the tones of the voice, and watching the face of the speaker and his gestures.

It was past nine when the performances ended; and while the audience were retiring, our friends remained to examine the interior of the temple, lit up as it was by millions of jets of flame. The effect of this illumination was to reveal beauties of design concealed before. Mrs. Jay spoke of this to St. Perpetua, who replied that there was not a pillar, arch, or ornament which was not contemplated and designed by the architect in its double relations to sunlight and artificial illumination.

·On coming out of the temple, Perpetua invited Calliste and Faustinus and our friends to ascend with herself, Angela and Tibertius, to witness from the furthest orb a wonderful comet, which had been reported as coming towards their planetary system. This was declined by Calliste, who said she had the promise of Mr. Schlemihl and Laurens to spend the evening with her in her own parlor; and turning to Mrs. Jay, she expressed the hope that she would go home with her. Angela begged Mrs. Jay's company on their excursion, and in this Tibertius united. It was a passage of wit and entreaty between Calliste and Angela, who should retain the society of Mrs. Jay; and it was gratifying to all to see the buoyancy and brilliancy already manifested by the beautiful nun. That cowed and depressed demeanor, seen in her bent figure on her approach to St. Perpetua, was gone, and now her step was volant, and her flashing eye full of gladness. The nun of the Sacred Heart of Jesus was lost in the Redeemed child of God.

Time flew fast amid scenes so various and beautiful; but there was no shadow cast over their brightest moments by the thought, that they were to come to an end. Eternity was before them; and every new joy brought with it the capacity for an advance to higher happiness.

There was no ebbing of the tide of existence, no weariness from excess of blessedness.

As Mrs. Jay and her friends were walking together in
the grounds of the palace, studying the beauty of the
statuary and temples, they saw a great convoy of angels
and Redeemed floating onwards to the palace. They
were evidently enjoying the splendors of the hour
The sun had just sunk into a sea of molten gold, while
silver-capped clouds rose like mountains intervening between the zone; so that this broad, illuminated belt
looked like a bow of promise resting on clouds of silver.

It was the closing day of the week, and these angels
and Redeemed whom they saw in the air were returning from distant worlds to share in the services of the
Lord's day at the temple of the palace. On earth this
is a day, with most Christians, of penitence and prayer;
but here the day was spent by all in public worship and
praise. In all worlds, as we have before said, there is a
Lord's day; and wherever the Redeemed of earth are
present, they tell to unfallen beings the story of man's
redemption; and this is their last and highest attainment—to preach the Gospel of the grace of God. This
was the joy of Paul on earth, and is his delightful theme
in heaven. In whatever world the Redeemed are placed
for their development and culture, all alike rejoice in the
hope of being at some time thus capacitated to glorify
their God and Saviour.

The next day was a high day at the palace; and it

was a beautiful sight to see the assembling of the angels, Redeemed and servitors, with buoyant steps and countenances lit up with devotion, thronging to the temple.

Every part of this vast edifice was full at an early hour in advance of the time for beginning the services, and the great masters of music were in their places, when Handel and St. Cecilia entered the choir, whereupon the sublime services of this sanctuary commenced by a choral anthem. This was followed by songs of praise, in which the orchestra and organ, and every one present, joined. This magnificent ritual of worship was the work of ages. The grandest conceptions of the love of God in the gift of his only Son, for the redemption of man, were conveyed to their souls by a liturgy, exhibiting in itself the utmost power of language ; which was intensified by the genius of the great masters, and made vocal by a vast audience, all alike glowing with the enthusiasm of love. Mrs. Jay and Peter sat overwhelmed with emotions of gratitude to God who had made them partakers of the divine nature. This service ended, the orator of the day ascended the forum. He was of a majestic height, and his face was noble. His eye threw rays of light over the audience as he surveyed them from the platform. There was in his bearing a consciousness of the loftiness of his theme, which swelled in his breast and gleamed from his eye. The attention of every one present was riveted. Stretching forth his hand, the orator began: "Hear, O heavens, and give ear O earth; for the Lord hath spoken. 1 have nourished and brought up children, and they have rebelled against me." Taking this for his text, he portrayed in words of flame the rebellion of man, from the earliest days to the death of Christ; and then he brought this home to every redeemed soul present, in their past history and present blessedness; showing the glory of God's grace in their salvation with a vividness, which, like a flash of lightning to the eye, shut out from their minds every other thought, and only God and Christ, and their soul's life, were present in their consciousness.

When the orator ceased there was a long pause. Like the apostles on the Mount of Transfiguration, his auditors were blinded with the excess of glory, which weighed upon their spirits like a heavy sleep, out of which they slowly awakened. And this was the eloquence of a human being!—a minister who had held a high place in the Christian world, and who since had been a student in the school of eloquence, and was now traversing the wide-spread universe of God, to tell of the glorious gospel of Jesus Christ.*

* The heavens as seen on a starry night are called the universe. Now, modern astronomy has shown us the shape of the firmament in which our sun is a star; and beyond and outside this our firmament, are already catalogued upwards of twelve hundred *nebulæ*, believed to be distinct firmaments; and of these there is no end.

Sir J. F. W. Herschell, in his Astronomy, chapter xii., § 626, says: "The nebulæ furnish, on every point of view, an inexhaustible field of speculation and con-

One afternoon of the following week, as Mrs. Jay and Peter were walking in the gardens, watching the coming twilight and listening to the singing of birds and of far-off choirs, they were joined by the orator, John Howe, the eminent chaplain to Oliver Cromwell, whose benignant smile as he approached them, encouraged Mrs. Jay to address him. With a courtesy full of graciousness he came up and inquired what had been the subject-matter of their conversation, that he might share in it.

"We were talking of the blessedness of the righteous, and of the text in John's epistle, 'Behold what manner of love the Father has bestowed upon us that we should be called the sons of God.'"

"A precious subject," replied Mr. Howe, "and one concerning which I delighted to speculate while on earth."

"I was expressing to my friend my astonishment that this topic is so seldom the subject of ministerial teachings at the present day; and that mere matters of method and of ritual are permitted to take the place of the great theme of the adoption of sinners into the family of God. I was myself, sir, a member of the Episcopal church, and

jecture. That by far the larger share of them consist of stars there can be little doubt ; and by the interminable range of system upon system, and firmament upon firmament, which we thus catch a glimpse of, the imagination is bewildered and lost."

Since this work of Sir J. F. W. Herschell was published, Lord Rosse has erected his great telescope, which has resolved many nebulous spots into vast firmaments of stars.

in the light of eternity I see no reason to change my preference for its liturgy; but I fear it is too common for Christians of all denominations to deem the shell as essential as the kernel itself."

"As it is," replied Mr. Howe, with emphasis; "for, madam, a man to be without a creed, a mode of faith, a formula of devotion, is to be without religion."

"But, reverend sir, on earth," said Mrs. Jay, "the scaffolding is too often regarded as an object of more interest than the temple. *Here* accessories are nothing, and Christ is all—his birth, his life, his works of mercy and his words of love, his death and resurrection, and the descent of the Holy Ghost; these are the themes of heavenly worlds, but how is it on earth? Is Christ all and in all? No, indeed! It is the General Assembly, the convocation of the House of Bishops, or the Convention of some sort—mere vehicles for promoting the interests of the several sectarian organizations, absorbing the talents and time of the ministry which should be consecrated to God and Christ."

"It is the infirmity of earthly natures. In the world there is no progress but what comes from conflict of opposing forces. There was no little of this in the days of the Protectorate, in which I largely shared."

"How does modern preaching compare with that of your times?" asked Peter.

"The ministry of my day, and of all days since the apostolic age, has been too often aside from the true power of the gospel of our blessed God and Saviour. Of late, recondite themes have taken the place of the simple story of the life and death of the Lord Jesus, which has come to be a twice-told tale. All this is wrong. The song of Moses and the Lamb is an ever new song in heaven; and the story of the incarnation of the Son of God is the one great theme which God designs shall be the power of God to the salvation of the soul. It is to be hoped that a day-spring from on high is about to dawn, when a symmetrical and beautiful union will exist in the Church of God of sympathy with man, and of high and holy aspirations after the indwelling of Christ."

"I beg you will pardon me, sir," said Peter, "for saying, that until this descent of the Holy Spirit, I do not see what our preachers can so well do as to make a careful and entire preparation of their sermons. I have believed, and do still believe, that the Holy Spirit blesses those labors of the ministry which are the result of long study and earnest prayer; and this in spite of all the success of modern evangelists, so-called, who reap the golden harvest from seed sown by men of whom the world has never heard."

"The question you have started, my brother, I have often sought to solve," replied Mr. Howe. "God has doubtless made the conversion of every man brought home to glory to be the result of all the influences attending his existence, from the creation of Adam and Eve to the moment of his regeneration by the Holy Ghost."

Mr. Howe now made some inquiries concerning their nativities, and of the age in which they had lived on earth; and next, of the present state of the churches in North America. He was well advised as to the condition of the churches up to the opening of the nineteenth century; and Peter and Mrs. Jay gave him a full narration of the present state of the churches.

At this point of their colloquy, they came to a place where the avenue on which they had been walking diverged, and Mr. Howe took leave of Mrs. Jay and Peter, with many kind expressions of the pleasure he had derived from meeting with them.

Perpetua joined them as they were turning into a new path.

"I am glad to have met you, my friends," said Perpetua; "for Tibertius and Angela desire us to go with them on a visit to a certain studio in the metropolis to-morrow. Now I hope you are disengaged, and can accompany them."

Mrs. Jay and Peter both said they were at liberty, and would gladly go with Angela and Tibertius. "How pleased I am to see Angela so happy here," said Mrs. Jay.

"Angela," replied Perpetua, "is fast regaining her soul's freedom, and I am under obligations to Tibertius for his devotion to her happiness. It is wonderful how perfectly their tastes assimilate. He is never weary of the task I have assigned him, and Angela is a delighted and docile pupil   To-morrow, then, we will go in company to the city?"

Mrs. Jay and Peter having assented to this engagement, Perpetua took leave of them to ascend into the air, and meet some friends of hers who beckoned to her to join them, while Peter and Mrs. Jay walked homeward to the Palace of Beauty.

CHAPTER XII.

THE dawn broke with a cloudless sky. Mrs. Jay and Peter met on the grand portico to welcome the coming day. The early hours are everywhere beautiful, but no words can convey the loveliness of that hour of prime— the freshness of the breeze, the fragrance of the morn, the music of birds; and looking up into heaven, the zone, which at night turned toward the planet its broadside, was now showing its edge, lessening in width, until at noon when it appeared but as a narrow belt of cloud across the sky; and now moons of various magnitude, and wearing different phases, were paling before the rising sun.

"To-day, Peter," said Mrs. Jay, "we are to visit the studios of the metropolis. I wonder I have never yet walked into them when we have been sight-seeing in the capital, for unlike our world, living artists are here held in highest regard."

"And for a very good reason, madam. In our world we look back to the days of Pericles for the highest development of art. Not so here, where artists of the present day are expected to reach to a new grace of form, or some unexpressed loveliness of the human face."

"Yes, that is so. With us, living artists are generally mere copyists, and their works are valued according to the success of their imitations. Now if a torso could be dug up at Athens, which could be recognized as the work of Phidias, how would the *cognoscenti* of the fashionable world—tourists of all lands—wonder after it? Men and women of recent full-blown fortunes, whose taste is in the bud, would stand in crowds at gaze before it; as if by the simple act of staring they could see anything else than a bruised and battered mass of marble. Do you not think so, Peter?"

"No doubt," replied Peter, amused at the thought as presented by his lady friend.

"But here," continued Mrs. Jay, "the ancient works are preserved to show the stages of progress from the infancy of art to the perfectibility of the skill of the present age. Now why is this not the case with the Fine Arts in our day?"

"Oh, because God never made for man such a climate

as that of Greece—never formed such a race as those of
Attica, and never built such a city as Athens: that is the
reason. One of these days—I should rather say when
many centuries have passed away—the race of man, elevated by Christianity, may reach a symmetrical development, when sculpture and painting shall attain a higher
perfection than in the days of Pericles."

"There is one thing in which we of earth have a
decided advantage over the races of all other worlds,
Peter, and it is this, that we are sinners saved. This
gives a power to the conceptions of our artists, and supplies subjects for the chisel and the pencil to which
these pure beings never can reach. Look at the works
of their great masters in the galleries of this palace, and
in the collections of the city, and compare them with the
works of the students from earth, and see what a world-
wide difference there is between the conceptions of these
different races."

" Certainly it is so, though I have not been aware of
this difference before. It is the difference between
beauty and passion; and now you have spoken of this
contrast, I think there is something of this to be seen in
the forms of the ancient and modern school of art.
Compare the Venus de Medici with the Greek slave.
The Venus is nothing but a pretty animal rising out of
the ocean awakening to existence; while the Greek slave
is a woman, conscious of her degradation, and despising
those who have bound her in fetters."

"Yes, Peter; it is sin and suffering that heightens our ideas of the grand and the beautiful. It is our pre-existent state which supplies our artists with splendid subjects for their genius—subjects which can never be fully understood and appreciated by the natives here, to whom sin is unknown; and who can have no adequate conceptions of what it is to be saved from sin and made one with God as Christ and God are one."

"No! my lady; nor have we, though redeemed and disenthralled. We know of our adoption; but what the privileges of adoption into the family of God may be, are mysteries forever revealing new and inconceivable wonders; for so soon as one mystery is solved, we meet with mysteries more wonderful and inexplicable, which in some sort are shadowed forth by those magical dissolving lights which change as one screen is removed and a new one takes its place. We can never find out God to perfection. But to return to our topic—the forms of beauty, grace and goodness we see here, are so lovely that I have not felt the need of any of the contrasts you speak of to heighten my appreciation of the works of native artists."

Angela now came out upon the terrace, and was welcomed with all affection.

"How glorious in this world!" exclaimed Angela, clasping her hands over her breast and looking up into the beautiful sky. "When I look about me, Mrs. Jay, and see what loveliness there is in all God's works—what beauty there is in his creatures around me, and go back in memory to earth, and recall the gloomy hours of my past life, and my fears that because I was so miserable God did not love me, my soul leaps up for joy that I am here; free from sin and sorrow forever."

"I am glad to hear you say so, Angela; for my friend Peter sometimes talks to me of our past life in a way to make one think he is sorry not to be still on the earth."

"Indeed!" said Angela, turning with a look of surprise to Peter who replied to this silent inquiry of hers, thus:

"I sympathize with you, Angela, in the joy of being free from sin and sorrow. I am right glad that the enigma of life with me is solved; and that I have safely waded through all the sloughs of despond in the course of my pilgrimage, and have seen the Celestial City. What I said to Mrs. Jay yesterday, was this—that I regarded my life on earth as a great privilege; and that those who are in possession of life, whatever may be the depth of their grief, ought to thank God for life to suffer; and I ask you, Angela, what you have to say to this?"

Angela replied, with enthusiasm: "I would not have had one day of trial—one pang of sorrow less than I was permitted to meet. Indeed, I could not have had one less; for all were needed to wean me from the world, and to compel me to set my affections on heaven. Yes! I bless God for all my afflictions as well as for all the many mercies which were mine. My pathway in childhool was full of hope and joyful anticipations; but it was grief which fitted me for an early departure from time, and opened to me eternal life."

The silver tones of the morning chimes now called them to the temple, and hastening down the stairway into the vestibule of the grand entrance, they walked out upon the green turf in company with hundreds of others; all with joyous and elastic steps, hastening to join in the glorious choral morning worship in the temple.

In this service all the congregation of the Redeemed joined in singing the song of Moses and the Lamb, with which the morning ritual opened; then followed anthems and hymns of praise, and an oration by some one of the Redeemed whose eloquence fitted him to address the assembly; nor was there ever a lack of gifted and glorious minds to discharge this duty to the delight of the audience. When the services were ended, the morning repast followed, and then the occupations of the day were entered upon.

In company with many others, Tibertius, Angela, Perpetua, Laurens, Mrs. Jay and Peter—ascended from the grand balcony of the palace into the air. Some were about to visit distant spheres, others remote regions of this world; and others again, to prosecute their studies at the libraries or studios of metropolitan cities, of which there were some thousands scattered in various countries on this globe, as large as that to which our friends were now going.

As they slowly ascended, it was a pleasant thing to those below to gaze upon them in their flight. Sometimes one would descend to pick up a flower, or to kiss a child in the arms of its mother. There was a constant change in these happy beings, and a playful conversation was kept up as they soared away. The most brilliant sallies were indulged in, and a war of wit finally arose between two doctors of medicine—a homeopathist and an allopathist, which kept the entire company in close order, and was a source of long-continued merriment.

The contest was concerning the fallacies of medical science as exhibited in their several modes of practice; and so much truth was told on this occasion, that it is to be regretted this colloquy cannot be here recovered for the benefit of those who are living, and are destined hereafter to become the victims of medical science whichever method · is followed; as was most satisfactorily shown to our voyagers. As they were now over the metropolis, Perpetua and her company here staid their flight; and all clustered around her and her friends, taking leave with loving regrets; some of whom expected to be absent for weeks or months, and perhaps years.

"Before we separate," said one of the doctors who had been maintaining this amusing controversy, "will you not, St. Perpetua, give us your judgment of our argument so far as you an I your friends have heard it?"

Perpetua looked around to see whom she should call upon for the verdict sought for, and bowing to Mrs. Jay, she said: "Perhaps that lady will do you this service;" but she declined and referred the query to her friend Schlemihl, who, after some hesitation, and with great modesty stated his views. So far as he could see into the discussion, medical science was of all sciences the most dubious and uncertain; and the question had been, and would be for ages to come, whether nature alone was the more reliable, or nature aided by the doctor. Mr. Schlemihl said, between doctors Do-much, Do-little and Do-nothing, he should certainly rely on the skill and science of Doctor Do-little. This doubtful decision gave new grounds for controversy to these doctors, who went forward earnestly discussing the vexed questions of their favorite science, while Perpetua descended with her friends and alighted on the portico of the gallery of Art.

On entering this vast hall, they were received by the attendants, artists of eminence, to whom is confided the supervision of this treasure-house of sculpture and painting. Tibertius and Angela led the way as they slowly walked forward stopping at groups of statuary, which were explained by their attendants, who gave the name of the artist and the age in which he lived, and other interesting facts; all which added greatly to the interest of their sight-seeing. It was a matter of remark made by Mrs. Jay and others, how wonderful it was, where all seemed faultless, that there was so palpable a difference in the works before them; and it surprised Angela and Mrs. Jay and Peter that their eyes even were so soon able to discriminate variations so very slight. And this feeling was increased when they came to a series of works where the same subject was represented by great artists of different schools, and of widely-separated ages; men who spent years striving to supply some defect or to heighten the power of expression of what had before been regarded perfect.

Peter remarked to Mrs. Jay, that such contests of art would never be known on earth; for though the form of woman had been and would be recast and sculptured by thousands, yet the Laocoön would probably remain alone; no modern sculptor would be likely to have sufficient rewards offered to induce him to venture to present that subject in a new aspect; though no one doubts the great artist who conceived that work, had in his mind other conceptions which another and superior genius might have made yet more eloquent of agony.

"Come," said Angela, when they had finished walking through one of the halls of sculpture; "now let us go and look into the studios. Tibertius has a work in hand which we must all admire."

In compliance with this invitation, after having made their acknowledgments to their courteous attendants, they left for the studios. Mrs. Jay thought they were very unwise in not going to the workshops first, and then to have visited this museum of the great masters. But Angela and Tibertius, who acted as leaders, said they had good reasons for the course adopted. Angela whispered to Peter, that in the studio they should visit, was to be seen the work of a young artist of earth—a mother and her firstborn son—who had thus recalled his recollections of his infancy and of his young mother. "It is such a sweet thought, realized in marble!" exclaimed Angela; "he was but a child when he was taken away, and when sent here to be perfected in the schools of sculpture, he determined his first labor should be to recover the looks of his mother; and he has thus attained to his highest hopes, and it is to him a crowning joy to have given life to marble and with such wonderful power that it is already regarded as a miracle of art; a work of inspiration and love."

"It is certainly," replied Peter, "a most beautiful expression of love; pray, why do you whisper this to me, Angela?"

Angela laid her finger upon her lip and turned away. Tibertius led them to his studio, where they all expressed their earnest admiration of his group of Jesus and the two Marys, which was his last labor of love and worship. They sat down on stools and benches, and remained for an hour in conversation concerning Christ and his affection for Lazarus and his sisters, of which Tibertius gave them many examples; which, had they too been written down with *all* the words and acts of our God and Saviour, the world could not have contained the books that would have been written.

Leaving his studio, Tibertius next led them to another, hid from sight by the shrubbery of the garden. The solitary artist was in the dew of youth, verging to manhood. He held a file in his hand and stood with his back to the entrance, gazing with a fixedness which absorbed his whole being and rendered him unconscious of the presence of visitors. Throwing down the file, the artist stretched forth his hands towards his work and cried out with a voice full of emotion: "It is done! my mother!"

"How like Mrs. Jay!" whispered Peter to Angela. This whisper reached the ears of the artist, and with a look of wild intensity he glanced from face to face, when Mrs. Jay, who had been stooping down to the figure of the boy, looked up at the artist and with a flash of perception, she rose and exclaimed: "My son!" . . . . "My mother!"

This reunion of souls filled all present with delight. Perpetua leading the way, the mother and son were left alone. Objects of interest were on all sides; but so entirely did they sympathize with Mrs. Jay, that everything lost its power to charm, and it was concluded to return to the studio of the new-found son. Here they met the happy son and mother. All the longings of his soul were now satisfied, and to Mrs. Jay he was a lost treasure unexpectedly restored, whose value had been enhanced beyond all expression. This was her son, and this work of art was from his chisel.

It was a pleasing and a salutary change for Mrs. Jay to receive the loving congratulations of her friends, and in these the son shared with his mother. Then it was that Tibertius and Angela told of their visit to this studio, and Angela's discovery of the resemblance to Mrs. Jay, and of their plans to bring about this happy meeting.

The party now separated. Tibertius, Angela and Perpetua left to make some visits in the city, Mrs. Jay gladly accompanied her son to his residence; and Peter, having nothing to do, rose into the air without any definite purpose, and in doubt whether he should wing his flight to some one of the worlds above him, or enjoy the loveliness of the landscape over which he was quietly floating, and the delicious atmosphere of the day. He fell into state of reverie, and so continued till he heard a voice calling to him. Rousing himself, he saw upon a cloud near him, Lucia, wife of Philo Publius, a bright and charming lady with whom he had met at the palace. With the instant volition prompted by her presence, Peter transferred himself to the silver cloud upon which this lady was seated, and was graciously welcomed to a seat on her air-cushioned sofa.

"I must seem very idle here, Mr. Schlemihl," said Lady Lucia; "but you see I have been aiding my husband in some observations on electrical currents;" and so saying, she held up an electrometer which lay in her lap.

"I am fearful I may interrupt you," said Peter.

"No, not so. I have made my last observation, and was about to descend; but since you have joined me, and I have some one to talk with, I will remain and enjoy with you this lovely day, and the pleasure of sailing over so beautiful a country."

"What observations have you been making, madam?"

"My husband," she replied, "was recently on our earth, and attended a meeting of *savans* at Montreal, in Canada, for the Advancement of Science, and heard a paper read which was written by a lady, upon tidal currents of electricity; and since his return he has been testing its universality in various worlds; and he tells me that the law she has discovered stands related to the most important phenomena yet to be resolved."

"Indeed; a lady! and a living lady! How glad I am to know the fact! And what does your husband say of the condition of science in America?"

"He was not gratified with what he saw and heard; for, in his judgment, there exists a clique who assume to be the arbiters of scientific reputation in North America. They possess commanding positions, and do what is possible to dwarf the development of scientific scholarship to their own proportions. He tells me that they have so little confidence in themselves, that no discovery is re ceived until it has been indorsed by European *savans*."

"May I ask if the laws of magnetism and electricity on this globe give the same phenomena as on ours?"

"Precisely, sir; my husband holds that electricity represents the deity in all systems and firmaments in its life-giving, diffusive and controlling power. He says, 'It is true of all worlds as of ours, that the experiment performed in a watch-glass, or before a blow-pipe, succeeds alike, in a great manufactory, on tons of matter, or in the bosom of a volcano, upon millions of cubic fathoms of lava.'"

"And the same law which globes a tear stealing down the cheek of infancy, governs and controls the ocean?"

"Certainly, sir. The student of natural philosophy encounters numberless cases in which this transfer of ideas from one extreme of magnitude to the other will be called for; as for example, Mr. Schlemihl, when you are asked *why* you cannot conceive the atoms of a grain of sand to be as remote from each other (proportionally to their sizes) as the stars of the firmament; and why there may not be going on in that little microcosm processes as complicated and wonderful as those of the great world around us.* The tremors of a stretched wire and

* So says Sir J. F. W. Herschell's "Intro. to the Study of Natural Philosophy," p. 130. The ingenious and unknown author of "The Stars and the Earth," a little tract published in England in 1846, gives this illustration: "Let us suppose, for example, that, from the present moment, all the measurements of the universe were reduced to the half of their size and that all distances were equally shortened, it would be impossible for us to perceive, or indeed to believe if it were told us, that

the upheavals of an earthquake differ only in intensity
of electrical action, and God's wisdom is both illustrated
and glorified by the oneness of manifestations of almighty
power."

This topic was discoursed upon for some time, when the
lady requested Peter to tell her the history of his life; a request constantly made in the society of the Redeemed, as
directly leading to the wonder-working providence of God
in the salvation of the soul. When this was completed
to the satisfaction of Lucia, Peter asked her as to the
age and country to which she belonged. Lady Lucia
replied that she was a Roman by birth, and had lived in
the early part of the second century. This led to some
remarks as to the character of those times, and as to
what was then regarded essential to a true faith. In
answer to Peter's inquiry, Lucia said she was the
daughter of a Christian named Carpophorus, who kept
what is now called a Savings bank in the Piscina Publica

any change had happened to us, or to the world around; and we might, like Gul-
liver's Lilliputians, fairly consider ourselves perfectly grown men. But if everything was lessened a million or a billion times, it would be as little noticed by us
as when the reduction of all measurements to one half of their size took place;
and if our system of fixed stars, with all that it contains, was suddenly contracted
to the size of a grain of sand, we should move and exist with the same freedom
of restraint, and with the same convenience, in that little world, as we now do in
this which seems so large to us." Coleridge has made a similar statement, thus:
"It is surely not impossible that to some infinitely superior being the whole universe may be as one plain—the distance between planet and planet being only as
the pores in a grain of sand, and the spaces between system and system no greater
than the intervals between one grain and a grain adjacent."

of Rome, and that her faith and that of others around her was simply this: "Jesus Christ, the Son of God, the Saviour of sinners."* Peter then complimented her as belonging to the age of martyrs, and spoke of his high veneration for the courage and faith of Christians in those days, when Lucia interrupted him, saying, "Oh yes, Mr. Schlemihl, I know all about it, and let me tell you, as an incitement to your love and gratitude to God, that he cast your life in pleasant places, and in a golden age; in a land of Sabbaths and Sabbath schools, of Bibles and a Christian literature. And I tell you, my brother, that there never was a truer faith—a faith so widely diffused and fittingly received into the hearts of men; never so near conformity to Christ; never so much true godliness and good will among men, as exists in our world at the present day. And how any person possessed of the epistles written by Cyprian, and others in later days, can talk of the pristine purity of the church in the second and third centuries, astonishes me. I assure you, my good brother, I am not surprised when I meet with it in young ladies just arrived from the

* The symbol of the early Christians, as yet to be seen in the catacombs, was, what is sometimes called by the Church of Rome, "the monogram of Christ," and is the figure of a fish. The Greek term 'ΙΧΘΥΣ, or *fish*, is composed of the initial letters of the sacred name and titles as written in the Greek language of our Divine Redeemer; in English thus, "Jesus Christ, the Son of God, our Saviour." This symbol of a fish St. Clement (A.D. 194) recommends to be worn as a ring, saying, "Such a sign will prevent them from forgetting their origin—'buried with Christ by baptism.'" This symbol is now becoming fashionable with high churchmen, and is wrought on altar cloths, etc.

Church of St. Barnabas, in Pimlico, London; but such language from you, Mr. Schlemihl, I did not expect."

Peter apologized for his ignorance as best he could, saying that all writers and preachers of the present day, spoke of the early ages as being full of the grace of God and the enlightenment of the Holy Spirit. And having said this, wishing to change the discourse, he asked of whom did she speak in alluding to ladies recently from St. Barnabas in Pimlico. She replied:

"You must first know, that my husband and I have been residents in West-end, London, with one of our children, who belongs to the nobility of England; and his sweet wife is a most eminent pietist of the Puseyite school. In this way we became personally acquainted with Pusey, Newman and the leaders of this attempt to restore to the English Church the dogmas of the Nicene age. My son and his lovely lady were distinguished for their piety and liberality to the poor, and frequently they drove to St. Barnabas, in Pimlico, on a Lord's day. In this church is to be seen the nearest possible approach to the ceremonial of the Papal Church.* I was accustomed to go with them, constrained by a fond desire to save them from being satisfied with the husks of religion. It is wonderful to me that such high and holy aspirations

* Father Gavazzi has lately addressed a letter to a friend of his in Dublin, in which he thus expresses himself:—"Last Sunday I was in St. Barnabas, Pimlico. Horrible! horrible!! horrible!!! All Popery transubstantiated into a so-called English service. It is a great shame for the bishops who support or tolerate it."

can be so mixed with such will-worship and human con-trivance; but God is great and his ways are past finding out. So much, Mr. Schlemihl, by way of preface—and to show you my acquaintance with English manners, and to assure you of my high appreciation of English worth.

" Last evening, I was standing near one of the doors of entrance, when a lady whose air and bearing showed her to be a lady of fashion from England, made her appearance in company with an angel with whom I was acquainted. The lady, with English instinct of aversion to a crowd, paused as she saw the throng of the Redeemed and our invited guests, as if she hesitated to enter. Whereupon I advanced with the frank courtesy of our present life to meet her. The lady slightly withdrew and made a low courtesy, which I returned with one more elaborate and formal. Thus we stood, when her angel, with a smiling air at this reproduction of the manners of West-end in heavenly worlds, led her towards me, and with greatest possible reverence to me, said, ' Permit me, Lady Alice De Vere, to present you to Lucia, one of Christ's con-fessors and martyrs of the second century.' Lady Alice advanced and took my hand, and bowing over it very low, kissed it. We were soon enlisted in conversation. She asked me many questions not altogether unlike those of your own just now, about the purity of the Holy Catholic Church of the second century; and begged me to present her at my convenience to St. Zephyrinus and

St. Callistus, 'the sainted bishops of Rome' of my own own age—just as if such men were to be seen in a heaven of holiness because they had been popes! She left me somewhat wiser than when she came; and I shall strive to labor with her, and without violence to her feelings, will save her from the idols of her imagination."

"Pray tell me who these saints of the church were, Lady Lucia, for I, being a 'dissenter,' never heard before of St. Zephyrinus and St. Callistus?"

"Oh, they are persons of no particular interest, except to saints, 'scarcely saved,' of the Oxford school."

"But what about these saints?" asked Peter, pertinaciously.

"Which saints, the ancient or the modern?"

"Those saints of the Roman calendar which are held in such request now-a-days by modern pietists."

"Well, my dear sir, they are saints in the calendar of the Church of Rome, and nowhere else. And as you are ignorant of their history, I will tell you of it. When Victor was diocesan of Rome, and he was a godly man, though his name is not on the calendar, Zephyrinus was one of his assistants, and on the decease of the patriarch Victor, Zephyrinus became bishop. He was a man who loved bribes, and was the first to compound church censures for money. This business demanded skill and a go-between, and Callistus was the person selected by him, and a most fitting person he was for that base occupation. He had been a trusted slave of my dear father, and acted as his cashier in the bank of the Fish Market, and was thus the holder of the earnings of the poor. Callistus absconded while my father was away, and taking with him as much gold as he could well carry, he fled from Rome. He was hotly pursued to Portus, where he had embarked in a ship about to sail, and which was moored in the middle of the harbor. When Callistus saw that he was about to be taken, seeing no way of escape, he threw himself overboard, and it was with difficulty he was saved and delivered up to my father with his treasure. He was taken home where he served an apprenticeship to a domestic tread-mill of that day. Not liking this service, he sought to get rid of his life, and a most ingenious way he took to accomplish his end; and this was by raising a riot in a Jewish synagogue, for which he was transported to the sickly parts of Sardinia. After the lapse of some time, Marcia, the mistress of Commodus, the emperor, wishing to be kind to the Christians, sent for Victor and asked what Christians had been transported to Sardinia, saying that she would beg the emperor to release them. Dear old Victor was delighted, and made out a list of them, but omitted the name of Callistus, well knowing his character and the crimes he had committed. Marcia obtained the letter of pardon, and Hyacinthus, a eunuch of the palace, and also a presbyter of the church, was dispatched to Sardinia to bring back the confessors. Hyacinthus delivered his list, and when Callistus found that his name was not on it, he made the governor believe it was an accidental omission ; for that of all on the island, no one was personally acquainted with Marcia but himself, and that he was the only person in whom she was interested. So successful was he that Hyacinthus was at last induced to demand his liberation, to which the governor, glad of this show of authority, readily acceded, and Callistus made his appearance once more at Rome. When Victor was informed of it, to save himself from censure (for my father was still alive), he was sent off to Antium. There he remained until after the death of my father, when Zephyrinus, who succeeded Victor, sent for him and made him his co-adjutor, and as such he soon became a ruling spirit in the church ; for, as Zephyrinus was both stupid and ignorant, he did what he pleased, and when his master died he became, as we now say, Pope of Rome. Such, Mr. Schlemihl, were some of the saints of my day, to whom the saints of your day are so ready to kneel for their blessing."

"I am extremely obliged to you for this interesting fact of the history of your times. It would serve to open the eyes of some blind folks if it were repeated on earth."

"No sir, no! Men and women love their delusions and would not believe it though it were told to them by Hippolytus himself."

"Hippolytus! may I ask, Who was he?"

"He was the great man of my age in the church--

the bishop of the port of Rome; and all I have told you
is recorded in a work of his ' On Heresies.' " *

The further discussion of this subject was suspended
by the coming of Publius, with whom they descended
and separated upon the steps of the palace. Here they
were met by Calliste and Angela. When Publius and
Lucia had taken leave, Calliste, addressing Peter re-
proachfully, asked him how he could have left Faustinus
and herself behind, and so deprived them of the pleasure of witnessing the reunion of Mrs. Jay and her son.
Peter professed his ignorance of the purpose of their
visit; and that when he entered the studio of the young
artist, and while Mrs. Jay was stooping to see the child
in the lap of the young mother, then it was he first saw
the resemblance, and said to Angela : " ' How like Mrs.
Jay !' At that instant the son and mother, with a flash
of recognition, embraced each other."

"It must have been delightful, and I wish I had
shared in your joy; but here I have been," said Calliste,
" all the day occupied with an English lady of rank who
needs the society of Perpetua more than our Angela."

Angela smiled lovingly, and said : "Lady Alice will
soon give up her idols, now that she is away from all the
influences which have chained her soul to ritualism."

Upon this, Peter repeated what he had just heard of
Lady Alice from Lucia, saying: " how hard it is for us

* This work was found in 1852 in MS., taken from monasteries of Mount Athos
and was first republished as a work by Origen.

to leave ourselves behind! Do you not think so, Angela?"

"No, for I have had no such experience; for so soon as I was enlightened, I was a willing convert to all the unspeakably precious revelations made to me by St. Perpetua, as well as all which have come to me from all I have seen and all I have heard."

"You are young and docile, Angela," replied Peter.

Calliste, now taking Angela by the hand, proposed to Peter that they should go and repeat to Faustinus the adventures of the day.

CHAPTER XIII.

Mrs. Jay is recalled to Earth by Flavianus, her Angel, to be present at the Marriage of her Daughter—She is accompanied by Faustinus and Calliste, Peter and her Son—Sights seen on the Journey—The Records of Eternity—A World on Fire—On reaching the Milky-way they have a Vision of Paradise before the Creation of Adam—Scenes passing before them to the Ascension of Christ—Flavianus explains how the Air holds a Record of all Events from the beginning of Creation—They alight at the Home of Mrs. Jay.

Days and weeks and months flew by and found Mrs. Jay and her friend Peter absorbed by the pleasures of their life in this world of loveliness. Their studies were pursued with delight; and in every new discovery, the harmonies of creation filled them with unspeakable joy, as they caught the clue leading them through labyrinths of wonders into the light of a higher law—one of greater simplicity, all alike tending to that one volition —the great decree in which the wisdom and power of the Creator is concentrated.

This perilous task, as it would have been to them once, was now a labor of love, full of gladness, reverence and devotion; shared by all holy beings, who, while they are forever approaching, never reach the infinitude of God's perfectability.

Their first study was, with Perpetua for a teacher, to reach the philosophy of the Sublime and the Beautiful, and they rose gradually to a true sympathy with Art, so that pictures they had once passed by unheeded, now riveted their attention in earnest study to obtain the full conceptions of the artist.

After a day devoted to the architecture of the temple, St. Perpetua and our friends returned to the palace and joined the happy groups sitting upon the balcony, talking over various topics of interest; and of these there is never any lack: for some work of art has reached its completion, some poem has been published, some new world has been visited, some eminent man of the early ages has arrived; and thus in these homes of the happy, topics of pleasant converse are forever occurring to give zest to their social life.

Persis now came with a message from Calliste, to Mrs. Jay and Mr. Schlemihl, requesting them to come to her. To this they at once assented, and insisted on taking their loved Perpetua with them. On entering the parlor of Faustinus and Calliste, what was the joyful surprise of Mrs. Jay to see her own angel, Flavianus, standing with her son in expectation of her coming. With a cry of joy, Mrs. Jay embraced her guardian angel, and then presented him to Perpetua and Peter.

"I have come to take you back to earth," said the angel.

Mrs. Jay started—"Take me back to earth! pray,

what have I done to be banished from this paradise of God?"

"Nothing, dear lady; but I have a mission to take you home that you may be present at the .marriage of your and my beloved Augusta."

"Married! my child to be married, and so soon! Oh, what infatuation and folly! She is only seventeen, Calliste; and she is to be married, all because I was not there to save her from making the wretched exchange of the pleasures of girlhood for the cares of married life. O, it is pitiable!"

"I see nothing so very dreadful," replied Calliste; "I think your dear child shows excellent judgment."

"To me it is madness. What folly to give up such a home as hers has been, and the love of her father, for this stranger, whom a year since she did not so much as know!"

"Mother," said her son, archly, "what is there so fearful in marriage?"

"You are a child of heaven, Willy, and happily, you know nothing of life."

"Are you not unlike all the rest of the world, my sister?" asked Perpetua. "I was charmed to be present at my son's wedding, and I think you will come back delighted with all you see and hear. Think, my dear Mrs. Jay, of mixing once more in the circle of your friends; seeing them and hearing them talk."

"It may, perhaps, be pleasant; but how can I but be

sorry that my husband is so soon to lose the society of his only child; and, indeed, that she can love any one so well as her father."

"God will provide!" said Perpetua, with a smile, and this encouraged Faustinus to say something about the leadings of the affections and the will of God. Even old Pindar, two thousand three hundred years ago, thus sung of the decrees of heaven :

———————"When the Gods lead
Short is the road, and swift the deed."

"I think," continued Faustinus, "your Augusta is but following in the footsteps of all her parents, from Eve down to Mrs. Jay herself. And who should marry but the young ? It is as God wills it, and wills it wisely and well."

"Sufficient !" said Mrs. Jay. "I see I have neither countenance nor sympathy from any one of you. When do we leave, Flavianus ?"

"To-morrow before sun-rising we depart, in order that we may reach your house as early as nine o'clock in the evening; and I doubt not I can make this voyage across the abysm a source of instruction, if not of pleasure. There are sights worth seeing as we go."

"You will let me take my son with me?" asked Mrs. Jay.

"Certainly."

"And allow me to follow," said Mr. Schlemihl.

"Not to please me, friend Peter," said Mrs. Jay.

"Then let me go to please myself; for I have a deep interest in the future of Augusta, and have no higher wish for her happiness on earth than to see her married to one worthy of such an angel."

"Thank you, Peter," said Mrs. Jay. "You have not forgotten the language of compliment."

"What else could he have said, madam?" asked Faustinus. "In what better phrase could love and friendship and high esteem be expressed?"

Mrs. Jay consented to receive the compliments of her friend Peter to oblige her friends, at their full value.

"Will you not go with us, Faustinus and Calliste?" asked Mrs. Jay. "You have not seen Rome for so many centuries, I should think you would revisit it with great interest."

"I should like to go very much, Mrs. Jay; and why not Faustinus?" asked Calliste.

"I will go, dearest, with all pleasure, if it pleases you; but we have few attractions to earth now."

"Yes, Faustinus, but we can never cease to be interested in the battle-field of the universe of God. Shall we go?" and Faustinus, with a smile, consented, to the great joy of Mrs. Jay and Peter. Then they asked Perpetua to go along, but she had duties which kept her at the palace.

Peter took his leave of the company to go and seek out Laurens, if, perhaps, he too would return to earth for a short stay ; and it was agreed to meet on the balcony of the east front before sunrise next morning.

*   *   *   *   *   *   *

The day broke with a clear sky. Our travellers stood admiring the beauty of the morning, when St. Perpetua and Laurens joined them to see them take their flight, and to bid them God-speed. Laurens wished Peter to visit his wife, and Perpetua had like requests of Faustinus and Calliste concerning her descendants residing in Italy. While thus occupied, quite a group of the Redeemed gathered around them, and each had some graceful word of parting. It was a matter of congratulation with all to be assured by Mrs. Jay that it was her irreversible purpose to return to the palace without loss of time.

"Come," said Flavianus, "the morning star is paling before the coming day ; let us go."

With a last kiss, Perpetua and Mrs. Jay separated, and in an instant the party rose with the swiftness of angels into the air. Having far surmounted the atmosphere of the world of Art and Beauty, Flavianus indicated the direction they were to take. To the eyes of Mrs. Jay and Peter, all was dark about them, while at immeasurable distances, above, below and around, lay firmaments, scattered like autumnal leaves, whose nebulous light wore every variety of form and intensity. The souls of all were alike hushed into silence in presence of such Omnipotence. It was an emotion too deep for words.

Thus they flew onwards, when, nearing a nebula, clustering with suns, Flavianus rested, while Faustinus and Calliste, who were some distance behind, came up; he then pointed out, in a vast system into which they were about to enter, a spot intensely bright.

" There," said he, " is a world on fire. In passing through this firmament, I shall lead you near that conflagration, which will show you the closing scene of your own earth." *

Soon they reached the verge of this system of suns, which lay scattered around and formed the broken edge of the nebula. Next, they were in the denser sections, and suns with their planets lay so near that the ellipses described by planets of one sun ranged within the planetary circles of another; and here it was that the central sun of a magnificent planetary system was being destroyed by fire, the flames of which, reaching high beyond its atmosphere, were kindling into flame the nearer planets and their satellites—so threatening the destruction of that entire planetary system.

The blaze of that vast conflagration shone far into space, with a baleful glare, on all sides.

" 'Tis fearfully grand!" exclaimed Calliste; a sentiment echoed by our travellers.

" How inexplicable, that this should ever happen!" said Mrs. Jay.

* Tycho Brahe, 1597, discovered in the constellation of the Ship, a world on fire,

"I suppose, my sister," said Flavianus, smiling as he spoke, "no such contingency would have occurred had you been the creator. Hereafter you will learn that these are but parts of his ways; but how little a portion is heard of him? and the thunder of his power, who can understand?"

"I am silenced, Flavianus," replied Mrs. Jay, submissively.

As they passed beyond the last star of this cluster of suns, Faustinus said to Calliste: "Here is one of the wonders of creation lying before us, and when we reach its verge of history, we will run down the line of its development."

This they did; and in doing so they spoke of seeing its various stages of progress, when great deeps were broken up, and mountains rising out of the beds of oceans, pierced high the heavens; and all this in the space of a half hour. Faustinus and Calliste, as well as Flavianus, were all absorbed, leaving Mrs. Jay and Peter to listen to what they were telling, without the least glimpse of the objects, vast and wonderful, which seemed within the scope of their vision.

"Do I go too rapidly, Calliste?" asked Flavianus.

"At times objects and events run so close together that I have no very clear apprehension of what I see."

"Pray, what events and objects do you speak of, Calliste?" asked Mrs. Jay; "for I see nothing but nebulæ, whose light is drawn out into streamers across the depths of space by the rapidity of our flight."

Flavianus answered Mrs. Jay by telling her that she was yet to be educated into the powers of her spiritual nature; and that he would this day give her her first lesson in reading the stories of creation and the histories of worlds; but as it was necessary to reach her house by nine o'clock, he must defer this pleasure till they had come within the nebula in which her sun would be seen but as one of the stars with which the skies are paved. "The scenes which are present to my mind," said Flavianus, "with the distinctness of reality, and which Faustinus and Calliste discern imperfectly, pass too rapidly for you to take cognizance of. I purpose you shall soon make your first essay in the development of this latent power; one of many which lie in your bosoms as yet unknown, waiting for development to confer delight." *

* Dante (Canto ii. Paradise) enters the moon under the guidance of his loved Beatrice, and like Mrs. Jay and Peter, his vision is dull:

> " Turning to me, with aspect glad as fair
> Beatrice spake : ' Gratefully direct thy mind
> To God, through whom to this first star we come.' "

Dante describes his sensations after landing :

> " Me seemed as if a cloud had covered us ;"

And asks Beatrice to explain the scenes about them. Beatrice " somewhat smiled," he says, as she replied,

> ————" Mortals err
> In their opinion, when the key of sense
> Unlocks not.''

After this, Mrs. Jay and Peter followed on in silence, wondering what new sense was about to be revealed in them. System on system first glowed in the depths of space, then filled the heavens with radiance as they took their way through the densest centres of magnificence; and by and by they looked back, and saw a firmament, but as filmy a cloudlet as any of the millions they had seen along their pathway.

Flavianus paused. "We are now nearing your home, and with all pleasure I shall redeem my promise, and show you the enduring records made in accordance with the laws of God, by which every look and action is perpetuated to all eternity. Do you not see that nebula, in form resembling a serrated leaf,* lying on the abyss of darkness?"

"That little flake of light!" cried Mrs. Jay.

"Yes, madam; and when we shall have reached the stars, only seen from earth by mortal eye when aided by the Rosse telescope, we shall there meet the rays of light

She compares his then condition of soul, to the ground covered over with snow, which when dissolved by the warm rays of the sun, is revealed; she says:

> ——————" So thee,
> Dismantled in thy mind, I will inform
> With light so lively, that the tremulous beam
> Shall quiver where it falls."

The word dismantled is here used, to throw open, to divest, to disrobe.

* So described and mapped by Sir W. Herschell. See "Nichol's Architecture of the Heavens," London edition, p. 21.

which left the earth on the day that Adam woke into life."*

"Will you please explain this mystery," asked Mrs. Jay.

"It will be best explained by what you will see;" and so saying, Flavianus set forward with such rapidity, that the stray stars of their own firmament, into which they were now penetrating, once more became mere streamers of hazy light to the sight of our travellers.

Flavianus now called upon his companions to halt. "We are now," he said, "in the highest spot of the Milky-way, near the Scorpion. The suns in sight were once to your vision the diamond dust of the skies. I will leave you for a moment, in order to find the line of reflected light from earth."

Flavianus soon rejoined them, saying, "I have found the line of rays." Taking Mrs. Jay and Peter by the hand, he cried out, "*See*, yonder is Eden!"

It was long before either Peter or Mrs. Jay could, so to speak, get the focus of vision; when they did, what was their delightful surprise to look down upon Paradise instantly before them in all its beauty! Receding with exact conformity to the laws of light, the objects in view

* STRUVE concludes, from the dimensions of his telescope, etc., that the smallest stars visible to him are at a distance of twenty-three thousand billions of miles, and require a period of time for the travelling of light to the earth as great as four thousand years.—*The Stars of the Earth*, p. 14.

stood before them, and so near, that the wing of a hum-
ming-bird, instead of being viewless from the rapidity of
its vibrations, could be examined, and its beauties all
seen.

"This is magical!" cried Mrs. Jay.

"This is real," replied Calliste, who, with Faustinus,
obeying the same laws of movement, in receding, saw
objects with like distinctness.*

"Where are Adam and Eve?" asked Mrs. Jay.

"They are not yet created," replied Faustinus; "but

---

* The author of "The Stars of the Earth" first developed these ideas of the
optical reactions of light. He says: "The pictures of every occurrence propagate
themselves into the distant ether, upon the wings of a ray of light; and although
they become weaker and smaller, yet, in the immeasurable distance, they still have
form and color; and as everything possessing color and form is visible, so must
these pictures also be said to be visible, however impossible it may be for the human
eye to perceive it with the hitherto discovered optical instruments." Again he
says: "Thus the universe incloses the pictures of the past, like an indestructible
and incorruptible record containing the purest and the clearest truth. And as sound
propagates itself in the air, wave after wave, and the stroke of the bell, or the roar
of the cannon, is heard only by those who stand nearest in the same moment when
the clapper strikes the bell, or the powder explodes; but each more distant spec-
tator remarks a still greater interval between the light and the sound, until the
human ear is no longer able to perceive the sound on account of the distance,
. . . . so in like manner, according to our ideas, the pictures of every
occurrence propagate themselves into the distant ether, upon the wings of a ray
of light," page 31. "Let us imagine an observer, with infinite powers of vision, in
a star of the twelfth magnitude. He would see the earth at this moment as it
existed in the time of Abraham," p. 33.

"Man is mortal, he thinks and he feels. These are three separate and different
truths, according to our ordinary ideas. But the difference only depends upon the
fact, that our mind is not able at once and completely to grasp the idea of man,
with all its consequences," p. 62.

I will advance and show you them as they were seen by their Creator on their wedding-day."

"That will be delightful," said Mrs. Jay.

When they next paused, there stood before them Adam and his Eve. She had just been led to her husband, and all that Milton by inspiration has pictured was present before them.

Mrs. Jay remonstrated against being hurried out of Paradise; but Flavianus advanced, and when he paused, the garden was no more. The rude homes of Adam and his families were seen scattered over a mountainous landscape, covered with flocks and herds. They saw Cain and Abel building their altars of stone on the brow of a steep hill which rose in sight of the dwelling-place of Adam. The offerings having been made, God answered Abel by fire upon the altar of his burnt offering.* "Come nearer," said Flavianus, and they beheld with terror, the look of horror which flashed over the face of Abel as he received his death-blow. They stood next before the ark. Astonishment and anxiety sat upon the faces of the multitude of those who had built it for Noah, and whom they had regarded as demented, now that they saw the strange march of wild and tame animals up the staging leading into it. When next they halted, all was a watery waste, and the ark was seen floating in the far distance.

Renewing their flight, Flavianus paused to show them

* So David was honored by God.—1 Chron., xxi. 26.

Abraham, with his only son Isaac, in the act of disbur-
dening his ass of the wood at the foot of Mount Moriah,
and placing it upon Isaac, while he took fire and his sacri-
ficial knife; when Isaac, as if the thought had first presented itself to his mind, said: "my father, here is the
fire and the wood, but where is the lamb for a burnt
offering." The words they did not hear; but they
knew by intuitive knowledge the thought spoken; and
Abraham, with grief in every feature, replied: "My
son, God will provide himself a lamb."

Reaching the top of the hill, Abraham, assisted
by Isaac, built an altar of stones and laid the wood in
order. Then it was, the father told his son the will of
heaven concerning him; words which drove the blood
from the cheeks of his boy, who, without a struggle,
submitted to be bound and laid upon the altar. This
childlike acquiescence, so instant and sudden, extending
even to giving up life itself, seemed to our travellers not
surpassed by the obedience of the father to the will of
Jehovah. They saw (for in effect they stood beside that
altar), the agonies of soul in Abraham as he lifted up his
arm; and Isaac, shrinking and shuddering, closing his
eyes in terror of the knife impending over him. Then
it was the divine glory shone down upon the type of
the Lamb of God, who was crucified two thousand years
after, upon that very spot. Leaving that wonderful
scene, they now paused to look down upon David with
his sling advancing to slay Goliah. This was an event of

singular interest to Mrs. Jay, who wanted to see more of David's life; but Flavianus moved rapidly on, saying: "We have the Son of David yet to see;" and when they next paused, they stood upon the plains of Bethlehem, beside the shepherds with their flocks; and lo, the angel of the Lord came down out of heaven and the glory of the Lord shone round about them. When the good tidings were told, a multitude of the heavenly hosts descending, sang the anthem of joy to all people and receding into heaven were seen no more. With joy they accompanied the shepherds and saw the babe lying in a manger. It was of all things, lovely to gather around the cradle of their Lord and Saviour, and catch his smile of innocency, and watch the face of the virgin mother gazing upon her firstborn son, with love mingled with awe. Calliste and Mrs. Jay were reluctant to leave a scene alike beautiful to all, but to Calliste and Mrs. Jay it was divine. Then followed in fast succession the adoration of the magi and the flight into Egypt, the baptism in Jordan, and the mysterious temptation in the wilderness, and the public ministry of their great God and Saviour to the day of his ascension.

Flavianus told them they must not linger on their way, at which both Peter and Mrs. Jay remonstrated. Flavianus answered: "We must proceed. You can at any time, and to all eternity, thus live over the life of your glorious Saviour from his cradle to his ascension; and not of his life only, but of your own and of all that have lived in all time and in all worlds. Do you not think, my sweet lady," said he, turning to Mrs. Jay, " that you will find full occupation in all the cycles of eternity? You once thought you would some time or other become weary—*ennuyed* of heaven itself."

" Oh, yes! but I was on earth then, and I had been taught to entertain repulsive ideas of a future state, in which (so I was led to believe) all the relationships of earth ceased ; that I should never again recognize my friends, or if I did, I should not feel any more of friendship for one than for another ; and then, I was to live in a state of beatific vision of God, and so be forever changing into his likeness ; forever thirsting after God ; which Dante describes as

> " ' The increate perpetual thirst, that draws
> Toward the realm of God's own form.' *

But I was a child then, and I spake as a child ; but

* DANTE: " Paradise," canto il.

" It is not, indeed, expressly asserted, but seems rather to be supposed and implied, in the expression and thoughts of most persons on this subject, that the heavenly life will be one of *inactivity*, and perfectly *stationary ;* that there will be nothing to be *done*, nothing to be *learnt*, no *advances* to be made ; nothing to be *hoped* for ; nothing to look *forward to*, except a continuance in the very state in which the blest will be placed at once. Now, this is far from being an alluring view to minds constituted as ours are. It is impossible for us to contemplate such a state—even with the most perfect assent of the understanding to the assertion, that it will be exquisitely happy—still, I say, it is impossible for such minds as ours to contemplate such a state, without an idea of tediousness and wearisomeness forcing itself upon them."—ARCHBISHOP WHATELY's *Future State*, p. 210.

now, I have put away such childish thoughts of God's plans for man's future development."

As they proceeded on their way, Mrs. Jay and Peter discoursed with their companions in travel of the wonderful law by which the actions of the past were recovered; and which had been revealed to them so unexpectedly since their entrance into their own firmament. With one consent, Peter and Mrs. Jay agreed to live along the lines of reflected rays of the life of Christ and of the great apostles, before they returned to their studies.

Flavianus spoke: "Not only has God, the Creator, constituted ether an imperishable record of the past by the reflection of light; but he has in like manner written our actions upon earth, air and ocean, which are the eternal witnesses of the acts done in each."

Peter, addressing Flavianus, asked: "Is the air itself one vast library on whose pages are forever written all that man has said or woman whispered?"

"Stop, Flavianus! pray do not reply to my friend Peter till he takes back his offensive words; 'men have said and woman whispered!' as if all the whispering and gossiping on earth were done by us women. Is that polite and kind, Peter?" asked Mrs. Jay.

"I beg Mrs. Jay's and Calliste's pardon, but I only made that arrangement of words because of their alliteration. I meant nothing more, dear Mrs. Jay," addressing that lady.

"Go on, Flavianus. I accept Peter's explanation as sufficient."

"The figure our friend Peter has called up, that the air is a vast library, I regard as happy, and as such I adopt it; for there, in unerring characters, is written the actions of all men for all time. There stands recorded the earliest as well as the latest sighs of mortality, with vows unredeemed, promises unfulfilled, perpetuating in their united movements of each particle the testimony of man's changeful will."

"What a thought it is, Flavianus," said Calliste, "that our actions, however secret, are thus made visible to the universe of God! And if this idea could but be brought home to the business and bosoms of men, what a change would come over the world!"

"How is it, Flavianus?" asked Faustinus; "can such ideas be brought within the scope of the mind of man?"

"Yes; it has been done by Mr. Charles Babbage, the eminent mathematician, in a tract which he has entitled, 'The Ninth Bridgewater Treatise;' one of the remarkable works of the present century. Mr. Babbage has been the first to present this great truth to the world, and he has shown how the principle of equality of action and reaction opens this vast treasure house of private and public history to the inspection of all intelligences."

"Will you please explain yourself so that I may apprehend how this can be, Flavianus?" asked Mrs. Jay. "I desire to know how Mr. Babbage has made this most occult of all questions plain to the apprehension of common people."

"With all pleasure, Mrs. Jay," replied her angel. "Mr. Babbage begins by saying, 'The pulsations of the air, once set in motion by the human voice, cease not to exist with the sounds to which they gave rise. Strong and audible as they may be in the immediate neighborhood of the speaker, and at the moment of their utterance, their quickly attenuated force soon becomes inaudible to human ears. The motions they have impressed on the particles of one portion of the atmosphere are communicated to constantly increasing numbers, but the total quantity of motion measured in the same direction receives no addition. Each atom loses as much as it gives, and regains again from other atoms a portion of those motions which they in turn turn up. The waves of air thus raised, perambulate the earth's and ocean's surface, and in less than twenty-four hours, every atom of its atmosphere takes up the altered movement due to that infinitesimal portion of the primitive motion, which has been conveyed to it through countless channels, and which must continue to influence its path throughout its future existence.'"

'Now, Flavianus, how can Mr. Babbage make such statements as these palpable? How are these aërial pulses, unseen by the keenest eye, unheard by the acutest ear, unperceived by the human senses, yet demonstrated to exist to the reason of mankind?" asked Mrs. Jay.

"In some few and limited instances they are shown to

exist by calling to our aid the most refined and comprehensive instrument of human thought; their courses have been traced and their intensities measured. Let us imagine a being whose knowledge of mathematical science in the apprehension of Newton, with all his enlarged powers, is boundless; such a mind could trace even the minutest consequence of every primary impulse; and if the slightest deviation was discovered, he would read in its existence the action of a new cause; and, through the aid of the same analysis, tracing this discordance back to its source, he would become aware of the time of its commencement, and the point of space at which it originated."

"I have no doubt, Flavianus, all you say is perfectly plain to the intellect of Calliste and Faustinus, and it may be of my friend Peter; but for myself," said Mrs. Jay, "I confess I want some familiar illustration within my comprehension."

"The waves of the air," replied the angel, "although in many instances perceptible to the organs of hearing, are only rendered visible to the eye by peculiar contrivances; but those of the water, dear Mrs. Jay, offer the illustration of transmitted motion you ask for. Every one who has thrown a pebble into the still waters of a sheltered pool, has seen the circles it has raised gradually expanding in size, and as uniformly diminishing in distinctness. He may also have noticed the perfect distinctness with which two, three or more series of waves each pursues its own unimpeded course, when diverging from the two, three or more centres of disturbance. He may have seen, that in such cases the particles of water where the waves intersect each other, partake of the movements due to each series."

"And from these premises what is your conclusion, my Flavianus?" asked Mrs. Jay.

" It is this: No motion impressed by natural causes, or by human agency, is ever obliterated. If the Almighty stamped on the brow of the earliest murderer the indelible and visible mark of his guilt, he has also established laws by which every succeeding criminal is not less irrevocably chained to the testimony of his crime; for every atom of his mortal frame, through whatever changes its severed particles may migrate, will still retain, adhering to it through every combination, some movement derived from that very muscular effort, by which the crime itself was perpetrated.

"Let me give you a further illustration. The soul of the negro whose fettered body surviving the charnel-house of his infected prison, was thrown into the sea, that his Christian master might escape the limited justice assigned by civilized man to crimes whose profit had long gilded their atrocity, will need, at the last great day of human account, no living witness of his earthly agony. When man and all his race shall have disappeared from the face of the planet, ask every particle of air still floating over the unpeopled earth, and it will record the cruel mandate of the tyrant. Interrogate every wave which breaks unimpeded on ten thousand desolate shores, and it will give evidence of the last gurgle which closed over the head of his dying victim. Confront the murderer with every corporeal atom of his immolated slave, and in its still quivering movements he will read God's denunciation: 'Thou art the man!'" [*]

They had now reached the orbit of the moon, at that moment rising in the eastern skies, over the home of Mrs. Jay. At the request of Calliste, they all landed to see that orb near, which had been so often looked upon by her with delightful admiration. It was a visit of interest to all our travelling party. Each had entertained his or her own fancies of the surface of the moon. It was a waste indeed, whose deep caverns and sugar-loaf mountains were alike desolate. Mrs. Jay searched in vain for those lovely beings described by Dante—

"Hither through failure of their vow exiled." [†]

As they were about to descend to earth, Mrs. Jay most earnestly entreated Calliste and Faustinus to go home with her and witness her child's marriage, but they thought at such a time she would be embarrassed by their presence, and with many expressions of love, they

---

[*] The words of Babbage have been carefully copied without any other change than was required to retain the shape of a dialogue. The author has used the second London edition, printed 1838.

[†] Canto III. "Paradise," line 29, Carey's translation.

declined. After long lingering, they separated, Faustinus and Calliste winging their way to Rome, and Flavianus and his party to the United States.

It was a clear, cold December night, and the stars shone with diamond brightness. The city now lay just below them, and its avenues and streets marked out in lines of light, and so near that they heard the bells striking the hour of nine.

"We have reached our place of destination in good time, my friends, and we will now alight;" so saying, Flavianus descended to the pavement in front of the well-known residence of Mrs. Jay.

CHAPTER XIV.

As our invisible guests entered the spacious hall of Mrs.
Jay, they paused; for at that instant Augusta and her
groom, with their attendants, were in the act of descending the grand staircase.

"How like an angel of light!" exclaimed Peter.

"Oh, that she were indeed an angel!" replied Mrs.
Jay.

William started forward to meet his sister, but Mrs.
Jay held him back; and when the bridal party had
entered the splendid saloon, Mrs. Jay and her party
followed.

There stood the minister in his robes, and beside him

the father, whose face was beaming with benevolence,
without one thought of himself, and that he was about
to give away the chief of all his earthly treasures. The
ceremony proceeded, and Mrs. Jay expressed to her
angel her pleasure in looking upon the young man,
whose bright eye was full of intelligence, while his features bore the marks of culture and refinement. The
radiant eye of Augusta fell upon the floor, and her long
eyelashes fringed her cheek, while she repeated in a low,
clear tone her vow of love and fidelity.

When the ceremony was concluded, and the bride-
maids clustered around the bride, Mrs. Jay and William
impressed their kisses with fervent love, unobserved.
Indeed, Augusta at this moment was not able to perceive
any difference in the kisses she received.

While the ceremony was in progress, the rush of carriages was heard, and as soon as it was over, a stream of
guests flowed into the rooms, eager to be presented to
the bride, and share in the gladness of the hour.

Mrs. Jay stood beside Augusta, listening with delight
while her numerous friends presented their congratula
tions. As her son had many questions to ask, his
mother's attention was fully occupied by him, until calling Flavianus, Mrs. Jay begged him to supply her lack
of service to William, as she wanted to be at liberty to
move among the crowd that now filled the house.

As for Peter Schlemihl, he was everywhere and interested in all that was said and done by those about him.

He was especially attracted by a beautiful young lady, splendidly attired, who, with her husband, having made their bows to the bride, now came to the spot where he was standing. Those about Peter presented to them their congratulations, and thus he was advised that they were now in their honeymoon. As they passed onwards, a maiden lady, whose diamonds bespoke a high rank in the circles of fashionable life, turned to a lady next to Peter, and said in a whispered tone, "There goes a foolish girl, who claims to have married for love, and counts the sacrifice she has made of splendid offers as not worth a moment's thought. I wonder that her father should have thrown away his child upon a man of no fortune; one who has nothing but his head to depend upon." In reply to this depreciating remark, the lady replied she thought if Mr. Morgan had no fortune of his own, his talents would create one all in good time.

"You are so kind and so hopeful, dear Mrs. Fairfield," replied Miss Judith Grey; "but I think I know some fathers who would not give up an only daughter without surer hopes of success."

"That life does not consist in the abundance of things possessed, we have the highest authority for saying, and the surest hopes are built on integrity, intelligence and industry." So saying, Mrs. Fairfield bowed and passed.

At this moment, a lady of forty, with a handsome face and a bright look, richly dressed, illuminated with diamonds came along, as Miss Judith stood with her lips compressed, a little vexed with the reproof conveyed in the reply of Mrs. Fairfield.

"What a pity, Mrs. Thomson, you had not come up a minute sooner, and you would have heard Mrs. Fairfield preach to me about the vast superiority of worth over wealth."

"Pray what was her text?" asked Mrs. George Thomson.

"Henry Morgan and his bride;" and then she repeated what had been said.

"What folly!" exclaimed Mrs. George Thomson; "and does Mrs. Fairfield think to blind us with such common-places? She can afford to be sentimental, but let a poor young man approach her beautiful daughter, and then we shall see the worth of all such pietistic preaching."

"I am sure it does not go for much anywhere, unless it be at the board of brokers; but in the circles of good society up town, it is in very bad repute." So said Mrs. Jonas Moreland, a lady of thirty; who had married an old banker, and had recently entered the upper circles, of which she was now forever talking.

"My dear Mrs. Moreland," replied Mrs. George Thomson, "I assure you it goes for nothing. Do I not know? Have I not sounded all the shallows and depths of fortune? Born under no kind auspices, I made the most of all the distinctions within my reach. I could not wait for wealth, and I therefore became a pietist, and reached the slippery pinnacle of perfection. This was a pin's-point to stand upon, but I held it with honor until fortune began to smile upon us; and then it was I fell from grace, just when I was pluming my flight into these third heavens."

"Oh, Mrs. Thomson, you are such a funny person; and you say things of yourself no one else would ever think of saying."

"No, Miss Judith, I understand myself and the people by whom I am surrounded. If we were all in heaven the course I take would not be in good taste; but neither Mrs. Fairfield, nor any of our up-town Christians, have any desire to reach a higher position than that they now occupy for a good while to come. I imagine we all think this world of ours good enough for us for the next twenty-five years."

"Tell me, Mrs. Thomson, what did you think of our late hostess; was she not a very proud person?" asked Miss Judith.

"Mrs. Jay was proud, Miss Judith, but not haughty. It was nature-born with her. That she was a proud woman you could see by the glance of her eye, and her bearing at all times and everywhere. Poor dear lady! She was very clever, and I always admired her. But she, too, had her weak points; and there is the evidence of what I say. Look at that broad canvas covered all over with brown paint. That was her pet treasure—a

real Rembrandt and no mistake. She confessed to me
it could only be seen in the strong light in which it had
been painted; and by the way, I can say that very many
of the pictures in our parlors are in the same bad fix.
Now to see that picture, our dear friend must have had
a hole cut in the wall of the house to let daylight down
upon it, and so have made the beauties of her gem visi-

wrong as to my taste in pictures; but in diamonds I rather think I surpass some eminent persons who cannot tell the difference between the true and the false, between the paste and the gem. I can tell the difference blind-fold."

"Pray, how! do explain this mystery."

"It is no mystery; I simply touch my tongue with the so-called diamonds, and my tongue tells me the difference as surely as my eye discovers the cheats I see all about me;" and so saying, Mrs. Thomson gave a look at a diadem crowning a lady passing at the moment.

"I love to hear you talk, Mrs. Thomson; you are so brave."

"Yes, and I love to hear myself. I am always excited pleasurably when I find myself surrounded by good society. And yet, alas! what is it? 'Vanity of vanities,' as Solomon said of his own age. Here we have for leaders, persons of both sexes, sadly ignorant of what they most affect. I love to hear them talk superfine. No one wears a more admiring look than I. When these oracles speak I am dumb; no courtier can bow so low as I; none assume a more deferential air, and, Miss Judith, like all the rest of the world, they love to be admired. These dowager dames laugh at me and talk of my aping their style. Yes, I do so, and they think the better of their style because I copy it; and excel most of them in their own way of manifesting the possession of wealth."

Peter stood listening with all his might, when Mrs.

Jay laid her hand on his shoulder, and roused his attention.

"Tell me, Peter, what do you think of all you have heard? Was not that a just critique upon my poor Rembrandt?"

"She is a bright woman, and I like her," answered Peter.

At this instant Mrs. General Wentworth came up, and bowing to Miss Judith and Mrs. Thomson, and after the usual compliments, said: "This is a very nice party, and Mrs. Jay would have enjoyed it, I am certain. How much we miss her bright beaming eye, her silver tones and sweet smiles!"

Mrs. George Thomson replied: "Yes, madam, her smile was beautiful, brightened as it was by the adornments of exquisite taste, and reflected from all these plate mirrors; and I think she appreciated all this."

"Oh, no, Mrs. Thomson! Mrs. Jay was superior to such things, and always preferred worth before wealth."

"My dear madam," replied Mrs. Thomson, "you do not know the value of money. You were born to wealth, married wealth, and have all your life long had every wish gratified; but I may speak what everybody knows, that my good husband has aided me to my present position. And let who will talk lightly of the worth of money, it won't be me. And why should it be discredited? It buys everything, shelters me in a home like this, with all its appliances of comfort—supplies me with a carriage and horses and servants—I am welcomed at Stewart's with smiles, and the looms of the world are at work for my adornment; and last, not least by any means, money pays for one of the best pews in the broad aisles of our best churches up-town, and aids me to keep a conscience void of offence. I can afford to be charitable, and have my name as manager of any number of societies; and when death comes at last, I shall have the consolations of religion and the benefit of clergy; and when buried, my disconsolate husband, before he marries again, will take good care to erect at Greenwood a tall obelisk or a broken shaft with a well written inscription, to keep alive my many virtues in the memory of the future Mrs. George Thomson, to whom my epitaph will stand as a perpetual exhortation, and my monument be forever a rock of offence. In one word, money secures to us all the best things of this life and the fairest hopes for the life to come."

"You are positively shocking, Mrs. Thomson," cried Mrs. General Wentworth as she passed on, with a pleased look and a tap of her fan.

Peter, who was interested in Mrs. George Thomson, followed her, listening to her clever sayings. She passed many ladies who ignored her presence, or who were unknown to her. Two matrons, whose bearing showed the unmistakeable marks of high culture and position, bowed to Mrs. Thomson; and the three paused, when Mrs. Thomson addressing the younger of the two, said: "This mansion, so magnificent and thronged with the talent, intelligence and beauty of our city, is like the palace in the fairy tale; it is incomplete, and why?"

Mrs. Butler answered: "It is so long since I was familiar with my nursery tales that I do not recall the story you have alluded to; but I presume my reply ought to be, what we all feel to be the great lack in this home—the absence of our beloved friend, Mrs. Jay."

"Do you not think she is here unseen?" asked Mrs. Thomson. "The two worlds may be much nearer than is dreamed of in the philosophy and theology of our times."

"It is possible our dear Mrs. Jay may be here. What do you say, Mrs. Griswold?" replied Mrs. Butler.

"I have believed, that at death we are at once transported outside of all our present states of feeling and thinking; and in transcendental blessedness cease to inquire after the concerns of this life."

"That cannot be, Mrs. Griswold," replied Mrs. Thomson. "Our identity is one, and our 'prevailing love' is forever predominant. All the theologies from Paul to Swedenborg teach us that. Now if you knew the 'prevailing love' of Mrs. Jay, you can tell us the emotions of her heart had she entered this room."

"Well, Mrs. Thomson, I am not competent to look beyond the present. I am no Seeress, nor do I wish to be. It is my desire that her dear child may follow in the footsteps of her mother, and become another Mrs. Fry, and that we may thus have the mother restored to us. Her visits to our city-prison were like angel visits, only in this: they were neither few nor far between."

"Oh, yes! so I have heard, Mrs. Griswold. Remember, madam, that Mrs. Fry and Mrs. Jay were both lovely women of fine presence, and who always dressed with richness and a beautiful simplicity; and when they entered the dimly-lighted wards of our prisons, they wore the appearance of angels of light. And I have no doubt it was a source of pleasurable satisfaction to them to have done so. Indeed, what a sense of joy must have flowed into their souls, when returning to their mansions, the wretchedness they had just left behind them was contrasted with home comforts."

"You judge hardly of human nature, Mrs. Thomson," said Mrs. Butler.

Mrs. Thompson replied, "Self-love and social are the same. In this I am sustained by the brightest and wisest of men."

Mrs. Griswold asked: "And do you regard Pope and Rochefoucauld safe judges of Christian conduct?"

"I could have cited St. Paul, ladies; but somehow Paul is now regarded as a little *passé* for our times."

"You are very severe upon us, Mrs. Thomson," said Mrs. Butler.

Mrs. Thomson made a low courtesy and said: "If I may be permitted so distinguished an honor, I will add: 'and upon myself.'"

"You certainly have a right to make the application,"

said Mrs. Butler; "but it would hardly have been polite for us to have said: 'Physician, heal thyself.'"

"To you, ladies," replied Mrs. Thomson, "I dare speak. It is only to those 'to the manner-born,' I venture to hold up life as it is, and not as it fashions itself. The hollowness of our globe those know best who best ring it."

Mrs. Butler, with a smile, said: "You certainly have your share of the most beautiful rings, dear Mrs. Thomson."

Mrs. Thomson, with a laugh, playfully held up her hand and flashed the light from her diamonds, saying: "Yes, ladies, I have had my rings, and every new ring has helped me to realize the hollowness of the world in which I live and move and have my being." So saying, Mrs. Thompson bowed and was lost in the crowded room.

"That is a bright person," said Mrs. Butler to her friend, "and is destined to become a leader among us; and I think society will be likely to advance under such guidance. I met her at Saratoga last summer and found her a most agreeable person. She loves to surprise you, and affects to despise what most she covets; but she is a woman of tact and talent. We must make her feel herself at home in our social circles, and then she will cease to be satirical."

"I will call upon her next week," said Mrs. Griswold, "and will send her cards for my next party."

The ball having been opened by the bride, she took the arm of Mr. George Howard, one of the groomsmen, and returned to the saloons, where she continued to receive with grace and frankness the congratulations of her guests. This young gentleman took the first moment he could secure to say in a low tone to the bride: "This night shall be made memorable to me by a declaration of my love for your friend Amelia. Can you so far oblige me as to detach her from Mr. Livingston, who has been her shadow all this evening. I purpose to have more hope or none before I leave this house. What do you advise, my dear *madam?*" emphasizing her new title to the ear of the bride.

"Action, action, action! Your admiration of my beautiful friend is not unknown to her lovely self, though it has been so silent and deferential. This is pleasing to us ladies to a certain point of time; and whether this be the hour of decision in your love affairs, you must determine for yourself. I will aid you as you desire."

Taking the arm of Mr. Howard, the bride was led up to the spot where Mr. Livingston and Amelia stood. This Mr. Livingston was regarded as 'a great catch;' but in despite of all well-concocted plans, had as yet refused to be noosed, and was now approaching thirty-five, having changed the object of his admiration with every season. This winter he had shown a most decided preference for Miss Amelia Fairfield, a lovely girl of eighteen, whose dark eyes shone with starry brightness, and her happy, bright laugh revealed the most beautiful teeth in all the world. She was tall and graceful, and her appearance on this evening was singularly attractive; for she was dressed with exquisite beauty and yet severe simplicity. After mutual expressions of kind regards, the bride said to Amelia: "Forgive me, if I claim Mr. Livingston as a truant from the ball-room; and I am now about to enlist him for Miss Jones, my beautiful bridesmaid for the next quadrille, and I will leave you, Amelia, in charge of Mr. Howard."

Mr. Livingston was not pleased, but he affected to be so, and was led away to the ball-room, while Mr. Howard with profound deference asked permission to lead Miss Amelia into the conservatory which opened into the parlors. With a consenting smile Amelia took the offered arm and was soon hid from sight amid fragrant flowers blooming in mid-winter, lighted up by shaded lamps which made a mimic moonlight.

It was a brief absence, when Peter who had been observant of all that had passed, saw Amelia and her lover return into the rooms. But what important events are crowded into a few minutes! The eyes of Amelia shone with a dimmed lustre, her cheeks wore a brighter color, and her air was changed. The manners of Mr. Howard were no less deferential; but there was a loving tenderness in his glance which he had never dared before. As it was true to nature, it did not offend, though the eyes of Amelia fell beneath his gaze This sweet embarrassment was ended at once by the appearance of her pretty cousin Kate, who ran up to her, saying: " Come, Amelia, hasten to the ball-room in time for the next quadrille. Mr. Livingston, who is now on the floor with Miss Jones, sent me after you, and I promised to bring you as soon as I could find you. Where have you been hid?"

" I do not wish to dance to-night, Kate."

" Do not wish to dance, Amelia! Did you not intend to dance? In the carriage on our way here, you said you would."

" Yes, I did so; but I have changed my mind."

" Pray, cousin, tell me, are you indisposed?"

" Indisposed to dance, Cousin Kate."

" This is odd! What has happened, cousin?"

" Pray am I not a woman?" asked Amelia, with an air of mock earnestness; "and have I not a right to change my mind?"

" Certainly, cousin; but you are not changeable; and you have either had a quarrel of some sort with Mr. Livingstone, or you are ill."

" Mr. Livingston and I parted just now, on good terms; and I assure you I am perfectly well."

At this moment, Mr. Livingston came up in haste, and with the air of one who had a claim to the hand which he took on the instant, saying, " Let us hurry, Amelia, or we shall be one moment too late."

"I shall not dance to-night, Mr. Livingston," said Amelia. "I have this moment declined Mr. Howard's kind invitation to dance with him."

"I presume Mr. Howard will withdraw his invitation in my favor, Miss Amelia," said Mr. Livingston, with the air of a man who demanded it as a right not to be denied him.

Amelia, with a tone of decision which anticipated any reply from Mr. Howard, said to Mr. Livingston, "I shall not dance, sir."

"That being a decree 'which changeth not,' I am released from all further attendance in the ball-room. Will you please make my excuse, Mr. Howard, and give the bride the reasons for my absence?"

This was said with an air of one who wished to be left alone with Amelia, and accordingly her cousin accompanied Mr. Howard to the ball-room.

Mr. Livingston was evidently not a little flattered by this decision made by Miss Amelia; for as she well knew his aversion to dancing, he regarded her declining of Mr. Howard's invitation and his own as a *gage d'amour* which he was in a happy mood to take up. And this he did with all the skill he could command, and at the end of half an hour or more he found himself greatly embarrassed what next to say. He had made the most of an offer of himself that he had ever before ventured upon, and Amelia had shown not the slightest comprehension of his purpose. "Did she need him to be more

explicit, and should he be so?" These were question
ings hard to be answered in a saloon where he was every
moment or two interrupted by some teasing young lady
or far-sighted matron, saying, "Good evening, Amelia;
how cosy you are in this snug corner;" or, "Mr. Livingston you absorb Miss Amelia, to the infinite misery of her
despairing lovers." Weary of such impertinence, Mr.
Livingston, losing his patience, said, "I wish all these
people were"—Amelia's inquiring look was upon him,
and quailing under it, he added—"at the antipodes,
Miss Amelia."

"I am most grateful for their attentions," replied
Amelia, quietly. Nor did she fail to detain all such
friends in pleasant chat, until Mr. Livingston could
with difficulty command his temper; so vexed was
he that the exclusiveness of attention, young ladies
especially, had always conceded to him, was now
denied.

Men of known wealth are apt to have an imperious
bearing of which they may be all the while unconscious.
From boyhood they have been accustomed to rule over
superior minds, who, with bare-headed debasement, bow
down before such golden calves. Mr. Livingston was
among the idolized of "good society," and it was all new
to him to have his attentions disregarded. It had been
the study of his life to pay only such civilities, as, however flattering to the lady of the hour, were perfectly
non-committal. And now, when he was himself reck-

less how far he went, or what form of phrase he adopted, he found Miss Amelia unaffected and utterly unappreciative. Having exhausted his patience, he rose to leave Amelia as Mr. and Mrs. Fairfield approached them, and after making his bows of recognition, he said to Mrs. Fairfield, "I am sorry to find Miss Amelia so much indisposed; she will neither dance, talk, nor listen;" so saying, he made a bow to Amelia and her parents, and addressed himself to a young widow near by, who, having laid aside her long black veil, had just reappeared in society. This lady was delighted with the warmth of Mr. Livingston's address, who expressed his pleasure at seeing her once more, and thus it was he exploded his resentment, hoping to pique Amelia; but she stood beside her parents with a look of pre-occupation and unconsciousness that was truly provoking.

Mr. Howard returning with Miss Kate to the parlors, led her up to the bride; and after some pleasant conversation, Augusta requested her husband to take care of Margaret while she went into the conservatory with Mr. Howard.

"Shall I offer you my congratulations?" asked Augusta, as she took a seat.

"Oh, I dare not tell you all I hope for, dear madam. I had some minutes with Amelia, who occupied the same seat you now do—it might be fifteen or twenty minutes.

15

I cannot say how long, but I told Amelia all that was in my heart. The fountains of the great deep were broken up, and words came full and fast. All that had been treasured up in my soul for months and years now found utterance, and though I felt my flight was Icarus-like, I was without fear."

"Grand!" exclaimed Augusta; "and what reply did she make?"

"Not one word, but she listened without one sign of weariness, and what could I hope for more?"

"Nothing! and you have shown your true appreciation of a woman's nature to be content with this silent acquiescence of her soul. And is this all you have to tell me? Have you not spoken with her since? That was near two hours ago."

"No, for Mr. Livingston has had her all to himself on a sofa in a corner. I have been in and out and around to catch a glance at Amelia. She has remained listening listlessly and rarely smiled. He has grown red in the face in talking earnestly to her, but what it is he has been saying I have no guess even. No young gentleman has dared approach Amelia, and you know Livingston claims the entire attention of the lady he is talking to, and is rude as a bear to any one who dares to interrupt his conversation."

"How skillful and wise love has made you, Mr. Howard? Let me lead you to Amelia, for this bear will not dare to growl in my presence."

"Thank you, dear Mrs. Henry, for such thoughtful kindness as you have manifested to me this evening."

"Oh, I have a wish that Amelia shall have this day as conspicuous in her calendar as it is in mine."

"How glad you make me! and how grateful shall I be if your hopes and my wishes are ever realized."—So saying, they left the conservatory and sought out Amelia.

They found her with her parents, who were about to go, and were happy thus to take leave of the bride. Augusta kept Mr. and Mrs. Fairfield occupied, giving opportunity to Mr. Howard to converse with Amelia. She had supplied him with a beautiful moss-rose bud, which he presented to Amelia, who admired it and hid it in her bosom. Mr. Howard was delighted, and eagerly sought for one glance, but none was given.

The parents took leave, and Peter, who had been an interested "looker-on in Vienna," saw Mr. Howard hand Amelia into the carriage. Returning to the entry, Mr. Howard held in his hand a lady's glove, accidentally dropped, which he hid away carefully in his vest pocket. This love affair helped to while away the evening to Peter.

Mr. Henry and his bride were now receiving and returning the salutations of departing guests. While Peter was standing near the bride, gazing on the scene before him, Mrs. Jay came up to him and announced her purpose to leave. Peter begged her to

stay until the last guest was gone, but she was impera-
tive, as was her wont, and William had not a word to
say, and as for Peter she told him he was at liberty to do
as he pleased.

"See, my beloved husband, Peter! Look at him! Was
ever such self-forgetfulness seen before! Can any filial
love and duty repay him such devotedness? Oh, that
he may find like nobility of nature in his new-found son!
and Augusta too, will she ever forget to love her father?
If he could but go with us; but alas! he must travel onwards to the tomb unaided and alone."

"You are too distrustful, dear madam. I will venture
everything on the truthfulness and devotion of your
child."

"Oh, Peter, this is all moonshine. In the body, custom, habit, cares, losses, changes of place and pursuits,
little by little, steal away our affections, and we are
changed. There's nothing but a constant Christian faith
can enable Augusta and her husband to fulfill the demands of duty and self-sacrifice; and how imperfectly,
our own lives will bear us witness."

"I have all faith in Augusta, and I shall have to the
end of life. Pardon me, Mrs. Jay, but do you leave because you have been piqued by what you have heard
said of you this evening?"

"No, Peter, not so. I have been most lovingly
remembered by my friends, whose commendations I do
not deserve; and even my faults have found their ad-

mirers. Mrs. George Thomson's admirable critique upon my pet picture was so true, that I wonder it never occurred to me. I hope God, in his infinite mercy, will bring each and all of these, my dear friends, neighbors and acquaintance, to the knowledge of the truth as it is in Christ Jesus. That they may all repent of their sins, and live by faith of the Son of God—the only Saviour of sinners, and the only Way to Heaven."

"So may it be." answered Peter.

"I am about to impress my last kisses, and to tear myself away. You, Peter, prefer to stay awhile longer, and on your return you will find me somewhere along the pathway of light, which renews to us the life of our glorious God and Saviour. William and I intend to dwell upon his every look and action, and to make them our most precious inheritance. I am sure you will feel yourself in haste to join us in this blissful study of the life of Christ."

So saying, Mrs. Jay, with lingering tenderness, took leave of her husband and daughter. Again and again did she renew her unfelt caresses. Flavianus made his appearance in the saloon, and taking the hand of William, said to Mrs. Jay, "I obey your will, madam."

"Flavianus, I am grateful to God that your love to me is to be continued to my child. May I soon be restored to my husband and my child, and then will be added one more to the company of happy families, united in the love of Christ, to be separated no more forever."

With "longing, lingering looks behind," Mrs. Jay and Peter followed Flavianus and William into the hall, and thence into the street. The moon had risen and was walking in brightness above them. The long row of carriages showed that many guests were still enjoying the pleasures of an evening party in December. They walked slowly down the pavement, their minds full of the recollections of the past and with anticipations of the future, till Flavianus stopped on the crossing of the next street.

"Here we separate," said Flavianus, and after kind adieux, Mrs. Jay and her son and their angel rose, and soon became a mere point of light, even to Peter's space-penetrating vision, " as far as angel's ken," and were seen no more.

On his return to the house, and as he was about to go up the steps, Peter chanced to look up, and saw the curtains of an upper room on fire. Rising to the height of the windows, he saw the sash had been drawn down from the top, and that the curtains had blown free from their fastening and had caught fire from the gas-burners.

Descending in a fright, Peter rushed into the saloons, and going up to Mr. Jay, he whispered in his ear that his house was on fire, in the front room of the third story. Mrs. Woolsey and son were at the moment taking leave of Mr. Jay and Augusta, and he was so absorbed, that he paid not the least attention to what had been told him. So soon as this lady and her son had withdrawn, Peter with all earnestness again told Mr. Jay his house was on fire; but in vain. Mad with excitement, Peter ran up the stairs into the ball-room, which was still thronged with the bright and the beauti ful, who were waltzing with the bouyancy of midnight hours. No sooner did one couple make a vacancy than others were ready to sweep across the floor. As it was the last dance, its close had been thus indefinitely prolonged by Munck and his band, so that it had become a contest which should give out, the band or the dancers. Nothing could exceed the joyousness and excitement of the ball-room as Peter rushed in, and reckless of consequences, having reached the very centre of the room, he cried out with all his might—Fire!

It was all a dream! no sooner was the word spoken than Peter awoke and found himself solitary and alone; the naked, barren, and wintry waste of life, shrouded in clouds and darkness, still lay untravelled before him.

APPENDIX.

APPENDIX.

APPENDIX A.

THE following article is taken from the "Boston Evening Transcript." June, 1858:

THE HUMAN RACE.

When Mr. Miller was exhorting our people to be prepared for the end of the world, and gave it as his deliberate opinion that "the day of judgment would be a thousand years," I published the following estimate in the "Boston Courier" (1843), first published in the "Quarterly Journal of Agriculture," London, and copied by the "Albion," New York, 1830. It may be an interesting chapter for the study of your correspondent, "A," and not an uninteresting one for your readers:

"INCREASE OF THE NUMBER OF MANKIND.—On the supposition that the human race has power to double its numbers four times in a century, or once in each succeeding period of twenty-five years, as some philosophers have computed, and that nothing prevented the exercise of this increase, the descendants of Noah and his family would have now increased (1830) to the following number:

1,496,577,696,626,844,588,240,573,268,701,473,812,127,674,924,-007,424.

The surface of the earth contains of square
    miles.............................   196,663,355
Mercury and the planets contain about... 46,790,511,000
The sun contains................ 2,442,900,000,000
                                               2,489,887,174,355

"Hence, upon the supposition of such a rate of increase of mankind as has been assumed, the number of human beings now living would be equal to the following number for each square mile upon the surface of the earth, sun, and all the planets,—61,362,000,000,000,-000,000,000,000,000,000,000,000; or to the following number to each square inch, 149,720,000,000,000,000,000,000,000,000,000."

This last number alone is infinite with relation to human conception. Merely to count it would require an incredible period. Supposing the whole number of inhabitants now upon the surface of the globe to be *one thousand millions*—which is believed to somewhat exceed the actual number—and supposing that this multitude, infants and adults, were to be employed in nothing else but counting—that each working 365 days in the year, and ten hours in the day, and to count one hundred per minute, it would require, in order to count the number in question, 6,536,500,000,000 of years.

—•♦•—

APPENDIX B.

CRINOLINE THE CAUSE OF THE COMMERCIAL CRISIS OF 1857.

MALE AND FEMALE LUXURIES.

During the past year the ladies of the United States have spent for silk $28,699,681, for embroideries $4,443,176, for trimmings and laces $1,129,754, for shawls $9,246,361, for bonnets and hats $2,246,928; while the men have wasted their substance in brandies and liquors, $3,963,725, in wines $2,381,252, and in cigars and tobacco $5,579,931.   Total spent by ladies, $36,519,538 ; by gentle-men, $11,924,908.

A GREAT LEAK.

Nothing can afford at a glance a clearer insight into the universal prevalence of luxury in the United States, than the fact that during the fiscal year ending June 30th, 1856, we imported silk piece goods to the amount of $25,000,000, other silk goods to the value of $6,017,115, laces $1,601,610, embroideries $4,664,353, making altogether over thirty-seven millions of dollars.   These are the things which run away with the wealth of the country.

ENGLISH VIEW OF AMERICAN AFFAIRS.

The London "Times" makes the following comments upon the condition of things in the United States :

"The commercial panic across the Atlantic is beginning to lead to a very rigid economic inquiry.   The money is gone, and who has spent it all ?   That is the question.   We need not add that the question is asked with considerable irritation and sharpness of tone, suffi-cient to account for any amount of reluctance in the culprit to come forward and confess.   Who has spent all the money ?   The hue and cry of New York offers an almost unlimited reward for his or her apprehension.   Whoever discovers the criminal will receive not only a pension of several thousand dollars for life, but also a civic crown ; he will be clothed in splendid apparel, and led on horseback through the streets of the city.   All New York is at present busy in searching for the gigantic spendthrift.   Where has he gone ?   What has be-come of him ?   Who saw him last ?   What train did he leave by ?   Has he fled to the Dismal Swamp, or to California, or to Nicaragua ?   Is he still in the city, evading pursuit ?   Everybody is looking into cupboards, behind doors, under beds, and in all holes and corners of upper and lower stories to see if he is there.

"When a man becomes a bankrupt, and cannot find out who is to blame for it; when he has decided that, of course, he himself has had nothing to do with it; that none of his clerks are in fault, or the post office, or the government, or the custom house—in lack of every other cause of the smash, he turns round upon his wife—'Yes: now I have got it. I always thought it would come to this. Now I see the consequence of having married an expensive woman.'

"This our contemporary, the 'New York Times,' tells us is the general explanation given in New York of the recent convulsion of the money market. Women are the burden of conversation, and the whole community is agreed that it has married a most expensive wife. All the New York merchants are turning round fiercely upon their domestic partners; the extravagant wives have done it all—it is the French silks, the crinoline and moire, the gloves and feathers, fans and furbelows, that have ruined them; these have taken the money out of the country.

"The American merchant's wife must return to rigid republican simplicity. One would imagine that there was a Jonah preaching repentance, and that the great American Tyre was going literally to clothe herself with sackcloth. There will be allowed Quaker bonnets alone, gowns of the plainest drab stuff, shawls of the same; those wives of the most opulent citizens who are permitted to use silk, will have it measured out to them by the mayor and corporation. The Legislative Assembly of the State will debate in the next session upon the subject of female dress, and, as soon as a committee has sat, examined witnesses, and made a report on the annual quantity of clothing and ornament which the commercial welfare of the community can spare, the ladies will proceed to lay down permanent restrictions, which will be a model of sumptuary wisdom, and supply an example for the legislation of other countries that may find themselves falling into mercantile confusion.

"Such is the repentance, not of Nineveh, but of New York, and certainly it is an instance of the same sword that wounded healing. Money is the corrupter, and bankruptcy is the converter.

"New York now finds that it has gone astray, that it has departed from the rigid simplicity of its Puritan founders, and it is anxious to return to drab again, in order that it may get rich again. This motive to national penitence would not indeed have satisfied the prophets, and the penance itself appears rather too vicarious a one."

APPENDIX D.

The following narrative is one of many which could be given. It is taken from the writings of the Rev. James B. Finley, an eminent minister in North Carolina, who was born in North Carolina, in the year 1781, and became one of the most zealous and efficient pioneers in the missionary cause during the early settlement of Kentucky and Ohio. He died but a few years since, at an advanced age. He was held in high estimation by all denominations of Christians, and was long known to the Christian world by the endearing name of Father Finley. In his Autobiography, page 375, we find the following:

"During my labors on the Dayton district, an incident occurred which I must relate, because it is due to the many to whom I promised an account of it, that it should be published in my biography.

"It was in the summer of 1842. Worn down with fatigue, I was completing my last round of quarterly meetings, and winding up the labors of a very toilsome year. I had scarcely finished my work till

I was most violently attacked with bilious fever, and it was with great
difficulty that I rallied from it. The disease had taken so violent a hold on
me, that I sank rapidly under its power. Everything that kind
attention and medical skill could impart was resorted to, to correct
the disease, but all was in vain, and my life was despaired of. On
the seventh night, in a state of entire insensibility to all around me,
when the last ray of hope had departed, and my weeping family and
friends were standing around, anxiously waiting to see me breathe my
last, to me an unearthly visitant entered my room. It
came to my side, and in the softest and most silvery tones, which fell
like rich music on my ear, it said, 'I have come to conduct you to
another state and place of existence.' In an instant I seemed to rise,
and gently borne by angel guides, I floated out upon the ambient
air. Soon earth was lost in the distance, and around us, on every side,
were worlds of light and glory. On, on, away, away from this world
to luminous worlds afar, we sped with the velocity of thought. At
length we reached the gates of Paradise; and oh! the transporting
scenes that fell upon my vision, as the emerald portals, wide and high,
rolled back upon their golden hinges! Then, in its fullest extent,
did I realize the invocation of the poet:

" ' Burst ye emerald gates and bring
To my raptured vision
All the estatic joys that spring
Round the bright Elysian.'

"Language, however, is inadequate to describe what then, with
unveiled eyes, I saw. The vision is indelibly pictured upon my heart.
Before me, spread out in beauty, was a broad sheet of water, clear as
a crystal, not a single ripple on its surface, and its purity and clear-
ness indescribable. On each side of this lake, or river, rose up the
most tall and beautiful trees, covered with all manner of fruits and
flowers, the brilliant hues of which were reflected in the bosom of
the placid river.

"While I stood gazing with joy and rapture at the scene, a convoy of angels was seen floating in the pure ether of that world. They had all long wings, and although they went with the greatest rapidity, yet their wings were folded close to their sides. While I gazed, I asked my guide who they were, and what their mission? To this he responded, 'They are angels dispatched to the world from whence you came, on errands of mercy.' I could hear strains of the most entrancing melody all around me, but no one was discoverable but my guide. At length I said, 'Will it be possible for me to have a sight of some of the just made perfect in glory?' Just then there came before us three persons. One had the appearance of a male, the other a female, and the third an infant. The appearance of the first two was somewhat similar to the angels I saw, with the exception that they had crowns upon their heads of the purest yellow, and harps in their hands. Their robes, which were full and flowing, were of the purest white. Their countenances were lighted up with a heavenly radiance, and they smiled upon me with ineffable sweetness.

"There was nothing with which the blessed babe or child could be compared. It seemed to be about three feet high. Its wings, which were long and most beautiful, were tinged with all the colors of the rainbow. Its dress seemed to be of the whitest silk, covered with the softest white down. The driven snow could not exceed it for whiteness or purity. Its face was all radiant with glory; its very smile now plays around my heart. I gazed and gazed with wonder upon this heavenly child. At length I said, 'If I have to return to earth, from whence I came, I should love to take this child with me, and show it to weeping mothers of earth. Methinks when they see it, they will never shed another tear over their children when they die.' So anxious was I to carry out the desire of my heart, that I made a grasp at the bright and beautiful one, desiring to clasp it in my arms, but it eluded my grasp, and plunged into the river of life. Soon it rose up from the waters, and as the drops fell from its expanding wings, they seemed like diamonds, so brightly did they sparkle Directing its course to the other shore, it flew up to one of the topmost branches of one of life's fair trees. With a look of most seraphic sweetness, it gazed upon me, and then commenced singing in heaven's own strains, 'To him that hath loved me, and washed me from my sins in his own blood, to him be glory both now and forever. Amen."

"At that moment the power of the Eternal God came upon me, and I began to shout, and clapping my hands, I sprang from my bed, and was healed as instantly as the lame man in the beautiful porch of the temple, who 'went walking, and leaping and praising God.' Overwhelmed with the glory I saw and felt, I could not cease praising God. The next Sabbath I went to camp meeting, filled with the love and power of God. There I told the listening thousands what I saw and felt, and what God had done for me, and loud were the shouts of glory that reverberated though the forest."